S0-ASX-325

THE CONTEST FOR CALIFORNIA IN 1861

HOW COLONEL E. D. BAKER SAVED THE PACIFIC STATES TO THE UNION

THE CONTEST FOR CALIFORNIA IN 1861

HOW COLONEL E. D. BAKER SAVED THE PACIFIC STATES TO THE UNION

BY

ELIJAH R. KENNEDY

WITH ILLUSTRATIONS

BOSTON AND NEW YORK
HOUGHTON MIFFLIN COMPANY
The Riverside Press Cambridge
1912

Published April 1912

TO MY OLD MATES
OF MILWAUKEE HIGH SCHOOL
AND MILWAUKEE UNIVERSITY

THOUGH BOTH INSTITUTIONS
HAVE CEASED TO EXIST
THEIR NAMES REVIVE THE JOYS OF
THE GOLDEN AGE

PREFACE

A PROFESSOR in one of our leading universities, said a New York paper I received one day at my hotel in London, — I quote from memory, certain that I do not quote literally, — visiting Washington, in one of the interesting rooms of the Capitol came upon a marble statue inscribed "Baker." Whereupon — so the story ran — this learned professor — young, I dare say, probably familiar with the names of the heroes of the Peloponnesian War — asked, "Who was Baker? What did he do to get in here?" These questions prompted me to write this book.

But, years before our learned professor asked his questions I had reflected that those of us who knew General Baker, who came under the spell of his incomparable charm, and who retain recollections of his power and influence and achievements, are becoming few; and if one of us is to enlighten the professor — and others no better informed — it must be done soon. I wish some one better qualified than I had undertaken the task. To write the history of an important episode is — being a plain business man I will venture to use a business man's expression and say, "out of my line." However, I feel that what I have done, though poorly, would better be done poorly than not at all. The defects in my book will be apparent to the few who shall read it. Those few may not all be aware, as I am, of how much more might have been brought in. Still, I trust I have put together enough to prove that the story of the secession conspiracy on the Pacific Coast deserved to be told. And until some one tells it better, let this stand. I shall be gratified if I have done something to rescue from an unmerited oblivion the name of Edward D. Baker, — as gentle and pure and unselfish and generous and eloquent and valiant a man as ever cheerfully gave his life for a noble cause.

A precious little book entitled "Sketch of the Life and Public Services of Edward D. Baker," written and published by Joseph Wallace (Springfield, Illinois, 1870), must always be the main source of knowledge of the events of General Baker's career, especially of his early life. I have borrowed from it freely. I have also made much use of Hubert Howe Bancroft's History. I have not always used quotation marks because I have generally preferred to condense statements or slightly alter expressions. Scrapbooks which I made while the stirring occurrences herein described were being daily reported in the newspapers have been of service; but I have not relied implicitly on scrapbooks. I have been aided by Winfield J. Davis, of Sacramento, recently deceased, and my old friend William H. Fleming, of Philadelphia, in collecting and verifying facts. In that matter I am under many obligations to Miss Carrie Baker Hopkins, of Seattle, a granddaughter of General Baker.

I am reminded — of what is purely a coincidence — that I am writing this preface on the Fiftieth Anniversary of the death of General Baker on the battlefield of Ball's Bluff.

E. R. K.

BROOKLYN, NEW YORK,
21st October, 1911.

CONTENTS

CHAPTER VII

CHAPTER VIII

CHAPTER IX

CHAPTER X

CHAPTER XI

CHAPTER XII

CHAPTER XIII

CHAPTER XIV

CHAPTER XV

ILLUSTRATIONS

THE CONTEST FOR CALIFORNIA IN 1861

HOW COLONEL E. D. BAKER SAVED THE PACIFIC STATES TO THE UNION

CHAPTER I

SOCIAL AND INDUSTRIAL CONDITIONS

I PROPOSE to describe the secession movement on the Pacific Slope, and to show how, mainly through the efforts and influence of Edward D. Baker, the plot to involve California, Oregon, and contiguous territories with the South, in 1861, was frustrated and the Pacific Coast was saved to the Union.

Social and industrial conditions on the Pacific Slope, especially in California, were unlike any that had ever been known in this country. Bancroft declares that society in California was "a gathering without a parallel in history."[1] It was a community of young men, effective for action but lacking the proverbial wisdom that develops only with the passing of years. There was an extensive representation of nationalities, — more so, even, than in New York; among many, ignorance of American institutions and ideas of government and entire

[1] Bancroft, vol. VI, p. 221.

absence of sympathy with American principles in religion and politics. Previous to the Civil War most manufactured articles were brought from the East, and there was but little of the sort of industrial population that grows up in manufacturing towns and is anchored to its comfortable cottages. Soil and climate were as favorable to agriculture and horticulture as the soil and climate of any state in the Union; yet the prosperity of the state was not based on its crops, as was the prosperity of Wisconsin, Minnesota, and Iowa, frontier states of the same period. The men of New York and New England who settled in the Northwest were the most enterprising of the communities from which they journeyed forth. The ranchmen of California were the boldest of the enterprising. They had come from the farms of the East, the plantations of the South, and in many cases from the prairies of the Northwest. In California they inhabited ranches. The very name indicated a changed environment and suggested fiery mustangs, dashing vaqueros, and other novel Spanish or Mexican features. The pioneers of the Northwest had their adventures by land and lake and river. The Californians had ten times as great. They sailed in cockleshells over two vast oceans, cut their perilous way through the deadly thickets of Panama and Nicaragua, weathered the boisterous Horn, or dragged for months across "the Plains" and over snow-capped mountains. Many of them, shipwrecked on the coast of Mexico, subsisted on roots and wild fruit for weeks while they trusted the guidance of the North Star as they forced their weary bodies toward their El Dorado. The emigrant to the Northwest was accustomed to work and inured to hardship. The California pioneer was experienced and developed in adventure. If a man had been "queer" or eccentric in the East his peculiarity was apt to run wild in the new community. The spirit of the country washed by the Mississippi was industry and contentment. The essence of California was a combination of mutability and recklessness. Cities were, to superficial appearance, like cities in other pioneer states. Churches flourished, — more generally, I should say, than they do at present. Schools were fairly well conducted. Newspapers treated coast affairs with talent, and in some instances displayed genius; but they were entirely without the advantages of telegraphic communication with the world outside, and they depended for exchanges on the mails that only once a fortnight came in the paddle-wheel wooden steamers that slowly ploughed their way up from Panama. Eastern newspapers often sold for a dollar each on their arrival; those that brought the tidings that California had been admitted to the Union as a state were snatched up at five dollars. Banks were frequently unstable — to the advantage of lawyers. Bench and bar compared favorably with the legal profession in any state of the Union. Theatres were no worse than they were in the Eastern States, and Forrest, Booth, Matilda Heron, and other stars sometimes appeared. Libraries were growing. Hospitals were established. The main roads, highways of the California Stage Company and the great freight wagons, were good. But the result of the infrequency of the mails and of the entire absence of telegraphic communication with other states and countries was the creation of a feeling of remoteness and separateness.

There was another element, — one never seen in "the States," — the miners; an element that did not settle down in one place to cultivate the arts and embellishments of civilized life; that was but little hampered with impedimenta in the way of families or property; that received the report of a "strike" of "pay dirt" one day, gathered its few utensils, and the next morning "vamoosed" and moved to the new "diggings." A writer of early days, a chaplain of the United States Navy, who spent some time in the diggings, says: "I have never met with one who had the strength of purpose to resist these roving temptations. He will not swing a pick for an ounce a day with the rumor of pounds ringing in his ears. He shoulders his implements to chase this phantom of hope." [1] Many miners were of the best men of Eastern and Southern communities; many were of the worst. Here they delved side by side in unavoidable intimacy. By day they worked in gravel or stood in cold and muddy water. By night they reposed on hard beds sheltered in ragged tents, or "bunked" by scores in

[1] *Three Years in California*, p. 292.

rickety cabins. They performed their ablutions at the same pump, ate poor food that had been badly cooked, and existed without any of the luxuries or comforts to which they had been accustomed. The Reverend Walter Colton, from whom I just quoted, mentions prices and the quality of food. "We pay at the rate of $400 a barrel for flour; $4 a pound for poor brown sugar; and $4 a pound for indifferent coffee. And as for meat, there is none to be got except jerked beef, which is the flesh of the bullock cut into strings and hung up in the air to dry, and which has about as much juice in it as a strip of bark dangling in the wind from a dead tree." [1]

The historian Hittell says: "The character of the population was peculiar. It was composed almost exclusively of men — usually young, vigorous, and adventurous. There was a roughness about the kind of life they were compelled to lead, the clothing they were compelled to wear, and the food they were compelled to eat, which soon told upon them. There was a sort of recklessness and abandon that became common and characteristic, while, at the same time, helpfulness and generosity and a disposition to be accommodating were encouraged. Every one went armed; no one was willing to submit to much imposition or imagined wrong; life and limb were cheap; but at the same time there was an undercurrent of kindness which developed into a sort of chivalry, of sympathy, characteristic of the

[1] *Three Years in California*, p. 279.

so-called diggings alone. The typical miner was a large, strong, physically perfect man, with long hair and uncut beard, a slouch hat, woolen shirt, coarse pantaloons stuck inside the legs of long, heavy, hobnailed boots and supported at the waist with a leathern belt to which were slung, ready for instant use, a revolver and a bowie knife. Airs and pretensions were his abomination; and this feeling was carried so far that, though refined and respectable at heart, he set what ordinarily passes for refinement at defiance. His talk was laconic and directly to the point; but he emphasized it with oaths. He played cards; broke the Sabbath; was always ready for a carouse; and despised the very name of restraint. He exhibited the same tendency in the names which he gave and by which various of the mining-camps were popularly known. Among these were such as Whiskey Bar, Brandy Gulch, Poker Flat, Seven-up Ravine, Git-up-and-Git, Gospel Swamp, Gouge-Eye, Ground Hog's Glory, Blue-Belly Ravine, Loafer's Retreat, Petticoat Slide, Swell-Head Diggings, Nary Red, Hang-Town, Shirt-Tail Cañon, Red-Dog, Coon Hollow, Skunk Gulch, Piety Hill, and Hell's Delight." [1] Equally humorous and disrespectful were many of the appellations applied to persons as substitutes for the names they had brought with them — as, Sandy Pete, Long-legged Jack, and Dutchy.[2]

Mr. Colton, who had been detailed to act as

[1] Hittell (San Francisco, 1885), vol. II, pp. 735, 736.

[2] Bancroft, vol. VI, p. 228.

alcalde of Monterey, left his office to a subordinate for a time, and who, as has just been stated, "roughed it" in the panoply of a miner, had a less favorable opinion of the class. Writing in his diary on the eighth of November, 1848, while the realities of mining were all about, he says: —

"Some fifty thousand persons are drifting up and down these slopes of the great Sierra, of every hue, language, and clime, tumultuous and confused as a flock of wild geese taking wing at the crack of a gun, or autumnal leaves strewn on the atmospheric tides by the breath of the whirlwind. All are in quest of gold; and with eyes dilated to the circle of the moon, rush this way and that as some new discovery or fictitious tale of success may suggest. Some are with tents and some without; some have provisions and some are on their last ration; some are carrying crowbars, some pickaxes and spades; some washbowls and cradles; some hammers and drills; and powder enough to blow up the Rock of Gibraltar. . . .

"But I was speaking of the gold-hunters here on the slopes of the Sierra. Such a mixed and motley crowd — such a restless, roving, rummaging, ragged multitude — never before roared in the rookeries of man. As for mutual aid and sympathy — Samson's foxes had as much of it, turned tail to, with firebrands tied between. Each great camping-ground is denoted by the ruins of hovels and shanties, the bleaching bones of the dead, disinhumed by the wolf, and the skeleton of the culprit still swinging in the wind from the limb of a tree, overshadowed by the raven." [1]

Once in a while human nature demanded entertainment, and "the boys" danced to the invigorating strains of the fiddle, bewhiskered men swinging around heavily booted other men for partners. Whatever taste for dancing the immigrants had brought with them from the States was enhanced by association with the natives, especially the señoritas. Chaplain Colton declares that "the dance and a dashing horse are the two objects which overpower all others in interest with the Californians." [2] He mentions meeting a native when an American force had taken possession of Monterey: "I met a Californian to-day with a guitar from which he was reeling off a merry strain, and I asked him how it was possible he could be so light-hearted while the flag of his country was passing to the hands of the stranger. 'Oh,' said the Californian, 'give us the guitar and a fandango and the Devil take the flag.'" [3]

Hittell describes a fandango at the Russian farm of Knebnikoff: "The occasion was the Saint's Day of Hélène de Rotschoff, wife of the Russian comandante. A party of about thirty persons, male and female, started in the morning, rode all day, and in the evening arrived at their destination; there they danced all night, all the next day, and all the following night; and the following, or third day, at

[1] *Three Years in California,* pp. 314, 315.

[2] *Ibid.,* p. 20.

[3] *Ibid.,* p. 191.

sunup, they started on the journey back home again. The distance ridden in this instance, counting both ways, was some eighty or one hundred miles; but for a dance lasting several days it was regarded an easy thing to go one hundred leagues or more.[1]

Letters from the States were a month old when they arrived. There was as yet no delivery of mails. In San Francisco the line at the post-office began to form the day before the steamer was signaled from Telegraph Hill. Places well forward fetched a hundred dollars or more. By the time the pouches were received at the post-office the assemblage of expectant men, women, and children stretched out for more than half a mile. If left in the mail letters usually reached the mines in three or four days. Wells, Fargo & Co., who for years competed with the Government, could be relied on to deliver letters a day earlier. But, often, when mail arrived at its destination the persons addressed were gone, — "prospecting" or "trying their luck" elsewhere. Thus men became isolated; home ceased to exercise its blessed restraints, and the pure influences of the family were weakened or altogether lost. Men became negligent of dress — of everything. The common apparel, as Hittell relates, was a pair of boots that extended above the knee, a pair of trousers tucked into the boots, a rough flannel shirt, and a broad-brimmed, soft felt hat. A man in a mining-camp possessed of a white linen shirt was often asked for the loan of his "boiled shirt" to

[1] Hittell (1885), vol. II, p. 507.

grace some social occasion. The emigrant to Wisconsin kept a shotgun or rifle to bring down game as food for his family. The California miner carried his pistol to shoot any man who tried to "jump" his "claim," who cheated him at cards, or who questioned his veracity. What with the absence of the natural refining elements of civilized society, the craze for gold, so often ending in embittering disappointment, and the depression caused by the prevailing chills and fever, men accepted solace in whatever form offered, — the flowing bowl, the gambling-den, and the company of lewd women.

Hittell refers at some length to the prevalence of gambling. Describing the convention which met to form the state constitution, he refers to the proposal to prohibit lotteries and the sale of lottery tickets. Delegate Price opposed the prohibition as impolitic, and said: "The people of California were essentially a gambling people and it was no use to endeavor to deny it. Every public house had its faro and its monte tables, licensed by law wherever there was any law. These tables were constantly crowded. Were lotteries more immoral than such establishments? Had any of the gentlemen who cast up their hands in horror of lotteries denounced gambling to their constituents?"

Delegate Halleck (afterwards the noted major-general) said that "though the people might be a gambling community it was not well to create a gambling state."

Delegate Moore opposed prohibiting lotteries because "he was in favor of the broad and general principles of religious freedom!" [1]

The prohibition was finally incorporated in the constitution; but ten years later I should say that every form of gambling, except the prohibited lottery, was as common as the licensed sale of drink.

But — and here the cities felt an influence that differentiated them from Eastern cities — the miner's great reaction from his hard and cheerless life was in an occasional trip to some city — best of all to "The Bay." His money was "gold dust," which was kept in buckskin bags and weighed out for payment on the basis of sixteen dollars for the ounce. He had come to town for a spree, and he was accommodated with entertainment of all sorts — except good sorts — as long as his dust held out. To meet the demands of such customers garish and resplendent establishments were maintained where every form of dissipation was purveyed. Gambling-houses were licensed by the municipalities. Other forms of vice flourished by general knowledge and without governmental tax or hindrance.[2] The miner's holiday at an end, he returned to his desperate vocation. Aside from these occasional

[1] Hittell (1885), vol. II, pp. 763, 764.

[2] Dr. Gaius L. Halsey, who went out from New York State at an early day, repeats some interesting statements in a volume of reminiscences published in 1902. A tent used as a gambling resort in one of the mining towns paid a rental of $40,000 a year. A two-story frame building chiefly used for gambling purposes rented for $120,000 a year.

debauches two things made his life endurable: quinine and a sense of humor, — humor which was often rude and uncouth. In many "camps" there was not one decent woman; yet respect for the sex survived. One of the early clergymen describes his arrival in San Francisco: "We drove through what is now Washington Street, and coming to the corner of the Plaza, then a sandy, empty lot, my attention was drawn to a group of Frenchmen marching along what was called the sidewalk. Their leader pointed to the sandy space. 'Voila, Messieurs, la place royale!' he cried, in the mean time taking off his hat when seeing ladies in a carriage. All followed his example and cried lustily, 'Vivent les dames!' Ladies were indeed scarce in San Francisco, and on our road up Washington Street, through Stockton, many were the men who ran to the front doors of their shanties to have a view of the remarkable occurrence."[1]

Stephen J. Field, long a justice of the United States Supreme Court, in an interesting volume of reminiscences describes an instance of this respect. When the settlers at Nye's Ranch found it necessary to have a local government they met to organize a city. "Some one proposed that a name should be adopted for the new town. One man suggested Yubafield, another Yubaville. [It was in Yuba County, on the Yuba River, a few miles below Yuba Dam.] A third urged the name Circumdoro (surrounded with gold, as he trans-

[1] *Checkered Life*, p. 337.

lated the word), because there were mines in every direction roundabout. But there was a fourth, a solid and substantial old man, evidently of kindly domestic affections, who had come out to California to better his fortunes. He now rose and remarked that there was an American lady in the place, the wife of one of the proprietors; that her name was Mary; and that in his opinion her name ought to be given to the town, and it should be called, in her honor, Marysville. No sooner had he made the suggestion than the meeting broke out into loud hurrahs; every hat made a circle around its owner's head, and we christened the new town Marysville without a dissenting vote." [1]

At the same time an *ayuntamiento* (town council) was elected and Mr. Field was chosen first alcalde. It was urged against Mr. Field that he was a newcomer,—he had been in the place only three days, while his opponent had resided there twice as long. But Mr. Field had bought land; his stability had been thus proved; and he had a majority of nine votes.[2]

"The alcalde," says Judge Field, "was a judicial officer under the Spanish and Mexican laws, having a jurisdiction something like that of a justice of the peace, but in the anomalous condition of affairs in California at that time, he, as a matter of necessity, assumed and exercised very great powers." [3]

Judge Field narrates several interesting incidents in his law practice and his experience as alcalde.

[1] *Early Days in California*, p. 25. Printed for private distribution.

[2] *Ibid.*, p. 24.

[3] *Ibid.*, p. 24.

He was especially embarrassed with men convicted of crimes. There was no jail, so he resorted to public flogging. It was bad, but not so bad as the only alternative — a lynch-law hanging. For the community demanded penalties for offenses.

Several of the alcaldes were men of learning, of wisdom, and of probity, but not all. An early judge located in San Francisco would sit in his court, on an old chair tilted back, with his feet perched higher than his head, on a small mantel over the fireplace, and in that position, with a red shirt on, would dispense justice.[1]

Tender regard for childhood was manifested as occasion offered, and Bret Harte's story of "The Luck of Roaring Camp" might have been founded on fact. "The appearance of a little girl would be heralded like that of an angel, many a rugged fellow bending with tears of recollection to give her a kiss and press a golden ounce into her hand." [2]

Creed Haymond, a few years ago general counsel for the Southern Pacific Railroad, remembered that bells were rung and a general jollification was held in Auburn, Placer County, when the first girl was born in the town. The girl grew up and became Mrs. Haymond. There were many settlements, camps, towns, in the mining districts, where there were no children. The intimacies of pioneer life, of which I have spoken, and the absence of restraining elements, gave the rough humor free scope for demonstration, broke down social barriers, dulled

[1] Hittell (1885), vol. II, p. 778. [2] Bancroft, vol. VI, p. 233.

self-respect, and thus naturally destroyed reverence for superiors. Indeed, to this jocund society there was no thought of superiors. James W. Coffroth, editor, lawyer, orator, state senator, a familiar name throughout California, was stopped in the road, one night, by a highwayman. Mr. Coffroth calmly remonstrated and told who he was. "Go on, Jim," said the road agent, "I would n't take *your* money."[1] Fancy a New York highwayman addressing Mr. Choate as Joe! Probably Mr. Coffroth was partly to blame for any lack of deference. He was telegraphed for to go to Columbia to defend a man accused of murder and was asked what he would take to fight the case. He telegraphed back, "Brandy-and-water for three days."[2] Of course he counted on receiving a good money fee, but the joy of conflict was uppermost in his mind.

With lack of respect was resourcefulness in devices for defeating adversaries and expedients for winning contests. When Richard H. Daly ran for judge of Calaveras County friends of the opposing candidate posted in a conspicuous place a bill purporting to be signed by Daly and bearing this legend: "Notis — i announce i am a candidate for Kounty Jug."[3] It was effective. The "boys" revolted at such illiteracy and elected the other man.

A petition was started asking that the state capital might be located at Campo Seco, Sonora County. Something of a joke it was considered elsewhere;

[1] *Bench and Bar*, p. 306. [2] *Ibid.*, p. 306. [3] *Ibid.*, p. 371.

but as the capital had been changed repeatedly (one evidence of mutability), and a proposal for another change was before the legislature, everybody in Sonora County signed it. The document never was presented. Friends of a convicted murderer got hold of it, cut off the top, attached the signatures to a recommendation for pardon, and the man received executive clemency.[1]

A remarkable instance of readiness to be diverted, even among persons in official station, a disposition to convert a serious duty into a frolic, occurred in 1861. The legislature was in session and a United States senator was to be chosen to succeed Doctor Gwin. Friends of James A. McDougall believed that gentleman's chances were improving daily, but as the time for the election approached they were not sure they had pledges enough, and they wished for delay. Lee and Marshall's circus was in town, so one of Mr. McDougall's zealous supporters engaged the entire company for a continuous performance until the signal should be given that matters were arranged. All members of the legislature were invited, and refreshments, both solid and liquid, were supplied free and in abundance. The legislative chambers were deserted, and the fun went on for a day and a night. "It cost me $1700," said the friend, "but we got the pledges." [2]

The comic and the tragic lie side by side in the human heart. At no time was it all fun among the

[1] *Bench and Bar*, p. 307. [2] *Ibid.*, p. 258.

pioneers. At the period I shall try to depict there was also conflict and tragedy. I was witness to instances. One such occurred in the then prosperous town of Camptonville, on the Fourth of July in 1862. There had been the customary exercises in the morning, — reading of the Declaration of Independence, an oration, and singing. In the afternoon there was nothing to be done. All places of business were closed, except the saloons, in most of which games were openly going on, — poker, faro, and red-and-black. Union men had their favorite resorts; Southerners took their liquor and made their bets in other places. One saloon was especially favored by the men from Georgia Bar, a mining-camp just outside the town. "Billy" McGee, a son of Massachusetts, loyal to the Union, was passing this last-mentioned resort. One of the loungers uttered a disparaging remark. Mr. McGee instinctively turned his face toward the speaker. Quite as naturally his right hand slipped around to his hip pocket. A person making such a remark as Mr. McGee heard would naturally anticipate resentment. It doubtless occurred to Mr. McGee that he who fires first, even if he does not fire best, has the chance of gaining an advantage. Mr. McGee fired first. The Georgian was disabled, but not quite killed. Mr. McGee submitted to arrest and was charged with assault with intent to kill. At the hearing before the justice of the peace ex-Judge Stidger was brought over from Grass Valley to prosecute. I was forced to uphold the case of the patriotic defendant. Apprehensive that I might prejudice Mr. McGee's case, I advised him to waive examination, give bail, and await the action of the grand jury, when he could employ for counsel some one already admitted to practice law. Mr. McGee and his friends rejected the idea. "What! let them damned rebels drive us out of court! Not much! Go ahead and put up the stiffest fight you know how to." Under such instructions I appeared — while all Camptonville looked on. For our first defense we pleaded that the discharge of Mr. McGee's pistol was accidental; but, knowing the justice to be a strong Union man, we placed our reliance on our second point. We argued that it was not only justifiable, but was as laudable to shoot a rebel in the street of Camptonville as if he were in uniform on the bank of the Chickahominy. Judge Stidger raged, and his secession sympathizers "imagined a vain thing," but Billy McGee was honorably discharged. In scores of places "Union" and "Secesh," common terms of the time, confronted each other as closely as in the main street of Camptonville.

I am portraying social conditions by illustrative incidents and references to representative men. Hubert Howe Bancroft gives a remarkable summary of crime and lawlessness. Stealing horses and cattle became so common as to diminish the value of those animals fifty per cent. Some farmers lost all their teams. One journal said there were more than one thousand men who made horse-stealing a regular business. Highway robbery was common. From 1849 to 1854 inclusive forty-two hundred murders were committed in California. In San Francisco there were twelve hundred, and only one conviction. Murder, says Bancroft, was to be so sheltered and defended that the bowie-knife chivalry might have their safety in their own hands, whatsoever lives they might choose to take. The worst men sought office and were supported by those who intended to use them for nefarious purposes. A Botany Bay convict was a constable in one town; the county judge was a drunkard and debauchee; his successor could not spell correctly. The judge of a district embracing three prosperous counties was declared to be the most dissolute man that ever wore the ermine. It was especially difficult to bring a case to trial if the accused was a Southerner. In one case where the courts refused a change of venue the legislature passed an act granting the change. Reckless legislation during the reign of the chivalry often obstructed justice and was fruitful of crimes. In such a state of affairs it is not surprising that in many localities the people occasionally resumed the sovereign power, in disregard of the faithless or inefficient men they had placed in office, and enforced justice, though they proceeded by unlawful means. There were numerous hasty lynchings, but usually, when the law's delay in dealing with criminals became intolerable, the mass of good citizens met together, elected officers, gave accused persons immediate trials, and, for such as were convicted, suitable penalties were promptly inflicted. Such proceedings were outside the law, but they were conducted in a decorous manner, for the public safety.[1]

The first vigilance committee in San Francisco was organized in 1851, and it dispensed justice several months. The "Great Vigilance Committee," of which William T. Coleman, the eminent merchant, was chairman, was formed in May, 1856. This committee, comprising several thousand members, hanged several rogues and banished or frightened away scores of others. The Governor of the state endeavored to suppress the committee, and for that purpose appointed William T. Sherman, then engaged in banking in San Francisco (afterwards the great Union general), major-general of the state militia. Sherman could do nothing, for nearly every militiaman had joined the Vigilance Committee. The Governor tried to obtain the aid of General Wool, commander of the Regular Army forces stationed in the vicinity of San Francisco, and of Captain Farragut, commandant of Mare Island Navy Yard, but neither officer felt it his duty to intervene.

There were many exciting occurrences. Perhaps the most interesting incident was the arrest and imprisonment of the chief justice of the highest

[1] Bancroft, vol. VII, chapter IX. Much of this is in Bancroft's own terms.

court in the state, David S. Terry. Terry had no sympathy with the committee, which he described as "damned pork merchants." One day in June he interfered with the committee police, who were making an arrest. "In the scuffle Judge Terry drew a knife and stabbed Hopkins, a committee officer."[1] Terry was incarcerated several weeks while his victim hovered between life and death. When it was deemed certain that Hopkins would recover there was an anxious debate over the disposal to be made of the eminent prisoner. Mr. Coleman declared that he was "a white elephant." Many insisted that he should be punished by the committee. Senator Broderick argued that the conviction and punishment of a man of such exalted official position would be likely to arouse the national authorities and thus perhaps lead to the dissolution of the committee. Broderick's counsel prevailed and Terry was discharged. Professor Royce (who is not responsible for all these details) concludes his lucid and admirable account of this great movement with this observation: "The first real test of the success of the committee in its one true work, which was to agitate for a reform in municipal society and politics, came at the autumn elections, when the people sustained the whole movement by electing city officers to carry on in a legal way the reform which had been begun without the law; and thenceforth, for years, San Francisco

[1] Royce, p. 462.

was one of the best governed municipalities in the United States."[1]

Nor were the benefits confined to San Francisco. Other cities were suddenly brought up to a fair state of civilization and order.

[1] Royce, p. 464.

CHAPTER II

POLITICAL CONDITIONS

In politics, also, conditions were unique and interesting. There were no citizens native to the state — there had not been time for California children to grow to maturity — except the Mexicans who remained after California was wrested from Mexico. Many of these were lawlessly deprived of lands by newcomers, and their appeals to the United States authorities for redress were long ignored. Back of that rankled resentment at the means by which California had been conquered and torn from its easy-going relation to Mexico. Not very ardent, these natives, for the Government at Washington. Many of the pioneer immigrants were equally disaffected, because the Government hesitated to confirm them in the possession of fertile acres and valuable lots they had got away from the natives. Mr. Colton, asserts also, that "from the day the United States flag was raised in this country she has been the victim of the most unrelenting oppression. Her farmers were robbed of their stock to meet the exigencies of war, and her emigrants forced into the field to maintain the conquest"; and he goes into details relative to the treatment of California by the National Government.[1] Other causes of dis-

[1] *Three Years in California,* p. 397.

content were insufficient mails and general neglect. Although California was ceded to the United States by the treaty which concluded the Mexican War, — February 2, 1848, — the United States for several years did nothing whatever toward providing a government for the country — except as President Polk, without authority, appointed a governor. Efforts were made to persuade Congress to act; but the South was determined that slavery should be permitted in California and the Northern representatives were equally determined that it should not; so Congress adjourned with nothing done.

Withdrawal from the Union was a familiar proposition long before the secession movement of 1861. Mr. Colton declared, in his book written previous to 1850, from which I have already quoted, that if Congress failed to assist an overland railroad project of that day "such a dereliction of duty, so apparent, would erelong, as a natural if not necessary consequence, create an independent nation on the Pacific."[1] Independence was broached, also, in the Great Vigilance Committee.

As soon as it became apparent that there was to be a struggle in Congress, and that the adoption of a bill organizing a government might be delayed a long time, the Americans in California began to discuss the subject of organizing a government for themselves. Hittell states that the first public meeting to espouse the purpose was held at San

[1] *Three Years in California*, p. 456.

José on the eleventh of December, 1848, and that it recommended the assembling of a constitutional convention in the following January. Colton says that at "the first great meeting on this subject, held in Monterey in January, 1849," he was called upon to draft resolutions setting forth the conditions of the country and providing for the election of delegates to a convention.[1] Similar meetings were held in San Francisco in December (the month preceding the Monterey demonstration), which resolved that Congress had been trifling with the subject of a government for California; that there was no more time to be lost; that immediate steps should be taken by the people themselves to provide a government; and calling on other sections to elect delegates to a convention.[2] However, it was not until the first of September, 1849, that a convention of elected delegates assembled to form a constitution. Many subjects that no longer survive to vex such assemblies were debated, — land titles, dueling, lotteries, gambling, slavery, — and reports of the proceedings are very interesting. The outcome was the form of a complete state government. Arizona and New Mexico, which came to the United States pursuant to the same treaty that attached this remoter possession to the Union, have remained territories to the time of this writing; their governors appointed by the President; with no senators; their delegates to the House of Repre-

1 *Three Years in California*, p. 456.

2 Hittell (1885), vol. II, pp. 706, 707.

sentatives permitted to speak but not allowed to vote. The Californians had no idea of waiting. Having provided for a state they went ahead as if their state was complete, and on the thirteenth of November held an election, when the constitution was ratified and a governor and legislature were chosen. Meantime Mr. Polk's term of office had expired and General Taylor had become President. Within a month of his assuming office President Taylor sent the Honorable Thomas Butler King, a Member of Congress from North Carolina, to the coast to assure the people of the President's intention to do all that lay in his power to promote their happiness and welfare. It is significant that Mr. King's instructions included details as to how he should coöperate with the military and naval officers in the event of an attempt to alienate any portion of the newly acquired territory "or to establish an independent government within its limits."[1] Apparently the Government in Washington feared that neglect of the distant people might have suggested to those people the desirability of independence. They were entitled to order; for all that the Government had done they might have weltered in anarchy and disorder. Notwithstanding the President's recommendation of favorable action on California's petition for recognition, there was a vigorous contest over the question. The number of slave states, and thus the slave state vote in the Federal Senate, had been

[1] Hittell (1885), vol. II, pp. 809, 810.

equal to the number of free states and their votes. If California were admitted as a free state the balance of power would be destroyed. John C. Calhoun, rousing himself from a mortal sickness, made his last great oratorical effort on this subject. Rising in his seat, in great pain, he said he was unable, on account of his physical weakness, to deliver personally what he had to say; and, turning to James M. Mason, of Virginia, asked him to read the speech he had prepared in writing. It was a masterly production in all the arts that go to make up a chaste and finished oration; but, like Calhoun's arguments in general, it was based upon fundamental fallacies. He was opposed to the admission of California as a state, and argued that it should be remanded back to the condition of a territory. It might be, he continued, that California would not submit to be remanded back to the condition of a territory. It might be that the so-called state, as it had organized without authority, would refuse to obey authority. This was possible, but it was not probable, and it would be time, when it refused, to decide what was to be done.

Daniel Webster answered Calhoun. He had always been opposed to the acquisition of more territory. He believed in the Spartan maxim: Improve, adorn what you have; seek no further. He had therefore opposed the annexation of Texas. But Texas had been annexed, and at the same time a solemn compact had been entered into in reference to slavery; not by him but by representatives of the Nation,—and he was in favor of living up to it. But, so far as California and the territory acquired from Mexico were concerned, slavery was excluded from them by the laws of nature. He had heard the South complain and he had heard the North complain. Both were partly in the right and both were largely in the wrong. So far as the restitution of fugitives from service was a part of the Constitution, recognized by the law of the land, it should be enforced, — fairly, squarely, and rigidly enforced; but so far as the exclusion of slavery from the new territories was concerned, or the loss of what was called the equiponderance of representation, the South had no right to complain.

Others also took part in the debate. Of these William H. Seward, of New York, was the most prominent. He was for admitting California unconditionally and at once. To him California, coming from the clime where the West dies away into the rising East; California, which bounded the empire and the continent; California, the faithful Queen of the Pacific, in robes of freedom gorgeously inlaid with gold, was doubly welcome. If statehood was not then granted it might never be granted. California might not abide delay. He would not say that it contemplated independence, because he knew it did not anticipate rejection. But either the Stars and Stripes must wave over its ports, or it must raise aloft a standard for itself. It would be no mean ambition, if it became necessary for its own protection, to found an independent

WILLIAM M. GWIN

nation on the Pacific. It was further away than the old colonies had been from England. It was out of the reach of railroads or unbroken steam navigation. Nor would it be alone. As California would go, so would Oregon go, and the whole Pacific Coast might be lost.[1]

Mr. Calhoun and President Taylor died while the question was pending, and it fell to Millard Fillmore, who succeeded General Taylor, to approve the bill admitting California as a state of the Union, which he did on the ninth of September, 1850.

While the debate was going on, John C. Frémont and William M. Gwin, who had been elected Senators, and Messrs. Wright and Gilbert, who had been chosen to the House, and who were in Washington waiting to be admitted to the bodies to which they were accredited, united in issuing a manifesto assuring Congress that California was loyal to the Union. Doubtless they were right. But the possibility of separation had been mentioned and even seriously discussed by prominent statesmen. It was in the air.

As population increased citizens who had migrated from Northern States were divided between parties, as they had been in the East. Nearly forty per cent of the population had come from slave states. They were not divided. They were solidly, fiercely on the side of the Democratic Party, — more Southern than the South itself. Concerning

[1] Hittell (1885), vol. II, pp. 814 to 818.

the peculiar institution of the South that for years supplied the chief incentive of parties, the feeling of this people was something like Senator Hoar's feeling about Benjamin F. Butler's funeral. The Senator was walking on Washington Street, Boston, one day, when a friend met him and asked if he was going out to Lowell to General Butler's funeral. "No," said the Senator, with a snap of emphasis. Then, as he was starting on, he added, "But I approve of it." The Southerners and their allies from the North were, also, effectively bound together by "the cohesive power of public plunder." During the administrations of Presidents Pierce and Buchanan every Federal official was required to be an unquestioning supporter of the groveling pro-slavery policy of these administrations, and was counted on to uphold the South to the last extremity. Over the oligarchy of subservient office-holders, the numerous company of obsequious expectants, and a mass of complaisant sympathizers — all comprising the Democratic Party — brooded the sinister figure of William M. Gwin, leader and autocrat. This astute, indefatigable, and unprincipled adventurer was born in Tennessee, practiced medicine for a time, and had represented a Mississippi district in Congress before he came to California, in 1848. In the Constitutional Convention of 1849 he took a leading part. His adroit persistence and command of resources won him an election to the United States Senate, where he took his place when California was admitted to statehood.

He retained his hold for ten years; and during that time, notwithstanding occasional instances of individual recalcitrancy, dominated the Democratic Party in the state. James A. McDougall was elected to Congress, but as he refused to fall in with the disunionist plans already meditated by Southern leaders, whose confidences were shared by Gwin, he was left at home at the end of his term. Every Federal official owed his position to Gwin, who maintained a system of espionage over his followers. This made him disliked, but it made him supreme — until his supremacy was disputed by David C. Broderick.

CHAPTER III

DAVID COLBRITH BRODERICK [1]

THIS remarkable man, the possessor of noble traits, who promoted correct principles, sometimes by reprehensible methods, was born of Irish parents, in Washington, District of Columbia, in the year 1820, in the birth month of Washington, Lincoln, and Baker. When he was six years old his family moved to New York, where the boy attended the public schools. He was not yet a voter when he began to take part in politics, and shortly after he became of age he was Tammany leader in the old Ninth Ward. In 1846 he was a candidate for Congress, but as certain Democrats ran another candidate against him a Whig was elected. Broderick, as did many active politicians, early joined the Volunteer Fire Department, and he soon became Foreman of Howard Engine Company No. 34, whose house was at the corner of Christopher and Hudson streets. The firemen had their rude etiquette, to violate which inevitably led to trouble. A fist fight involving members of two companies was an occur-

[1] Bancroft makes the middle name Colbert, as does Lynch, Broderick's latest biographer. Broderick's successor in the Senate gives it as Colbreth. See *Cong. Globe*, 1st Session, 36th Congress, part 1, p. 748. Shuck spells it Colbrith, and I am assured this is the manner used by Mr. Broderick in signing his will. — E. R. K.

rence at nearly every important fire. During many years after the Civil War there was an attendant of the United States Court in New York City (a man whose first name was the same as Broderick's), whose nose had been broken in one of these contests, and who, when he could be persuaded to tell the story, evinced some little pride that his fracture was the result of a blow from a speaking-trumpet in the hands of "Dave Broderick." In 1841 Broderick kept a saloon called "Subterranean Hall," and the following year a place called "Republican Hall." He was not a consumer of his own goods, and during his entire life was almost a total abstainer from liquors. When he was keeping the latter-named place it was noticeable that he was becoming serious and was reading a good deal, — history, politics, and even poetry. A man who knew him at that time told me he once saw Broderick come rushing out in his shirt sleeves from his lodging over the saloon, repress a disturbance, throw the disturbers into the street, and then return to his books.

At last there came a time when Broderick decided to change his vocation and put his past out of sight. When leaving New York he said to his friend Sickles,[1] "I will never return unless as United States Senator." He arrived in San Francisco in June, 1849. William M. Gwin, shortly before he went to California, remarked to Stephen A. Douglas, "I will be back in a year as Senator." So when Baker was leaving the national capital, in 1849,

[1] Later Major-General Daniel E. Sickles.

after it was determined that he was not to become a member of President Taylor's Cabinet, the Colonel declared he never would return to Washington unless he came as a senator. How many, I wonder, left the East for the land of Golden Dreams with that same determination! How few of us became Senators! But how many returned to the States!

Directly Broderick landed in San Francisco he obtained a position in the United States Mint. There being a great scarcity of coin "Broderick formed a business relationship with an assayer and at once began the manufacture of five and ten dollar gold pieces or 'slugs,' the intrinsic value of the metal contained in each coin relatively being only four dollars and eight dollars. These bore an inscription consisting simply of the date, location of coinage, and the value in dollars. They readily passed current in the community, for they were far more convenient and comfortable than parcels of gold dust, even if every one knew that the intrinsic value was something less than the face value. Tradespeople received and paid them freely. Only the last holders could suffer." Broderick "added to assaying the manufacture of jewelry and himself used a sledgehammer in the stamping-press." [1]

The newly arrived citizen immediately plunged into politics. He also took the lead in organizing a fire department and was elected foreman of Engine Company No. 1. It may be doubted whether worse

[1] Lynch, p. 49.

political conditions ever prevailed in any city in the United States than those in San Francisco at this time. Broderick determined to improve them. One man who stood by him was William Walker, later the noted filibuster of Nicaragua. Another, who appreciated him from the first, was Stephen J. Field. But the men who held the offices, or hoped to, the men who held positions and expected promotion, frowned on this audacious and meddlesome newcomer; so Broderick was forced to take up with such fellows as he could persuade to join him. Among his henchmen were two notorious prize-fighters, — McGowan and "Billy Mulligan." To a friend who criticized the employment of such agents Broderick replied, "You respectable people I can't depend on. You won't go down and face the revolvers of those fellows who stuff the ballot-boxes and steal the tally-lists, so I have to take such material as I can get hold of. I have to keep these fellows to aid me." [1] Meantime Broderick gave little time to social intercourse but devoted every possible hour to study. A writer pronounced him a "lone, strange, extraordinary man." He seldom smiled, indulged in no pleasantries, was never gay but often gloomy. He gave his confidences to few and mourned that he had no kindred left on earth. The few friends who were admitted to intimacy loved him fervently. Such as were not on his side were generally bitter in their antagonism. Broderick himself was a good hater as well as a faithful friend.

[1] Merrill's Statement as quoted by Bancroft, vol. VI, p. 678.

His predominating trait was intense earnestness. His life was full of adventures.

He had not been long in San Francisco when he was elected to the state senate. He immediately became one of the foremost members and was chosen president *pro tem.* The governor having resigned and the lieutenant-governor become governor, the legislature elected Broderick lieutenant-governor — scarcely a year after his arrival in the state. It is conceded that he made a most excellent presiding officer. He was an untiring worker, but the thing that attracted most notice during his first session had nothing to do with his public duties. Stephen J. Field was at the time a member of the assembly from Marysville. He had been challenged to fight a duel by another assemblyman named Moore, — a Southerner. Judge Field disapproved of that method of settling disputes, but the sentiment in political circles approved of it, and as a public man he felt it incumbent upon him to stand as a champion of his party, and fight. He could find no one to act as his second, several pleading that they did not know the code. While in this predicament the Judge chanced to walk into the senate chamber one evening, where he found Broderick sitting at his desk, writing. The two were acquainted, although but slightly. Broderick looked up, and said, "Why, Judge, you don't look well; what is the matter?" Judge Field answered, "I do not feel well, for I have n't a friend in the world." Broderick replied, "What is it that worries you?"

When the matter had been explained Broderick said, "My dear Field, I will be your friend in this affair. Go and write a note to Moore at once and I will deliver it." Drury Baldwin was Moore's "friend," and upon him Broderick called with Judge Field's note. Baldwin replied that his principal had given up doing anything further in the matter. Broderick then declared that Field would rise in his place in the House, and after giving a statement of all that had passed, call Moore a liar and a coward. "Then," said Baldwin, "Judge Field will get shot in the same moment." "In that case," replied Broderick, "there will be others shot." When the House met the next day Field was in his seat, prepared to do as Broderick had said, who sat behind him with several of his personal friends, all armed. Just as Field rose Moore also rose, and the Speaker recognized him. He made a complete apology, — and there was no more challenging during that session.[1]

Judge Field in his reminiscences tells of another incident, which occurred the following spring. Broderick called on the Judge at his hotel, in San Francisco, and the two were taking wine at the bar, when Broderick suddenly threw himself before Judge Field and with great violence pushed him out of the room. Judge Field was astonished and indignant, and demanded, "What does this mean, Mr. Broderick?" Broderick explained that Vi. Turner, a well-known desperado, had drawn from

[1] *Early Days in California*, p. 77.

beneath his Spanish cloak a navy revolver and leveled it at Judge Field, seeing which, Broderick threw himself between them and carried off the intended victim.[1]

During an election day Broderick was watching at the polls in one of the San Francisco districts. Disputes were frequent, and the feud vigorous and vindictive, between the contending Democrats. Colonel Balie Peyton confronted Broderick, and a violent altercation ensued over the ballots. Peyton thrust his hand in his hip pocket and the handle of a pistol appeared. But Broderick, who had his right hand in his trousers pocket, remarked coldly and deliberately, "Move, Colonel Peyton, and you are a dead man." Peyton then knew that Broderick had his hand on a derringer which carried an ounce bullet, and which was small enough to be fired from his pocket without drawing, — a most deadly weapon in a street brawl. Peyton stood motionless until Broderick said, "There is no need for us to kill each other or to have a personal difficulty. Let us take a boat on the bay or a walk under the trees, and talk over this matter. If we cannot agree, then I am ready to fight to the death or to any extent that you may elect." Peyton consented, and a few minutes' conversation apart made them friends for life.[2]

Like many Tammany men, Broderick was a good judge of real estate, and his sagacity in this enabled

[1] *Early Days in California*, p. 82.

[2] Lynch, p. 85.

him, together with his other engagements, to acquire what for that time was considered a large fortune. But all the time his aim was for the Senatorship. More than once he contested. Once he succeeded in preventing Gwin's reëlection, but, unable to control a majority of votes, he brought about an adjournment of the session before any choice was made, and for a year there was but one Senator from California. When the legislature met in 1857 there were thus two Senators to be elected. Gwin expected the greater prize; Broderick determined to try for it. It is plain that there was finally a deal between the two, against the field. Broderick got the long term; Gwin was chosen for the vacancy. When the new Senator presented himself to President Buchanan he was frigidly received. He said to a friend, "It was cold without but icy within." Gwin may have observed his pledge to allow Broderick to control the patronage, but Gwin's friends, intimate and influential at the White House, were determined to thwart Broderick in any purpose he may have cherished of building up a machine in California to displace that established and managed by Gwin. The political divisions at the capital had long been accompanied by social segregation. Formal calls were sometimes exchanged between Southerners and such Northerners as had the temerity to differ from them respecting politics, but there was no sociable feeling between the two sets. Senator and Mrs. Gwin were in the political secrets and exclusive social circles of the "chivalry." It was believed that the Gwins spent seventy-five thousand dollars a year in maintaining their lofty rank and state. A fancy-dress ball given by them was the most elaborate function of the sort that had ever been seen in Washington. Bancroft declares, what was generally believed at the time, that Gwin was paid by the steamship companies to thwart or hinder the construction of the overland railroads.[1] The fraternity of chivalry took up the cause of Gwin and snubbed Broderick, — despising him, also, because he was the son of a stonecutter and had himself "worked at a trade." Broderick subsequently gave them ampler reason to dislike him.

On the fourth of March, 1858, Senator Hammond of South Carolina made the speech in which he characterized the laborers of the North as "white slaves" and "mudsills."[2] A fortnight later Mr. Broderick replied to Mr. Hammond in a speech that won plaudits for the California Senator all over the North and West. Replying to Mr. Hammond's characterizations Mr. Broderick said: —

"Many Senators have complained of the Senator from South Carolina for his denunciations of laborers of the North as white slaves and the mudsills of society. . . . I suppose, sir, the Senator from South Carolina did not intend to be personal in his remarks, to any of his peers upon this floor. If I had thought so I would have noticed them at

[1] Bancroft, vol. VII, p. 264.

Cong. Globe, vol. 36, 1st Session, 35th Congress, p. 962.

the time. I am, sir, with one exception, the youngest in years of the Senators upon this floor. It is not long since I served an apprenticeship of five years at one of the most laborious mechanical trades pursued by man, — a trade that from its nature devotes its follower to thought but debars him from conversation. I would not have alluded to this if it were not for the remarks of the Senator from South Carolina, and the thousands who know that I am the son of an artisan and have been a mechanic would feel disappointed in me if I did not reply to him. I am not proud of this. I am sorry it is true. I would that I could have enjoyed the pleasures of life in my boyhood days; but they were denied to me. I say this with pain. I have not the admiration for the men of the class from whence I sprang that might be expected; they submit too tamely to oppression, and are too prone to neglect their rights and duties as citizens. But, sir, the class of society to whose toil I was born, under our form of government will control the destinies of this nation. If I were inclined to forget my connection with them, or to deny that I sprang from them, this chamber would not be the place in which I could do either. While I hold a seat here I have but to look at the beautiful capitals adorning the pilasters that support this roof to be reminded of my father's talent, and to see his handiwork." [1]

The greatest distinction of Senator Broderick, which has permanently established his fame, was

[1] Appendix, *Cong. Globe*, vol. 37, 1st Session, 35th Congress, p. 193.

his opposition to the outrageous attempt of President Buchanan and the pro-slavery party to force the Lecompton Constitution upon the unwilling people of Kansas. Only three Democratic Senators opposed this, Douglas, Stuart of Michigan, and Broderick. In the debate Mr. Broderick unmistakably disclosed on which side his sympathies lay in the conflict between freedom and slavery, and which course he would be certain to take as the paths separated and the lines became more and more sharply drawn. In his speech on the twenty-second of March he said: —

"In the passage of the Kansas-Nebraska Bill the rampart that protected slavery in the Southern territories was broken down. Northern notions, Northern ideas, and Northern institutions were invited to the contest for the possession of these territories. How foolish for the South to hope to contend with success in such an encounter. Slavery is old, decrepit, and consumptive; Freedom is young, strong, and vigorous. The one is naturally stationary and loves ease; the other is migratory and enterprising. There are six million people interested in the extension of slavery; there are twenty million freemen to contend for these territories, out of which to carve for themselves homes where labor is honorable."

Senator Broderick bitterly resented not only President Buchanan's treatment of him personally, but the President's subserviency to the slave power, at the time referring especially to the attempt to force the Lecompton Constitution upon Kansas. He said: —

"It is notorious that the people of a neighboring state were permitted to vote at this election, at such precincts and as often as they desired. The names of people are recorded in the poll-lists as having voted who had been dead for months. But why enumerate these disgusting details? The facts are before the people. They are known to the President. He continues to keep the men in office who are charged with the commission of these frauds. The result of all their enormity is before us in the shape of this Lecompton Constitution indorsed by him. Will not the world believe he instigated the commission of these frauds, as he gives strength to those who committed them? This portion of my subject is painful for me to refer to. I wish, sir, for the honor of my country, the story of these frauds could be blotted from existence. I hope, in mercy, sir, to the boasted intelligence of this age, the historian when writing a history of these times will ascribe this attempt of the Executive to force this constitution upon an unwilling people to the failing intellect, the petulant passion, and trembling dotage of an old man on the verge of the grave." [1]

An incident of this period throws a strong light upon the character of Broderick. Stephen A. Douglas, the famous Senator from Illinois, had been the leader of the Anti-Lecompton movement by such Democrats as refused to follow the Southern chiv-

[1] *Cong. Globe*, vol. 36, 1st Session, 35th Congress, p. 193.

alry. Bancroft, quoting F. F. Low (a prominent man of California), repeats the story, thoroughly believed in Washington, that Douglas at one time came near yielding to the Administration. Congressman John Hickman, hearing that Douglas intended to back down, went to Broderick's room and told him of it. Broderick, thunderstruck, raged like a lion. He refused, at first, to believe the story; then in his imperious way he ordered Hickman to find Douglas and bring him to his room. When Douglas came he found Broderick pacing the floor. "Mr. Douglas," said he, "I hear you propose to abandon the fight." Douglas answered, "I see no hope of success; they will crush us; and if they do there is no future for any of us, and I think we can agree upon terms that will virtually sustain ourselves." Broderick replied, "You came to me of your own accord, asking me to take this stand. I have committed myself against this infernal Lecompton Constitution. Now, if you desert me (with an oath), I will make you crawl under your chair in the Senate." Douglas resolved to stand firm and not to support the English Bill, on which he was wavering.[1]

Although Broderick and Gwin had taken opposite sides on the stirring question mentioned, the junior's treatment of Senator Gwin usually was decorous and free from rancor. "The latter was not very assiduous, while Broderick never missed a session or a committee meeting. Gwin rather

[1] Bancroft, vol. VII, p. 259.

carped at Broderick's oratorical accomplishments, while the latter replied that whenever the former commenced to read one of his dreary exhortations the chamber was deserted by all save the speaker, Broderick, and one more Senator. Broderick remained through courtesy and the other man through pity." [1] Some of Broderick's detractors started the story that his speeches were written by George Wilkes, — as absurd as the scatter-brained nonsense that would attribute Shakespeare's works to Francis Bacon.

Mr. Lynch fairly summarizes as follows: —

"As a senator Broderick not only advocated the enfranchisement of labor, but stood for the Homestead Law; for the endowment of mechanical and agricultural colleges by Congress; for the construction of a railway from the Missouri River to the Pacific Ocean; for the prosecution of peculators in all departments of the Government; and for general reform and retrenchment in public affairs. Among the special objects of his animadversions were grouped Indian agents, venal surveyors of public lands, jobbery by postmasters, and the rascally revenue collectors of the Administration, sparing not even Buchanan himself." [2]

A general election for state officers in California occurred in September, 1859. The break between the pro-slavery organization of the Democratic Party and the element that followed Douglas and Broderick was complete. Broderick, in hopes of

[1] Lynch, p 191. [2] *Ibid.*, p. 191.

attracting anti-slavery support, persuaded his followers to nominate a member of the new Republican Party for governor and also privately aided the canvass of Colonel E. D. Baker, one of the two candidates for Congress. However, the Republicans nominated a complete ticket and the pro-slavery party won a decisive victory. Milton S. Latham was elected governor. Latham was largely responsible for the scheme to cut the state in two, with the expectation that the southern half would be given over to slavery. He boasted that California possessed resources not belonging to any other state of the Union, and declared it was qualified for independence. In a public address he had asked: "Why should we trust to the management of others what we are able to do ourselves? Why depend on North or South to regulate our affairs? — and this, too, after the North and South have proved themselves incapable of living in harmony with one another?" [1]

For reasons of prudence the idea of uniting with the South — as Virginia and some of the later states to secede joined the Confederate Government at Montgomery — was kept in the background. California was to rebel if the South led the way, but was at first to unite with contiguous states and territories and set up the Pacific Republic. It was this Latham was preparing the public mind for, in his speeches and declarations.

[1] Bancroft, vol. VII, p. 260.

"For the first time Broderick canvassed the state, addressing the people. Very likely his sojourn in the Senate and contact with ready and fluent orators had furnished him with courage and a certain aptitude. He spoke frequently in a clear, sonorous voice, distinctly heard. His enunciation was deliberate and his elocution good. He seldom gesticulated and never played cadence with his sentences,—the orator's charm. Not a jest, not a smile, but intensely resolved; grand, gloomy, and peculiar, as Shiel said of Napoleon. He accused Gwin of several public transactions as Senator which were prompted by venal ambitions; he delved into details on these matters; challenged Gwin to a public debate before the populace; and summed up his sins and crimes with the phrase 'dripping with corruption.' Gwin, who was also active in the campaign, replied with vigor and acerbity, and the conflict became bitterly personal and acrimonious. Latham, who had been a candidate for Senator when Broderick and Gwin were elected, and who was now leading his campaign for the governorship, made a second antagonist of Broderick. He was of the North with Southern prejudices and predilections, and supported Gwin, for therein lay advancement; but he was neither loved by the one nor hated by the other to a pernicious degree."[1]

In a meeting at Shasta Broderick said: "I now return to Gwin, and I shall be brief. I will give you

[1] Lynch, pp. 76, 77.

the copy of the letter that I believe led to the death of W. L. Ferguson.[1] Do you believe it was for nothing that Ferguson's desk in the Senate Chamber at Sacramento was broken open immediately after his decease? On his deathbed Ferguson told General Estell where he could find the letter. A curse has followed that letter, and I now give it to the public that the curse may return to its author, — that its disgrace and shame may burn the brand upon his forehead even as plainly, as palpably as the scarlet letter burned upon the breast of Hester Prynne. Let Dr. Gwin or any of his set deny its authority and I will prove that he wrote it, letter for letter, column for column."[2]

The letter, written by Gwin to Broderick, was dated the eleventh of January, 1857. In it he made the following pledge: —

"Provided I am elected you shall have the exclusive control of this patronage, so far as I am concerned; and in its distribution I shall only ask that it may be used with magnanimity and not for the advantage of those who have been our mutual enemies and unwearied in their efforts to destroy us."[3]

A quarrel with graver results sprang up between Senator Broderick and David S. Terry. Terry, although chief justice of the supreme court of the

[1] A brilliant young member of the legislature, who, although a Democrat, had offended the "chivalry" and had been disposed of in a duel.

[2] Lynch, p. 196.

[3] *Ibid.*, p. 156.

state, saw no impropriety in making an active stumping tour. He was born on a cotton plantation in Kentucky and spent part of his youth on another in Mississippi. Thence he went to Texas and joined the forces of Sam Houston. Later he studied law and was admitted to the bar. He served under General Taylor in Mexico, and after the war entered California at the head of a company of Texans. He settled in the city of Stockton and began the practice of his profession. He at once became active in politics and was a rabid Southerner. At the beginning of the Civil War he went East and enlisted in the army of the Confederacy. He raised a regiment in Texas, and at one time was on the staff of General Bragg. After the collapse of the rebellion he resided for a time in Mexico, but in 1869 he returned to California and again took up the law. For a second wife he married the claimant of the Sharon estate. He was shot to death by Special Officer Nagle, who had been detailed to guard Justice Field, of the United States Supreme Court, and who saw Terry approaching the Justice with the evident and undoubted purpose of shooting him.

In the campaign of 1859 Judge Terry was especially abusive of the opponents of the regular Democratic organization. In one of his speeches, referring to the Douglas Democrats, he described them as "A miserable remnant of a faction, sailing under false colors, trying to obtain votes under false pretense. . . . They are the followers of one man, the chattels of a single individual whom they are ashamed of. They belong, heart and soul, body and breeches, to David C. Broderick. They are yet ashamed to acknowledge their master, and are calling themselves, forsooth, Douglas Democrats. . . . Perhaps I am mistaken in denying their right to claim Douglas as their leader. Perhaps they do sail under the flag of Douglas, but it is the banner of the Black Douglass, whose name is Frederick, not Stephen." [1]

Senator Broderick read this in his morning paper while breakfasting at the International Hotel in San Francisco, and remarked that he had at one time upheld Terry as the only honest man on the supreme bench, but he now took back his former opinion. Even in a community where the duel was frequent this remark was far short of sufficient ground for a challenge. However, there were immediately upstart efforts to embroil Broderick. It was common belief throughout the state that the chivalry had determined to make away with him, and it was agreed that Terry, who was a dead shot, would make a sure thing of it if he undertook the job. Terry, who had but a short time to serve before the expiration of his term of office, resigned, and at once sent his challenge. Mr. Lynch has been at great pains to ascertain and collate every fact relative to this, the most sensational tragedy that ever occurred on the Pacific Coast. The purpose of this book does not require that his elaborate narra-

[1] *Bench and Bar*, chapter XXI.

tive should appear in full, but I am mainly indebted to him for the account I shall give. It appears that Broderick's seconds, although cool, brave men, were entirely without experience in arranging a duel, and did not know that a man should be groomed for one as carefully as a horse is groomed for a race. The pistols were the Lafoucheux type, a well-known Belgian make, with barrels twelve inches in length. The stock or breech construction was different from that of American dueling-pistols. Hence the man who had never handled them nor adjusted the stock to his hand would be at a disadvantage. They had been used in an earlier duel in the state, when it was developed that the hair trigger of one of the pistols was so light and delicate that the pistol would be discharged even on a sudden jar or motion, without touching the trigger. When the duel was decided upon, Terry went to the owner of these pistols and together they practiced with them until the chivalrous judge doubtless became aware of the tricky fault in one of them.[1] At the meeting, which occurred in San Mateo County, about ten miles from San Francisco, Terry's seconds won the selection of weapons. Article VIII, providing for the choice of pistols, was not fulfilled, as Broderick's seconds did not demand it. Terry's seconds, aware of the difference in the pieces, selected one for their principal. Brod-

[1] These pistols subsequently came into possession of a friend of mine in New York City who corroborates the statement of the defect in one. —E. R. K.

erick's seconds stated in a public letter the day after the duel that had they known that one of the weapons was lighter on the trigger than the other they would not have permitted the duel. The day after, on his deathbed, Broderick said that he did not touch the trigger of the pistol as he raised it, but that the sudden movement in elevating his arm from the vertical position caused the weapon to explode and the bullet plunged into the ground. After Broderick's fall Terry said to Calhoun Benham, one of his seconds, "The wound is not mortal. I have hit two inches too far out." Broderick was shot on Tuesday morning and died Friday morning, the sixteenth of September. As he lapsed into death's lethargy he exclaimed, "I die; protect my honor." [1]

The death of Broderick and all the circumstances leading up to the occurrence aroused intense excitement throughout the state. Terry was arrested, but was admitted to bail. Trial was postponed from time to time, but was finally set down for a day in June, nearly ten months after the shooting. Then a change of venue to another county was granted. On the day fixed for the trial the witnesses for the prosecution were embarked in a sailing boat for the location of the court-house and were becalmed on San Francisco Bay, so that they were somewhat late in arriving. The district attorney did not request or even suggest a postponement or

[1] Some details are taken from the books of Oscar T. Shuck, of the San Francisco Bar.

a brief delay, but declared that he could not secure the attendance of his witnesses and therefore moved a *nolle prosequi*, which the presiding judge (who was afterwards impeached and removed for disloyalty) promptly granted. Terry was immediately released. The witnesses arrived shortly after.

Senator Broderick's funeral, on the eighteenth of September, drew together much the greatest public assemblage that had at that time ever taken place on the Pacific Coast. The state and city governments, the militia and the fire department, civic bodies and fraternal orders, almost the entire population of San Francisco, and thousands from other towns, united in the demonstration. No one but Colonel Baker could have been thought of to declare the general grief and utter the sentiments of the people. Baker's oration was equal to the occasion. Edward Stanly, one of the most eminent lawyers and highly respected citizens of California, said, "I have read no effort of that character, called out by such an event, so admirable, so touching, so worthy the sweet eloquence of Baker. It should crown him with immortality."

George Wilkes, a prominent publicist of the period, wrote: "At the foot of the coffin stood the priest; at its head, and so he could gaze fully on the face of his dead friend, stood the fine figure of the orator. . . . For minutes after the vast throng had settled itself to hear his words the orator did not speak. He did not look in the coffin, — nay, neither to the right nor left; but the gaze of his fixed eye was turned within his mind and the tear was upon his cheek. Then, when the silence was most intense, his tremulous tones rose like a wail, and with an uninterrupted stream of lofty, burning, and pathetic words he so penetrated and possessed the hearts of the sorrowing multitude that there was not one cheek less moistened than his own." Mr. Wilkes adds that when Colonel Baker had finished "the multitude broke into a general response of sobs."

Colonel Baker, after a few words of introduction, declared that it was not fit that such a man should pass to the tomb unheralded; it was not fit that such a life should steal unnoticed to its close; it was not fit that such a death should call forth no rebuke or be followed by no public lamentation. It was this conviction which impelled the gathering of this assemblage. "Around him are those who have known him best and loved him longest; who have shared the triumph and endured the defeat. Near him are the gravest and noblest of the state, possessed by a grief at once earnest and sincere; while beyond, the masses of the people whom he loved and for whom his life was given gather like a thundercloud of swelling and indignant grief."

The speaker here briefly narrated the main events of Broderick's life, and continued:—

"Up to the time of his arrival in California his life had been passed amid events incident to such a character. Fearless, self-reliant, open in his enmities, warm in his friendships, wedded to his opinions, and marching directly to his purpose, through and over all opposition, his career was checkered with success and defeat; but even in defeat his energies were strengthened and his character developed. . . . From that time there congregated around him and against him the elements of success and defeat, — strong friendships, bitter enmities, high praise, malignant calumnies; but he trod with a free and a proud step that onward path which has led him to glory and the grave. It would be idle for me at this hour and in this place to speak all that history with unmitigated praise; it will be idle for his enemies hereafter to deny his claim to noble virtues and high purposes."

After referring to some of the chief acts of legislation, Federal and state, in which Broderick had participated, Colonel Baker said: —

"It is impossible to speak within the limits of this address of the events of that session of the legislature at which he was elected to the Senate of the United States; but some things should not be passed in silence here. The contest between him and the present Senator[1] had been bitter and personal. He had triumphed. He had been wonderfully sustained by his friends and stood confessedly the first in honor and the first in place. He yielded to an appeal made to his magnanimity by his foe. If he judged unwisely he has paid the forfeit well. Never in the history of political warfare has any public man been so pursued; never has malignity so exhausted itself.

[1] William M. Gwin.

"Fellow citizens, the man whose body lies before you was your Senator. From the moment of his election his character has been maligned, his motives attacked, his courage impeached, his patriotism assailed. It has been a system tending to one end — and the end is here. What was his crime? Review his history — consider his public acts — weigh his private character — and before the grave incloses him forever judge between him and his enemies. As a man — to be judged in his private relations — who was his superior? It was his boast — and amid the general license of a new country it was a proud one — that his most scrutinizing enemy could fix no single act of immorality upon him. Temperate, decorous, self-restrained, he had passed through all the excitements of California unstained. No man could charge him with broken faith or violated trust. Of habits simple and inexpensive, he had no lust of gain. He overreached no man's weakness in a bargain and withheld from no man his just dues. Never in the history of the state has there been a citizen who has borne public relations more stainless in all respects than he. But it is not by this standard he is to be judged. He was a public man and his memory demands a public judgment. What was his public crime? The answer is in his own words: 'I die because I was opposed to a corrupt administration and the extension of slavery.' Fellow citizens, they are remarkable words, uttered at a very remarkable moment; they involve the history of his senatorial career and of its sad and bloody termination.

"When Mr. Broderick entered the Senate he had been elected at the beginning of a presidential term as the friend of the President-elect,[1] having undoubtedly been one of his most influential supporters. There were unquestionably some things in the exercise of the appointing power which he could have wished otherwise; but he had every reason to remain with the Administration which could be supposed to weigh with a man in his position. . . . But when in his judgment the President betrayed his obligations to his party and country — when in the whole series of acts in relation to Kansas he proved recreant to his pledges and instructions — when the whole power of the Administration was brought to bear upon the legislative branch of the Government in order to force slavery upon an unwilling people — then in the high performance of his duty as a senator he rebuked the Administration by his voice and vote and stood by his principles. It is true, he adopted no halfway measures. He threw the whole weight of his character into the ranks of the opposition. He endeavored to arouse the people to an indignant sense of the iniquitous tyranny of Federal power, and, kindling with the contest, became its fiercest and firmest opponent. Fellow citizens, whatever may have been your political predilections, it is impossible to repress your admiration as you review the conduct of the man who lies hushed in death before you. You read in his history a glorious imitation of the great popu-

[1] James Buchanan.

lar leaders who have opposed the despotic influences of power in other lands and in our own. . . .

"Fellow citizens, let no man suppose that the death of the eminent citizen of whom I speak was caused by any other reason than that to which his own words assign it. It has been long foreshadowed — it was predicted by his friends — it was threatened by his enemies; it was the consequence of intense political hatred. His death was a political necessity poorly veiled beneath the guise of a private quarrel. Here, in his own state, among those who witnessed the late canvass, who know the contending leaders; among those who know the antagonists on the bloody ground — here the public conviction is so thoroughly settled that nothing need be said. Tested by the correspondence itself there was no cause in morals, in honor, in taste, by any code, by the custom of any civilized land — there was no cause for blood. . . .

"In the contest which has just terminated in the state, Mr. Broderick had taken a leading part; he had been engaged in controversies very personal in their nature, because the subjects of public discussion had involved the character and conduct of many public and distinguished men. But Judge Terry was not one of these. He was no contestant; his conduct was not in issue; he had been mentioned but once, incidentally, — in reply to his own attack, — and, except as it might be found in his peculiar traits or peculiar fitness, there was no reason to suppose that he would seek any man's blood. . . .

"Fellow citizens, one year ago to-day I performed a duty such as I perform to-day, over the remains of Senator Ferguson, who died, as Broderick died, tangled in the meshes of the 'code of honor.' To-day there is another and more eminent sacrifice. To-day I renew my protest; to-day I utter yours. The 'code of honor' is a delusion and a snare; it palters with the hope of a true courage and binds it at the feet of crafty and cruel skill. It surrounds its victim with the pomp and grace of the procession, but leaves him bleeding on the altar. It substitutes cold and deliberate preparation for courageous and manly impulse, and arms the one to disarm the other. It may prevent fraud between practiced duelists, who should be forever without its pale, but it makes the mere 'trick of the weapon' superior to the noblest cause and the truest courage. Its pretense of equality is a lie; — it is equal in all the form, it is unjust in all the substance. The habitude of arms, the early training, the frontier life, the border war, the sectional custom, the life of leisure, — all these are advantages which no negotiation can neutralize and which no courage can overcome.

"But, fellow citizens, the protest is not only spoken in your words and in mine; it is written in indelible characters; it is written in the blood of Gilbert, in the blood of Ferguson, in the blood of Broderick; and the inscription will not altogether fade.

"With the administration of the code in this

particular case I am not here to deal. Amid passionate grief let us strive to be just. I give no currency to rumors, of which, personally, I know nothing; there are other tribunals to which they may well be referred, and this is not one of them.[1] But I am here to say that whatever in the code of honor or out of it demands or allows a deadly combat where there is not in all things entire and certain equality, is a prostitution of the name, is an evasion of the substance, and is a shield blazoned with the name of chivalry to cover the malignity of murder.

"And now as the shadows turn toward the east, and we prepare to bear these poor remains to their silent resting-place, let us not seek to repress the generous pride which prompts a recital of noble deeds and manly virtues. He rose unaided and alone. He began his career without family or fortune, in the face of difficulties. He inherited poverty and obscurity. He died a Senator in Congress, having written his name in the history of the great struggles for the rights of the people against the despotism of organization and the corruption of power. He leaves in the hearts of his friends the tenderest and the proudest recollections. He was honest, faithful, earnest, sincere, generous, and brave. He felt in all the great crises of his life that he was a leader in the ranks; that it was his high duty to uphold the interests of the masses; that he

[1] These, so far as they ultimately became established historical facts, are mentioned on pages 51 and 52.

could not falter. When he returned from that fatal field, while the dark wing of the Archangel of Death was casting its shadows upon his brow, his greatest anxiety was as to the performance of his duty. He felt that all his strength and all his life belonged to the cause to which he had devoted them. 'Baker,' said he — and to me they were his last words — 'Baker, when I was struck I tried to stand firm, but the blow blinded me, and I could not.' I trust it is no shame to my manhood that tears blinded me as he said it. Of his last hour I have no heart to speak. He was the last of his race; there was no kindred hand to smooth his couch or wipe the death damp from his brow; but around that dying bed strong men, the friends of early manhood, the devoted adherents of later life, bowed in irrepressible grief 'and lifted up their voices and wept.'

"But, fellow citizens, the voice of lamentation is not uttered by private friendship alone; the blow that struck his manly breast has touched the heart of a people, and as the sad tidings spread, a general gloom prevails. Who now shall speak for California? — who be the interpreter of the wants of the Pacific Coast? Who can appeal to the communities of the Atlantic who love free labor? Who can speak for masses of men with a passionate love for the classes from whence he sprang? Who can defy the blandishments of power, the insolence of office, the corruption of administrations? What hopes are buried with him in the grave!

"But the last word must be spoken, and the

imperious mandate of Death must be fulfilled. Thus, O brave heart, we bear thee to thy rest. Thus, surrounded by tens of thousands, we leave thee to the equal grave. As in life no other voice among us so rang its trumpet blast upon the ear of freemen, so in death its echoes will reverberate amid our mountains and valleys until truth and valor cease to appeal to the human heart.

"Good friend! true hero! hail and farewell."

Haun, the person who was appointed to succeed Broderick in the Senate, in announcing his predecessor's death spoke of him as "having fallen in an unfortunate conflict, which was engendered by the use of unguarded expressions by the deceased, personal in their character, towards another distinguished gentleman."[1] Senator Crittenden, of Kentucky, in his remarks, said, "In this body, so far as I could judge, and so far as my testimony may go, his conduct seemed to be that of an upright, bold, faithful public servant. . . . He spoke what he thought and he spoke it like a man. He was a man, and we shall not look upon his like again."[2] Senator Seward, of New York, also paid a fine tribute to the memory of the deceased Senator. He said in part: "Mr. President, the great national event of our day, I think, is the extension of our empire over the interior of a continent, from the border of Missouri to the Pacific Ocean. He who shall write its history will find materials copi-

[1] *Cong. Globe*, 1st Session, 36th Congress, part 1, p. 748.

[2] *Ibid.*, p. 748.

ous and fruitful of incidents upon the integrity of the American nation and destiny of the American people. He will altogether fail, however, if he do not succeed in raising Houston and Rusk and Broderick to the rank among organizers of our states which the world has assigned to Winthrop and Villiers, Raleigh and Penn, Baltimore and Oglethorpe. . . . I never have known a man more jealous of his honor, or one who could so ill endure to be an object of pity or compassion in misfortune or disappointment. I leave him, therefore, in his early grave, content to confine my expressions of grief within the bounds of sorrow for the loss of a friend, than whom none more truthful and honest survives; a senator, than whom none more incorruptible ever entered these halls; and a statesman, who, though he fell too soon for a nation's hopes, yet, like Hamilton, left behind him noble monuments well and completely finished."[1]

[1] *Cong. Globe*, 1st Session, 36th Congress, part 1, pp. 748, 749.

CHAPTER IV

INKLINGS OF SECESSION — EARLY MOVES IN THE GAME

GWIN, having seen his party triumph and his most troublesome opponent removed by assassination, arranged for a continuance of the espionage upon his army of office-holders and returned to the national capital. Speaking in the Senate, on the thirteenth of December, 1859, shortly after his arrival, he said:—

"I believe that the slaveholding states of this confederacy can establish a separate and independent government that will be impregnable to the assaults of all foreign enemies. They have the elements of power within their own boundaries and the elements of strength in those very institutions which are supposed in the North to be their weakness. . . . I say that a dissolution of the Union is not impossible, that it is not impracticable, and that the Northern States are laboring under a delusion if they think that the Southern States cannot separate from them either violently or peaceably; violently if necessary. They can take possession of all the public property within their limits and prepare against any aggression from the non-slaveholding states or any power that may choose to infringe upon what they conceive to be their rights.

DAVID COLBRITH BRODERICK

It is because I believe they can separate, and that they will separate in the event to which I have alluded, that I have referred to the speech of the Senator from Alabama as a warning to every man who loves this Union that now is the time to present the question in its true form, and that the election of a Republican President is the inevitable destruction of this confederacy."

Doctor Gwin reminded the Senate that although the recent elections had been favorable to the Republican Party in "every state on the Atlantic border" (a careless error, oblivious of the Carolinas, Georgia, and Florida), the Pacific States had not fallen in with that trend. Looking back upon the larceny of United States Government properties by the seceding states, it is obvious that Gwin was fully aware of the purpose of the secession leaders and came near making an indiscreet disclosure of that purpose. In closing his speech he referred again to the probability that the Southern States would "take possession of all the government establishments that are within their borders, as in my judgment they will, in the event of the election of a Republican President, *before his installation.*" He added, "By waiting they put themselves in the power of the Federal Government; but by preparing for the event in advance they put it out of the power of any government on the face of the earth to inflict on them what they conceive to be a serious or fatal injury." [1]

[1] *Cong. Globe,* 36th Congress, part 1, pp. 124–126. The italics are mine. — E. R. K.

There is, I repeat, in these remarks an unintended but very palpable disclosure of Gwin's knowledge of the plans of the Southern leaders, — plans that were carried out in South Carolina and the other Southern States which seized upon the fortifications, mints, and other properties of the Federal Government. Doubtless his confidence that California would stand with the South was based upon the knowledge of conditions on the coast to be created partly through his instrumentality.

As early as May, 1858, Henry A. Wise, who was governor of Virginia at the time of John Brown's foray, had exposed the plot to dissolve the Union. In a letter to a friend he said: "The truth is that there is in the South an organized, active, and dangerous faction, embracing most of the Federal politicians, who are bent upon bringing about causes of a dissolution of the Union. They desire a united South, but not a united country." [1]

The state of affairs that was reached two years later is succinctly set forth in the comprehensive and masterly "History of Abraham Lincoln" by his two secretaries: "Two agencies have thus far been described as engaged in the work of fomenting the rebellion; the first, secret societies of individuals, like 'The 1860 Association,' designed to excite the masses and create public sentiment; the second, a secret league of Southern governors and other state functionaries, whose mission it became

[1] Nicolay and Hay, vol. II, p. 302.

to employ the governmental machinery of states in furtherance of the plot. These, though formidable and dangerous, would probably have failed, either singly or combined, had they not been assisted by a third, of still greater efficacy and certainty. This was nothing less than a conspiracy in the very bosom of the national administration at Washington embracing many United States Senators, Representatives in Congress, three members of the President's Cabinet, and numerous subordinate officials in the several executive departments. The special work which this powerful central cabal undertook by common consent, and successfully accomplished, was to divert Federal arms and forts to the use of the rebellion and to protect and shield the revolt from any adverse influence or preventive and destructive action of the general Government." [1]

The three agencies described were at work, also, in California and Oregon.

Governor Wise went on to explain that the radical Southern leaders were determined to force such nominations at the next Democratic National Convention as to make the election of those candidates impossible, and thus give them a pretext for carrying out their threats of secession. The political struggle of that time, the most grave and momentous in the history of this nation, is nowhere more cogently described than in the "History of Abraham Lincoln," already referred to. I condense

[1] Nicolay and Hay, vol. II, p. 314.

much of chapter XIII, volume II, which shows how the Southern extremists were supported by their allies from the Pacific Coast.

When Jefferson Davis submitted to the United States Senate, in February, 1860, resolutions designed as an authoritative statement of the Administration and extreme Southern party doctrines, the Pacific Representatives voted for them. It was not alone Senator Gwin's affiliations with pro-slavery leaders, and Senator Lane's equally cordial affiliations, nor the public declarations and private assurances of these men, that inspired the Southern leaders with confidence that California and Oregon would be on their side in the conflict they were forcing. Latham and Denver, at the moment rivals of Gwin in the party in California, succeeded in naming most of the delegates from their state to the Democratic National Convention in 1860; yet when the Committee on Platform, unable to agree, brought in two reports, — one favoring Douglas's view that the people of each territory should settle the question as to whether slavery should exist within their borders; the other advocating the Southern claim that slaves were property and that owners had the right to undisturbed possession of their property everywhere in the territories, — the delegates from California and Oregon stood up and were counted for the latter report,—the only free states that took that position. Senator Hammond, of South Carolina, discussing the comparative war strength of North and South, on the fourth of

March, 1858, had said, "I do not speak of California and Oregon; there is no antagonism between the South and those countries and never will be."[1] The developments of the following two years appeared to justify his mention of them as distinct from all the other free states and to verify his prophecy. The subsequent incident, that the two Pacific States, with the Democratic vote divided between Douglas and Breckinridge, gave Lincoln small pluralities, failed to impair Southern confidence in the sympathy and support of "those countries." If, as seemed likely, — it took many days for Eastern news to reach the Pacific Coast, — Mr. Lincoln had been elected, the prophecies and pledges of Gwin and Lane were to be fulfilled. Nor was that fulfillment to be left to Providence. Work was to be done — on the coast and at the national capital. To understand that, more of the conditions in those remote states must be described.

Excepting a brief dalliance with Know-Nothingism, California had always been a Democratic state, and men of Southern birth and Southern principles had controlled its affairs. Nearly all the leaders and officials, high and low, elected or appointed, were Southerners, or, what was less respectable, subservient to Southern interests. From the day Federal office-holders were first sent out to the coast nearly every man had to be satisfactory to the South. At an early period, as shall presently appear, there had been some exceptions to this rule,

[1] *Cong. Globe*, Appendix, 1st Session, 35th Congress, p. 70.

but they had been forgotten. The Whigs, as long as their party existed, made a little noise at election times, but effected no results. When the Republican Party sprang up there were many in California and Oregon who instantly responded to its summons to support the cause of liberty. But it was held in contempt by the dominant party as a harmless minority. A few citizens who assembled at one of its first meetings in Marysville were laughed at and driven out of the hall they had hired for a public meeting.

One advantage of the climate of California is the certainty that during the dry season there will not be rain, even a shower. People may assemble in open places with no risk of being scattered or disturbed by a storm. And as a public meeting in a street is less expensive than in a hired hall, — and in hot weather more comfortable, — many public meetings used to be held out of doors. I attended one such at the corner of the two most important streets of Marysville. A Republican from Sacramento was speaking, when there was an alarm of fire, — rapid tolling of bells, hoarse bellowing of coatless men running through the streets, and a general waking-up of the town. The old-fashioned engines, drawn by scores of brazen-throated firemen, dashed through the streets, scattering the throng that was gathered about the speaker's stand. There was no fire. The alarm, and the rush and shouting of the men drawing the engines with their clanging bells, was a jocular expression of disapprobation of the purpose of the meeting, a playful amenity, sanctioned by usage, and not seriously resented by the minority party. After chasing off toward the conflagration that was neither real nor even plausibly supposititious, the strenuous defenders of the city's property returned with the engines to their houses, again disturbing the political meeting, but replenishing the attendance with a considerable number of boys who had been deceptively lured away at the first alarm. In the course of time the number of Republicans increased, but when their party ceased to be despised it began to be hated. After the election of 1859 the Lecompton Democrats had all the Federal officials, all the officials of the state, and nearly all officials in counties and cities. Through the conflicting candidacies of Breckinridge and Douglas Lincoln got the electoral vote; Gwin and company had everything else.

The work for secession at this period, and at all times, was, naturally, to a great extent carried on in secret. The traitors were too shrewd to make and preserve evidence inculpatory of themselves further than was absolutely requisite for information between various sections. There were some records. How they were destroyed shall be told in its place. There were some of us who were more or less aware of the disloyal work, — not distinctly, definitely, but sensibly, — but we are growing fewer. Charles R. Street, editor of the Marysville "Express," conducted a sort of exchange or clearing-house for correspondence between disloyalists in all parts of California. Street, whose brother was postmaster at Shasta, said that Congressman Burch declared that all the representatives in both houses of Congress from Oregon, Washington, and Arizona supported the secession movement, and that Latham, just elected Senator, also favored it. Gwin and Latham have been already quoted. Congressman Burch declared that he was in favor of the Union, but should the Union be dissolved he favored a Pacific Republic. Scott, the other Congressman, wrote, "If this Union is divided, and two separate confederacies are formed, I will strenuously advocate the secession of California and the establishment of a separate Republic on the Pacific Slope." [1]

Two days after Christmas, 1860, things had gone so far that Street in a letter informed a friend that they were looking for a military commander for the California forces, and had sounded General Shields as to his willingness to accept the position. Disloyal associations and companies were springing up all over the state. A secret order called the Knights of the Golden Circle embraced quite eighteen thousand men in its membership. There was an active propaganda in the North, but the movement was strongest in the southern counties. The Bear Flag — graceless emblem of California before the state was admitted to the Union — was floated in Los Angeles, Sonoma, San Bernardino, Stockton,

[1] Bancroft, vol. VII, p. 277.

and other places, and palmetto flags — exotics from South Carolina — were raised even in San Francisco. Influential newspapers supported the secession movement. The Tulare "Post" denounced loyal guards as "bloodhounds of Zion," and incited such bitterness against the United States troops stationed near its office that some of the paper's readers assaulted a small detachment of soldiers and killed two of them. As late as January, 1861, many journals not actually disloyal were undecided what course to take. After Jeff Davis had been placed at the head of the Southern Confederacy, W. A. Scott, the most noted preacher in San Francisco, — save one who shall be mentioned hereafter, — asserted that Jefferson Davis was no usurper but "as much a president as Abraham Lincoln"; and, having been accustomed to pray for the President of the United States, amended his petition so as to refer to "the Presidents of these American States." Since President Buchanan retained Floyd, Cobb, and Thompson in his Cabinet —men known to everybody to be traitors—it was assumed that the President was aware of their treason and approved of their dastardly proceedings. Gwin exulted to have such an impression abroad. As all official correspondence from Washington came to men holding their places through the favor of Senator Gwin, these were the persons in touch with officialdom at the capital; and as the Cabinet radiated treason, disloyalty permeated every grade of the civil service, and, alas, much of the military. Every mail from the East brought additional encouragement and incitement to the secession cause.

Directly after New Year's Day, in 1860, the new legislature met at Sacramento. The state capital had wandered around somewhat, — a sort of political movable feast for some of the country members, — but had finally settled down at the point where the American River pours its turbid flood into the Sacramento. There were bitter debates, in which extreme secession sentiments were uttered. Crittenden, assemblyman from El Dorado, asserted that there were thirty thousand men ready to take up arms in the event of the secession of the Southern States if the Federal Government should attempt to enforce its laws in California. Relying on the assurances of Gwin and others, Floyd, Buchanan's Secretary of War, sent seventy-five thousand stand of arms out to California for just such use as Mr. Crittenden's men were ready to make of them, — such use as the Charleston men made of the United States muskets which Floyd sent for safe storage to the city where the rebellion began. The death of Broderick carried dismay into the ranks of the Democrats who had not bowed the knee to the Gwin Baal. Broderick was by nature and habit and practice a leader and a fighter. The disloyal element had "got rid of him." James A. McDougall, one of the most eminent members of the San Francisco Bar, succeeded — not to Broderick's place, nobody could quite fill that but — to the rank of leader of the Douglas, Anti-Lecompton wing of the Democratic Party. Mr. McDougall was devoted to his profession and not the partisan champion that Broderick had been. In Illinois he had already obtained eminence and had been attorney-general of the state. We shall hear more of Mr. McDougall. One thing was certain, he had courage.

I was present one night in the theatre in Marysville to listen to a speech by Senator Gwin. He was defending himself against charges that he had thwarted the passage of legislation favorable to government support of the building of Pacific railroads. Quoting from a pile of volumes of the "Congressional Globe" which he had on a table ("the Devil can cite Scripture for his purpose"), Doctor Gwin declared that in an earlier session of Congress, when he had been blamed for the loss of the Pacific Railroad Bill, it was not he who was to blame, but "a young member of the House of Representatives." Then there rose from one of the seats in the parquet the small but sturdy figure of a man, who, with remarkable distinctness, ejaculated, "Doctor Gwin, that is false." I remember very well how Senator Gwin leaped back, startled with such an astounding contradiction. Recovering himself, and observing who it was that had dared thus to affront him, he exclaimed, "It is true, fellow citizens, and that is the man!" At this the entire assemblage was in a turmoil. Those were days when "lie" was a fighting word. I dare say there were a hundred and fifty pistols on which men laid their hands. Then it appeared that Mr. J. Y. C. Ridge and Mr. George C. Gorham, editors of the Douglas Anti-Lecompton Democratic paper of Marysville, were standing on either side of Mr. McDougall. They were well known, and their intrepid character and their skill with firearms were understood. Mr. McDougall answered Senator Gwin's denial with another startling declaration: "Doctor Gwin, you are a liar." With this the turmoil rose into a state of frenzy that I have never seen equaled in a public meeting. Mr. McDougall, having said all that was practicable for the time, started with his two friends to leave the theatre. The superb exhibition of bravery by this trio, and a prudent respect for their skill with the common weapon of the country, led the crowd to draw apart and allow them to pass out.

A few days after the session of the legislature began, Governor Latham, who had been inaugurated less than a week before, was chosen United States Senator in place of the lion-hearted Broderick. It was said at the time that the leaders could not trust Latham to continue as governor. It is certain that a year later he turned against the men who elected him, made Union speeches in several cities, and afterwards in Congress lent a prudent support to some of the measures of President Lincoln. But, alas, his conversion was not permanent.

By the election of Mr. Latham to the Senate, John G. Downey, the lieutenant-governor, became governor of the state. He was young but accustomed to calculating chances. Would Downey, it was asked, stand firm for the secession cause? — not after that cause had triumphed, as its devotees believed it would triumph, but right then, in 1860 and 1861? — in the event of the election of "an abolition President"? Would Downey, if need be, accept the presidency of the Pacific Republic? Men who were living in those days remember well how sharply the line was drawn between loyal and disloyal, especially after Beauregard's forces bombarded Fort Sumter. The cleavage was more distinct in California than in states where there was no organized party espousing the cause of the South. Yet as late as May, 1861, when it was known that Sumter had fallen, Downey was prating about the Government's confining the exercise of force to "defending the national capital, preserving property, defending its forts and arsenals, and collecting the revenues." After the cotton states had associated and established a government and put armies in the field to fight the Government of the United States, Governor Downey denounced the use of force by President Lincoln, which, he said, "is understood to mean the invasion of the South by an army having in view the subjugation of Southern States and holding them as conquered provinces." He asserted that it was the purpose of the Government to incite "servile insurrection with its train of horrors," and declared that the Government was determined on "the obliteration of state lines and the confiscation of individual property." [1] Governor Downey claimed, and has always since maintained, that he was a Union man. Hittell, in his excellent "History of California," recounts many facts bearing upon that matter. He says "Downey's Unionism . . . was not of the kind by which the Union could be preserved," and adds that "if he had only managed to steer as clear of entanglements on the Union question as he had on the bulkhead" (a matter local to San Francisco), "he might have had anything he asked" of the state.[2] Loyal men did not talk like Governor Downey. Disloyalists, wherever found on both sides of the Rocky Mountains, used his phrases. The terms of his utterances were the common coin of traitors and rebels South and East. The ascription of infamous purposes to Abraham Lincoln's administration was, as everybody in the world concedes now, as everybody ought to have known in 1860, based on disloyal, malignant invention.

[1] Letter of May 16 to John Dougherty and A. Hayward.

[2] Hittell, vol. IV, p. 274.

CHAPTER V

GWIN'S WORK — ALBERT SIDNEY JOHNSTON PUT IN COMMAND ON THE COAST

SHORTLY after election day in 1860 Senator Gwin started for "the States." Mr. Lincoln had been elected President. The secession determination was accordingly being carried along in hostile acts, and in the most radical states steps were being taken to fulfill the threats made during the political campaign. There was no time to be lost. Buchanan was still President. What was more to the purpose, Floyd was Secretary of War. The Pacific Coast had been divided into two military departments and each was commanded by a loyal officer. Before Senator Gwin left California it was confidently and boastfully asserted that one of his first duties on arriving at the capital would be to have a "friend" placed over the Regular Army force of the coast. I am not aware of any documentary evidence that Senator Gwin undertook that matter.[1] There may be such. In this especial matter documentary evidence is not essential. The occurrences prove the influences.

(1) Senator Gwin arrived in Washington about the third of December.

[1] Although Senator Gwin left memoirs he said nothing of his relation to the rebellion. — E. R. K.

(2) It took nearly a month for a letter to go from Washington to California. Allow a few days for Gwin to impress Floyd.

(3) On the fifteenth of January, 1861, official orders from the War Department were received in San Francisco relieving the two loyal officers of their commands, consolidating the entire coast into one department, and placing Colonel (Brevet Brigadier-General) Albert Sidney Johnston in command.

The blow — for blow it seemed — was not unexpected by friend or foe. It raised the secessionists to a high pitch of confidence. Loyal men were dumfounded; but what could they do? The Federal office-holders — postmasters, mail-carriers, customs officials, marshals, judges, and the host of minor place-holders and attendants — were, with few exceptions or none, in sympathy with the South. The state officers and about all of their subordinates were of the same mind, together with nearly half the members of the legislature. And now, as the threatened crisis was drawing near, the Regular Army, with its control of the fortifications, garrisons, and munitions of war, was turned over to an officer undoubtedly designated by Senator Gwin. It mattered not that Captain Winfield Scott Hancock was stationed in the southern part of the state and that Lieutenant Philip H. Sheridan was at a post in Washington Territory. There was no way by which these two, and others who would be faithful, could coöperate; and they were subject to the command of General Johnston.

The General is said to have subsequently declared that he had no knowledge of a plot to carry California out of the Union. It seems incredible. Not only was the sentiment of sympathy with the South openly and defiantly expressed on the stump, in editorial columns, in hotels, clubs, and private houses, by the chief men of the Federal and State Governments, but the fact that disunion organizations were actively promoting their cause was known to everybody. Everybody except General Johnston. Oregon, Nevada, Arizona, and the northern counties of California were the field of a lively secession propaganda. The southern counties seethed with sedition. Men of prominence, some of whom had filled state offices, held frequent meetings and concocted rebellion in sight of the frowning batteries of Alcatraz. Still, General Johnston was a gentleman. His subsequent course may be deplored; but, while he could violate his oath of allegiance, his word must be accepted. This, however, is obvious: since General Johnston was unaware of a plot he could not be expected to take measures to repress a plot. But the plot existed, and if the military force of the National Government was not to restrain or quell it, who was? Certainly not Governor Downey and his disloyal associates. So the preparations for secession went on, and California and the rest of the Pacific States and Territories were slipping unhindered away from the Union. While Floyd remained in the War Department he lent most effective aid to the scheme. When he fled, and the influence of General Winfield Scott became paramount in military circles in Washington, the change, at first, did nothing for California. Buchanan was still President, and Gwin and Lane were his advisers concerning affairs in their states. Then, General Scott trusted in the fidelity of General Johnston and tendered him a major-general's commission in the Regular Army. Later Scott learned that Jeff Davis had offered Johnston a major-generalship of the Southern forces, and Scott ordered the arrest of Johnston. But at this critical stage in California General Johnston was permitted to remain in command of all the army forces in that remote department.

Read the history of Texas at the same period: the surrender of forts, posts, munitions, troops, by the infamous General Twiggs, and consider what might have been the fate of California and the entire Pacific Slope. For General Johnston, too, was a victim of the deadly poison of "state sovereignty." Sincere, you may say; yes, sincere, and therefore the more dangerous. His was the sincerity that subsequently led him, on whom his old commander set such hopes, to death at the head of his rebel brigades at Pittsburg Landing.

Doctor Gwin felt sure his friends in California would carry out his arrangements. He had said in the Senate that if the Southern States went out of the Union "California will be found with the South." Being challenged for this declaration he denied having made it, but added, "If the Union is ever broken up, the eastern boundary of the Pacific Republic will be, in my opinion, the Sierra Madre and the Rocky Mountains." [1]

There is other evidence of the Senator's confidence that "his state" would secede at this time. Mrs. Clay, wife of the Senator from Alabama, in her ingenuous and charming book of reminiscences describes the scene on Monday, the twenty-first of January, 1861, when the Senators from several seceded states bade farewell to the venerable body of which they had been members. "As each Senator, speaking for his state, concluded his solemn renunciation of allegiance to the United States, women grew hysterical and waved their handkerchiefs, encouraging them with cries of sympathy and admiration. Men wept and embraced each other mournfully. At times the murmurs among the onlookers grew so deep that the serjeant-at-arms was ordered to clear the galleries; and as each speaker took up his portfolio and gravely left the Senate Chamber sympathetic shouts rang from the assemblage above." [2]

About a month after the Clays had left Washington Mrs. Clay received a letter from a friend at the capital which throws light on the feeling and disposition and relation of California's senior Senator: "For days I saw nothing but despairing women leaving suddenly, their husbands having resigned and sacrificed their all for their beloved

[1] Bancroft, vol. VII, p. 59. [2] *A Belle of the Fifties*, p. 147.

states. You would not know this God-forsaken city. Our beautiful Capitol with all its artistic wealth desecrated, disgraced with Lincoln's low soldiery. . . . The Gwins are the only ones left of our intimates, and Mrs. Gwin is packed up, ready to leave. Poor thing! Her eyes are never without tears."[1]

[1] *A Belle of the Fifties*, pp. 151, 152.

CHAPTER VI

IF THE COAST HAD SECEDED! — GWIN AND BAKER GO TO WASHINGTON

If California and Oregon had seceded, whether they joined the Southern Confederacy or set up a Pacific Republic, Washington, Arizona, and contiguous territories would inevitably have been drawn into the movement. They were ripe for it. And if that section had rebelled the course of American history might have been sadly changed. While Southern armies threatened St. Louis, Louisville, Cincinnati, and Washington, with Generals Frémont, Halleck, Buell, Rosecrans, and McClellan continually calling for more troops and the Government unable to respond, it is impossible to see where forces to suppress a rebellion on the Pacific Slope could have been found. But if, by depleting other departments, an army had been collected, it would have been extremely difficult and enormously expensive to move it to that remote field. There was not a railroad in California, — except, I believe, one between Sacramento and Folsom, a distance of twenty miles, over which one mixed train, passenger and freight, ran every day under the genial conductorship of "Uncle George Bromley," later the patriarch of the San Francisco Bohemian Club. There was not in the States a railroad extending farther west than the middle of Missouri. If a force had been marched across the continent, much of the distance through deserts devoid of water and forage for men and animals, part of the way over high mountains covered with snow, the passes defended by the enemy, menaced night and day by savage Indians easily incited to hostilities, it would have been months on the road, its numbers would have been decimated by sickness, desertion, and death, and such of the men as reached their destination would have arrived physically and mentally exhausted. Their base of supplies would have been quite two thousand miles away, without a telegraph wire or other means of quick communication. Troops sent by the way of Panama could not have left New York until transports had first been sent around Cape Horn to await them at the Isthmus; and in the mean time the rebels, following the course of their kindred at Charleston, Savannah, Mobile, New Orleans, and other places, would have prepared the fortifications they had seized from the Government to repel the transports, as the Star of the West was repulsed from Charleston Harbor when she tried to succor the garrison of Fort Sumter. A naval expedition must have weathered Cape Horn, — a longer voyage than from England to South Africa. But we possessed no available naval force. Such as we had was thoroughly occupied on the Atlantic and Gulf Coasts. And transports capable of conveying any considerable number of troops could not have been instantly called into service. Mr. Lincoln's Secretary of the Navy did wonders, converting old tugs, East River ferryboats, and excursion steamers into war vessels; but Gideon Welles was not the Count of Monte Cristo, nor was he capable of creating something, and a great deal, out of nothing. If, however, after months of preparation, a fleet could have been dispatched to California, in what condition would it have arrived, tossed and battered by the tempests of a four or five months' voyage? And what port could it have entered?

Senator Gwin, as I have said, left for the East early in November, 1860. Reverdy Johnson, of Maryland, and Judah P. Benjamin, of Louisiana, — two of the foremost lawyers in the country, who had been to California as counsel in a lawsuit, — were returning to the States at the same time. The gallant Colonel Frank W. Lander was also on board the steamer Sonora. But, for the scheming California Senator, Nemesis was a passenger in the person of Edward D. Baker. California and Oregon had voted for Lincoln. It was considered probable that he had been elected. The South had long been resolved in such an event to break up the Union. Gwin had declared that California would be found with the South. He was going to complete the arrangement. We have just read of his master stroke.

CHAPTER VII

EDWARD D. BAKER — EARLY LIFE — LAWYER — LEGISLATOR — BEATS LINCOLN FOR THE NOMINATION AND IS ELECTED TO CONGRESS — COLONEL IN MEXICAN WAR

So now we have come to where we must consider the man for whose deserved but neglected fame this book is mainly written. At the time when the life of the nation was in peril from treason, the only loyal man from the Pacific Coast in either house of Congress. Years before he had been the only Whig in Congress from the State of Illinois. Whose fortune it was to be, as he continues to this day, the only man since Congress was established to speak in military uniform in both the House of Representatives and the Senate. As brave and as eloquent, I suppose, as any man who ever lived in any land in any age. After Alexander Hamilton, and scarcely excepting Carl Schurz, of the millions of citizens who have come to America from foreign lands, the one who rendered the most important service to our country. In the exalted profession of the law, foremost in the communities where he resided. Before assemblies of the people, the most captivating orator of his time. Gifted in poetical expression. In legislative bodies, wise in counsel and preëminent in debate. A man of action as well as a man of words. A pioneer in building the Panama Railroad. In three of the nation's wars an intrepid soldier and a skillful commander.

The Honorable Edward Stanly was one of the most respected men in California. Earlier he had represented a North Carolina district in Congress when Baker sat for the Springfield district of Illinois; a man on whom Abraham Lincoln set the stamp of his approval by calling him from California to become Military Governor of North Carolina. At the funeral of General Baker, in San Francisco, Mr. Stanly pronounced Baker "one of the most remarkable men of modern times." And if of modern, why not of all times? It is more to be preëminent in modern times than in ancient.

The impression Baker made on other men is described by the Honorable Samuel D. Woods, long a member of Congress from California: —

"General Baker was gracious and winning and the choicest of companions by reason of his abundant kindness of spirit and his richness in human touch and sympathy. He was of noble presence, classical in feature, and with the manners of a prince. He had great conversational gifts and in the hour of good fellowship became a fountain bubbling over with wisdom and wit. Free from vanity, unconsciously he became the centre of any group by common consent; and the hours flew on rapid feet while he poured out his soul from the affluence of his gifted nature. He was a natural orator, with every grace of speech, and on great occasions, when his soul was stirred, he spoke as one inspired. Words fell from his lips in joyous association and with the melody of music. He was a magician, and under his touch common things became beautiful. He called up from dull natures, from cold hearts, unsuspected sweetness, and lifted high natures into altitudes of lofty feeling. When his own nature became flooded with the splendor of his dreams he was beyond resistance, for he spoke as one having authority from the oracles." [1]

Edward Dickinson Baker was born in London, in February, 1811. His father was of a family of Quakers, a man of good education and known for his literary taste. His mother was a sister of Captain Thomas Dickinson, a naval officer of distinction who fought with great gallantry under Collingwood at Trafalgar.[2] The father, anticipating better careers for his children in the New World, left the old home when Edward was four years of age, and landed in Philadelphia. The family spent ten years in that interesting city, during part of which time Mr. Baker taught school. He used to lead the son to noted places, narrating incidents that had made them renowned, and thus vividly impressing the lessons of history. The War of Independence was then much nearer the people than the War for the Union is now, and the events and outcome of the former exercised a greater

[1] *Life on the Pacific Coast,* Funk and Wagnalls, p. 155.

[2] Wallace, pp. 10, 11.

influence on the minds of people than the events of our Civil War exercise upon the population of today. The father was once expounding the Constitution of the United States to his son — how many fathers do that for their sons nowadays? — when the boy learned that only a native-born citizen was eligible to the Presidency, — a provision deemed essential at the time it was adopted but no longer necessary to national security. The boy wept. He had been brought to this land of opportunity, and here he was precluded from aspiring to the highest place. As the exposition went on, and he was told of the functions of a United States senator, he formed a determination to be a senator, a purpose he deeply cherished from that moment.

The financial circumstances of the family were evidently unprosperous, — the Bakers all had superior talents but were not money-getters, — and the father found it expedient to look for employment for his boys that held out encouragement of early returns. It was natural to recall the great woolen industry of England, and Edward was apprenticed to learn the trade of a weaver. But this failed to satisfy either parent or child. The adventurous father heard the call of the West, and in 1825 moved to New Harmony, Indiana. He remained here less than two years, and then went farther west, to Belleville, St. Clair County, Illinois, whither the oldest son, Edward, preceded the family, on foot. Belleville at that period was the most important town in the state, the home of many leading men, renowned for wealth, refinement, and the hospitality of its inhabitants. Here, again, the father was established as a teacher, in which profession he was quite successful. By this time the son had given evidence of intellectual gifts that raised high hopes in the family. The boy had a passion for reading. His marked taste for literature attracted the attention of Governor Edwards, whose home was in Belleville, and he gave him free access to his extensive library. What Baker read he ever after knew. What he once acquired he always retained. No conscious effort of memory was necessary to arouse the teeming apartments of his mind. He read much, and all he ever read burst forth the instant it became germane to any subject on which his intellect was engaged. For several months he drove a dray in the city of St. Louis, to earn money to enable him to go on with his schooling; but it must be said that he never obtained any considerable amount or degree of systematic education. Neither did Benjamin Franklin, Abraham Lincoln, or Horace Greeley. If other Bakers, Greeleys, Franklins, and Lincolns ever appear it may be unnecessary to devote all the early, formative years of their lives to forcing or conferring upon them systematic education. But unless a father is certain his son possesses the intellectual endowments of a Lincoln, a Greeley, a Franklin, or a Baker, it probably will continue to be best to send the boy to college. Young Baker read widely, and by the power of genius appropriated and adapted and utilized to their utmost potency the information of history, the sagacious lessons of biography, the substantial foundations of scientific knowledge, the polish of *belles-lettres*, the patriotic uplift of oratory, and the glowing inspirations of poetry. Many years after, Colonel Baker had finished the conduct of a suit at law in Sacramento, where, attracted by the reputation of the advocate, crowds filled the courtroom. But they were not satisfied merely to hear an argument on the question of liability on a promissory note. They demanded something more and shouted for a speech. Colonel Baker promised that if they would let him go to his hotel for supper he would lecture, in the evening, on "Books." It was a theme on which he had never spoken, but his address was declared entrancing. "Baker," said Justice Baldwin, of the Supreme Court, — "Baker, you know everything about books — except law books." Colonel Baker was then among the leading lawyers in California.

Baker was but nineteen years of age when he was admitted to the bar, in Illinois. His youthfulness caused him to be looked on with distrust, and his success was at first indifferent. In the spring of 1832 he enlisted as a private soldier in the Black Hawk War. Others of note in that movement for the defense of Western homes were Robert Anderson, afterwards the patriotic defender of Fort Sumter, Jeff Davis, and Abraham Lincoln. Baker served until the campaign was ended by the decisive battle of Broad Axe River. In some newspapers of that period Baker was afterwards called "Major," but I have been unable to ascertain whether he actually obtained that title in the war or afterwards in the militia. Wallace narrates this incident to illustrate his youthful daring: "When his regiment was mustered out of service, near Dixon, on the upper waters of the Mississippi, instead of returning home overland, with his comrades in arms, he procured a canoe from some friendly Indian, and, accompanied by a single companion, boldly descended the Father of Waters a distance of about three hundred miles, to a convenient point in Calhoun County, where he landed his frail bark and then proceeded on foot to his home in Carrollton." [1]

In 1835 Baker moved to Springfield, then a town of fifteen hundred people, and began to seriously apply himself to the work of his profession. He must have been rated a competent lawyer, for among his partners at different times were Albert T. Bledsoe, subsequently Assistant Secretary of War of the Southern Confederacy, Josephus Hewitt, Esq., and the venerated and highly esteemed Judge Stephen T. Logan. To be something of a lawyer at that time and in that place Baker had to be something of a man, for among his contemporaries were Lincoln, Douglas, McDougall, Shields, Logan, Trumbull, Stuart, McClernand, and others of scarcely less learning and eloquence. Baker was once in a case when Stephen A. Douglas, O. H.

[1] Wallace, p. 14.

Browning, Richard Yates, William A. Richardson, D. B. Bush, William R. Archer, and James A. McDougall were also engaged on one side or the other.[1] To contend with such men Baker was forced to the utmost exercise of his mental powers.

Orville H. Browning, who became United States Senator from Illinois after the death of Stephen A. Douglas, said of Baker: "When I traveled upon the same circuit with him and others who have since been renowned in the history of Illinois, it was no uncommon thing, after the labors of the day in court were ended and forensic battles had been lost and won, for the lawyers to forget the asperities which had been engendered by the conflicts of the bar, in the innocent if not profitable pastime of writing verses for the amusement of each other and their friends; and I well remember with what greater facility than others he could dash from his pen effusions sparkling all over with poetic gems. If all that he thus wrote could be collected together it would make no mean addition to the poetic literature of our country."

Baker himself did not set so high an estimate on his rhymes and made no effort to preserve them. After his death Colonel John W. Forney gave the following short piece by Colonel Baker to the public: —

[1] *The Illini; A Story of the Prairies*, A. C. McClurg & Co., p. 137. The author, General Clark E. Carr, calls attention to the fact that six of these men became United States Senators: Douglas, Browning, Richardson, and Yates, from Illinois, — Yates having also been governor, — McDougall from California, and Baker from Oregon.

TO A WAVE

Dost thou seek a star with thy swelling crest,
O wave, that leavest thy mother's breast?
Dost thou leap from the prisoned depths below,
In scorn of their calm and constant flow?
Or art thou seeking some distant land,
To die in murmurs upon the strand?

Hast thou tales to tell of pearl-lit deep,
Where the wave-whelmed mariner rocks in sleep?
Canst thou speak of navies that sunk in pride
Ere the roll of their thunder in echo died?
What trophies, what banners, are floating free
In the shadowy depths of that silent sea?

It were vain to ask, as thou rollest afar,
Of banner, or mariner, ship, or star;
It were vain to seek in thy stormy face
Some tale of the sorrowful past to trace.
Thou art swelling high, thou art flashing free,
How vain are the questions we ask of thee!

I, too, am a wave on a stormy sea;
I, too, am a wanderer, driven like thee;
I, too, am seeking a distant land,
To be lost and gone ere I reach the strand.
For the land I seek is a waveless shore,
And they who once reach it shall wander no more.

Doctor Jayne, of Springfield, who knew all the extraordinary men of that extraordinary period, declared that "none of them began to compare with Colonel Baker as a public speaker." When the corner-stone of the new capitol of the state was laid, on the Fourth of July, in 1837, the committee of arrangements considered Abraham Lincoln, Stephen A. Douglas, John A. Logan, Lyman Trumbull, James A. McDougall, James Shields, and John A. McClernand, and finally chose Baker, who was then but twenty-six years of age, to deliver the oration. This choice and the eloquent character of the oration first brought the young lawyer into public notice throughout Illinois. The brief reports that remain of the oration indicate that, while it was eloquent, it also naturally indicated the youthfulness of the orator, whose closing was in verse of his own composition: —

> If, with the firm resolve to wear no chain,
> They dare all peril and endure all pain;
> If their free spirits spurn a chain of gold,
> By wealth unfettered and to ease unsold;
> If, with eternal vigilance they tread
> In the true paths of their time-honored dead: —
> Long as the star shall deck the brow of night,
> Long as the smile of woman shall be bright,
> Long as the foam shall gather where the roar
> Of ocean sounds upon the wave-worn shore —
> So long, my country, shall thy banner fly,
> Till years shall cease and Time itself shall die.

At this period Baker began to be active in political speaking. There were times when neither wit nor argument would move a crowd; when physical courage alone sufficed to control the turbulent spirits. "It was on such an occasion, one evening, that Lincoln's friend, Edward Dickinson Baker, who already gave promise of the brilliant career that lay before him, addressed a hostile audience in the Springfield courtroom. The meeting-room happened to be directly below the law office of

Stuart and Lincoln, in which the junior member of the firm lay listening through a trapdoor that opened above the platform. The speaker, as he warmed to his subject, denounced, with the impetuous eloquence that afterward made him famous, the dishonesty of Democratic officials. 'Wherever there is a land office there you will find a Democratic newspaper defending its corruption,' he thundered. 'Pull him down!' shouted John B. Weber, whose brother was the editor of the local administration sheet. There was a noisy rush toward the platform, and, for the moment, it seemed as if Baker, who stood pale yet firm, would be punished for his temerity. Then, to the astonishment of the advancing crowd, a lank form dangled through the scuttle and Lincoln dropped upon the platform, between them and the object of their anger. After gesticulating in vain for silence, he seized the stone water-jug and shouted, 'I'll break this over the head of the first man who lays a hand on Baker!' As the assailants hesitated, he continued, 'Hold on, gentlemen; let us not disgrace the age and country in which we live. This is a land where freedom of speech is guaranteed. Mr. Baker has a right to speak and ought to be permitted to do so. I am here to protect him, and no man shall take him from this stand if I can prevent it.' The crowd receded, quiet was restored, and Baker finished his speech without further interruption." [1]

[1] Lincoln, *Master of Men*, p. 56.

Baker's official career began in 1837, when he was chosen for the general assembly, from Sangamon County. During the years of his service, for he was reëlected several times, he was neglectful of irksome committee work, but was always thoroughly prepared when there was debate on pending measures.[1] In the session of 1839–40 a memorial was presented preferring charges against the Honorable John Pearson, Judge of the Seventh Judicial District of the state, and praying for his impeachment. A resolution to that end was offered. The subject assumed a partisan character and was warmly debated, the Whigs generally favoring, and the Democrats opposing, the measure. The House, by a party vote, decided against impeachment. Mr. Baker, alive to the importance of preserving unblemished the purity of the judicial ermine, drew up a protest against the action of the majority which was signed by himself, Abraham Lincoln, a colleague, and the minority members generally. The document expressed exalted views of the function of the judiciary and would be an honor to a veteran legislator to-day.

In the famous "Tippecanoe and Tyler" cam-

[1] Edward Everett said of Rufus Choate: "In the daily routine of legislation he did not take an active part. He shunned clerical work, and consequently avoided, as much as duty permitted, the labor of the committee room; but on every great question that came up while he was a member of either house of Congress he made a great speech; and when he had spoken there was very little left for any one else to say on the same side of the question." *Life and Writings of Rufus Choate*, vol. I, p. 267. Very like Baker. — E. R. K.

paign, in 1840, Baker stumped Illinois and neighboring states. In the same year he was elected to the state senate, where he served four years, making ten in all in the Illinois legislature. It is the testimony of his contemporaries that he was universally conceded the highest rank.

On the twenty-seventh of April, 1831, when only twenty years of age, Baker was married to Mary Ann Lee, an accomplished and well-to-do widow of Springfield, with whom he lived in the happiest of relations until his tragic death. Shortly after his marriage he joined the Reformed or Christian Church (the members of which are often spoken of as "Campbellites"), his wife being already a devout member.

In 1844 Baker sought the nomination for Congress in the Springfield District. Lincoln was also a candidate, but Baker won. There can have been nothing but honorable rivalry between the two, for in 1846 Lincoln named his second son Edward Baker. Baker had for his opponent John Calhoun, afterward notorious in the pro-slavery brutalities in Kansas. Baker was elected, and was, as already stated, the only Whig in Congress from the State of Illinois. Among his colleagues were Stephen A. Douglas, John A. McClernand, John Wentworth, Orlando B. Ficklin, Robert Smith, and Joseph P. Hoge.

In February, 1846, Mr. Baker addressed a lengthy letter to the people of his congressional district on the subject of the English grain laws and

ABRAHAM LINCOLN

the influence their repeal was likely to exert upon the agricultural interests of this country. The letter disclosed an intimate acquaintance with the laws of political economy and attained a wide circulation through the press. Notwithstanding his public duties Mr. Baker found time to lecture in Baltimore for the benefit of a Sunday school, his subject being "The Influence of Commerce upon Civilization." The Baltimore papers spoke of the lecture in very complimentary terms. Colonel Baker never found it necessary to supplement his professional income by fees for lectures, as so many of our public men have been forced to do, and his rostrum addresses were few and the occasions of their delivery far between. However, he had several topics on which he sometimes spoke. Among them, besides the two that have been named, were "Art," "Robert Burns," "Life and Death of Socrates," "The Sea," and "The Plurality of Worlds."

When the Mexican War broke out Baker hastened from Washington to his home in Illinois and quickly raised a regiment of volunteers which he led to the Rio Grande. He soon discovered that the troops stood greatly in need of tent equipage and munitions of war. After a few months in camp, during which he drilled his regiment and brought it to a high state of efficiency, he was chosen by General Taylor as bearer of dispatches to the War Department, and proceeded to Washington. Congress was in session, and as he had not resigned his seat in the House he availed himself of his privilege, as a member, to speak. By general consent one of the most important bills was made a special order for the twenty-eighth of December to enable Colonel Baker to discuss it. Having brought no civilian clothes with him he spoke in his military uniform, — and so rapidly that the reporters were unable to make a good report. The speech was almost entirely impromptu, entirely without notes, as nearly all his speeches were. It created a profound impression and exercised great influence upon his fellow Whigs. The members were much impressed by Colonel Baker's recitation of a poem in memory of his comrades who had died in the unhealthy camp on the great river, — the fact having been whispered through the House that the poem was their fellow member's own composition.

Where rolls the rushing Rio Grande,
  Here peacefully they sleep;
Far from their native Northern land,
  Far from the friends who weep.
No rolling drum disturbs their rest,
  Beneath the sandy sod;
The mould lies heavy on each breast —
  The spirit is with God.

They heard their country's call, and came
  To battle for her right;
Each bosom filled with martial flame,
  And kindling for the fight.
Light was their measured footstep when
  They moved to seek the foe.
Alas! that hearts so fiery then
  Should soon be cold and low!

They did not die in eager strife,
  Upon a well-fought field;
Not from the red wound poured their life,
  Where cowering foemen yield.
Death's ghastly shade was slowly cast
  Upon each manly brow;
But calm and fearless to the last,
  They sleep in silence now.

Yet shall a grateful country give
  Her honors to their name;
In kindred hearts their memories live,
  And history guards their fame.
Nor unremembered do they sleep
  Upon a foreign strand;
Though near their graves thy wild waves sweep,
  Thou rushing Rio Grande.

At the close of his speech, Colonel Baker by unanimous consent of the House introduced a joint resolution authorizing the Secretary of War to take measures for better clothing of the troops, which forthwith had all three readings and was passed.

The historians of Lincoln say: "Immediately after making this speech, Baker increased the favorable impression created by it by resigning his seat in Congress and hurrying as fast as steam could carry him to New Orleans, to embark there for Mexico. He had heard of the advance of Santa Anna upon Saltillo, and did not wish to lose any opportunity of fighting which might fall in the way of his regiment. He arrived to find his regiment transferred to the department of General Scott; and although he missed Buena Vista, he took part in the capture of Vera Cruz and greatly distinguished himself at

Cerro Gordo."[1] General Scott, with the bulk of his force, was directly in front of Cerro Gordo, which was a height and strongly fortified. He detached General Twiggs's division for a flank movement on the enemy's left. Twiggs ordered General Shields with his Illinois brigade to charge. The Mexicans discovered the movement and their battery opened fire with grape. The gallant Illinoisans were not dismayed but rushed forward with a shout. As they were in the thickest of the fight General Shields fell, badly wounded. That disconcerted the troops. There was a halt, a shudder, that began among those nearest the General and rapidly spread through the brigade. In another moment there would have been a retreat, probably a rout. Colonel Baker instantly took in the situation. Flashing his sword, he shouted to his own regiment, "Come on!" and ordered the whole brigade to advance. The brave fellows sprang forward to follow such an intrepid leader and drove the Mexicans pell-mell out of their fortifications. This movement on their flank led to a diversion of Mexican troops from the centre, as General Scott expected. Taking advantage of this weakening of the enemy's centre, Scott moved the main body of his army forward and gained one of the most brilliant victories of the campaign. General Twiggs in his report speaks of "the command of the brigade devolving upon Colonel Baker, who conducted it with ability." General Scott said, "The brigade so

[1] Nicolay and Hay, vol. I, p. 255.

gallantly led by General Shields, and, after his fall, by Colonel Baker, deserves high commendation for its fine behavior and success." The General continued Colonel Baker in command of the brigade.

Shortly after this battle the term of enlistment of Baker's regiment expired. The men preferred not to reënlist, but returned to Illinois and were mustered out of service. Baker was thus left without a command, so he at once resumed the practice of law. At this time the state presented Colonel Baker with a sword in a magnificent gold scabbard.

CHAPTER VIII

BAKER'S SUCCESSES — IN POLITICS IN THREE STATES — IN CONGRESS AGAIN — SUPERINTENDS CONSTRUCTION OF PANAMA RAILROAD — LIFE IN SAN FRANCISCO — POPULARITY AS ORATOR

BAKER had an insatiate appetite for action, an eagerness for influence on affairs, but he was unwilling again to be a rival of Lincoln for political honors. I believe Lincoln felt that Baker, with the glamour attaching to his military career, might with greater ease than previously have secured the nomination for Congress from the Springfield District. But the magnanimous and warm-hearted friend chose to move out of the district and settle in Galena. This other district had always been strongly Democratic, but Baker in 1848 announced himself an Independent Whig candidate for Congress, spoke everywhere, and was elected by a thousand majority, after residing in the district only three weeks. It was a personal candidacy, a personal canvass, and a personal victory. At the end of his term he declined to be a candidate again and the district reverted to Democracy. In 1848 he was also a candidate for Presidential Elector, and he and Lincoln were the chief stump speakers for General Taylor in Illinois. Baker's efforts extended also to Iowa, Wisconsin, and Minnesota. After General Taylor's election to the Presidency, Baker was urged for a position in the Cabinet. Lincoln tried to bring it about and the Whig members of the legislatures of Illinois, Iowa, and Wisconsin joined in his support. The effort failed and Baker was chagrined and disappointed. However, he was a Congressman-elect and he entered upon his duties with ardor. The House, that term, comprised an unusual number of men whose renown had extended beyond the borders of their own states. In the prolonged contest for Speaker of the House Baker received some votes, but he himself supported Mr. Winthrop, of Massachusetts, who was finally elected.

During the first session there was an acrimonious debate on the question of admitting California to statehood. The Southern Congressmen strove to reject the application of the new commonwealth. Colonel Baker advocated its admission. Mr. Venable, discussing the subject, mentioned Baker's foreign birth. Colonel Baker, referring to Mr. Venable's endeavor to keep California out of the Union, retorted, "I tell the gentleman, if he means to intimate that it is so great a disgrace to have been born in a foreign country, that I imagine the disgrace to be infinitely greater when a man desires to make one portion of his country foreign to another portion." The chivalrous Mr. Toombs also regarded it as not beyond the limits of the high courtesy he professed to refer to the fact that Colonel

Baker had not been one of the emigrants previous to 1776. Colonel Baker replied: "I do not see what the birthplace of an individual so humble as myself can possibly have to do with California; and perhaps I ought to be obliged to the gentleman for dignifying me by connecting my name for a moment with such a controversy. But no man feels altogether satisfied to have his position studiously misrepresented, and I appeal to the candor of the gentleman, with whom my associations have hitherto been agreeable if not friendly, to inform me what my ancestors, up to Father Adam, have to do with the admission of California into this Union. Whether they came from Great Britain or anywhere else, it can make but little difference so far as this question is concerned. But, while I acknowledge the grace and magnanimity with which my colleague [Mr. Harris] has spoken for me, I desire to say, also, for myself, that if any gentleman on this floor, directly or indirectly, means to impute to me that, because my first breath may have been drawn in a foreign land, and because my eyes first opened to the light of another sky I am not in mind, heart, feelings, purposes, and intentions, as true to the land of my childhood, and the land of my choice, as the man who dares impugn me, he says what is from the beginning untrue in word and act and thought and deed, — that which is utterly and entirely untrue. Sir, I have proved it, as my colleague has said; I have bared my bosom to the battle on the Northwestern frontier in my youth and on the Southwestern frontier in my manhood. I have earned somewhat of the good will of my country. In the councils of my state for a period of ten consecutive years, and in her service here, my constituents have confided in my devotion to their interests and my attachment to the Union. I have only to say that if the time should come when disunion rules the hour and discord is to reign supreme,[1] I shall again be ready to give the best blood in my veins to my country's cause."[2]

Colonel Baker favored some, but not all, of the compromise measures designed to allay the angry excitement of the South, but he took no active part in the debates. On the nineteenth of December he introduced and secured the passage of a resolution inviting Father Mathew, the great temperance advocate, to a seat on the floor of the House. He vigorously defended Secretary Ewing, of the Cabinet, against insinuations that he had exercised powers not legally belonging to his department. He spoke eloquently in favor of detailing thirty navy seamen to serve in the expedition being fitted out by Moses H. Grinnell, of New York, to aid in the search for Sir John Franklin. In the course of his remarks Colonel Baker said: —

"I will grant aid to Mr. Grinnell now as readily as I would have done to Columbus if I had been a citizen or legislator of Spain in the reign of Ferdinand and Isabella. It is this generous love of glory

[1] An expression of Mr. Toombs's.

[2] *Cong. Globe*, vol. XXI, part 2, pp. 1198 and 1200.

which I admire. It was this which prompted the 'world-seeking Genoese' to the noblest enterprise of any age and kept him firm amid terrified mariners and on an unknown and stormy sea. It is this which kindles high hearts to all great enterprises; and, sir, when this love of glory seeks its accomplishment in noble discovery and princely munificence, I not only admire, but honor it; and I am honored in being allowed to aid it.

"But, sir, the whole American people have an interest in these expeditions. It is no longer true of England, that she is the 'mistress of the ocean.' We, too, hold our 'march upon the mountain wave' — our keels vex every sea; and whatever opens new channels of commerce adds to our wealth and dominion. And yet I am disposed to place the support of this measure upon higher ground. It has been said that literature belongs to no age and no country. It may be repeated of discovery and invention, as the benefit is for all ages and all countries — for the world, and for the whole family of man. So I trust an enlightened statesmanship will send forth, in the name of this great nation, messages of consolation and succor to the absent — not alone to relieve them, but also to assure all who may succeed them in the paths of adventurous peril that they shall be neither neglected nor forgotten.

"Sir, should the sacredness of misfortune be overlooked? If these men had sought the Northern seas for mere private gain, even then the greatness of their danger would reach the American heart. The noble woman who looks out upon the 'melancholy main' with eyes shining with hope, yet dimmed with tears, does not and cannot appeal to us in vain. For one, I shall respond to the call. Here is a public-spirited American merchant, who, with a munificence equaling the merchant princes of Florence, equips his vessels and proposes to traverse the unknown regions of the North to restore distinguished men to the world and husbands and fathers to their homes. He asks the protection of our name and our laws. Sir, let him have them. Let us put our flag at the masthead, our laws upon the deck, our protection around the ship. It may be our stars may first gleam upon those watching eyes. Think you, sir, they will not hail them with a wilder joy when they come to tell them that America conducts the search?"

Doubtless the most notable act of Colonel Baker during this session was his beautiful eulogy when the commemoration service was held in the House shortly after General Taylor's death:—

"The late President of the United States has devoted his whole life to the service of his country. Of a nature singularly unambitious, he seems to have combined the utmost gentleness of manner with the greatest firmness of purpose. For more than thirty years the duties of his station confined him to a sphere where only those who knew him most intimately could perceive the qualities which danger quickened and brightened into sublimity and grandeur. In the late war with Great Britain he was but a captain; yet the little band who defended Fort Harrison saw amid the smoke of battle that they were commanded by a man fit for his station. In the Florida campaign he commanded but a brigade; yet his leadership not only evinced courage and conduct, but inspired these qualities in the meanest soldier in his ranks. He began the Mexican campaign at the head only of a division; yet as the events of the war swelled that division into an army, so the crisis kindled him into higher resolves and nobler actions till the successive steps of advance became the assured march of victory.

"Mr. Speaker, as we review the brilliant and stirring passages of the events to which I refer it is not in the power even of sudden grief to suppress the admiration which thrills our hearts. When, sir, has there been such a campaign, when such soldiers to be led, and when such qualities of leadership so variously combined? How simple, but yet how grand, was the announcement, 'In whatever force the enemy may be, I shall fight him.' It gave Palo Alto and Resaca to our banner. How steadfast the resolution that impelled the advance to Monterey! How stirring the courage which beleaguered the frowning city, which stormed the barricaded street, which carried the embattled heights, and won and kept the whole! Nor, sir, can we forget that in the flush of victory the gentle heart stayed the bold hand, while the conquering soldier offered sacrifices on the altar of pity, amid all the exultation of triumph. . . .

"Mr. Speaker, the character upon which Death has just set his seal is filled with beautiful and impressive contrasts: — a warrior, he loved peace; a man of action, he sighed for retirement. Amid the events which crowned him with fame, he counseled a withdrawal of our troops. And, whether at the head of armies or in the chair of state, he appeared as utterly unconscious of his great renown as if no banners had drooped at his word, or as if no gleam of glory shone through his whitened hair."

During this term Colonel Baker took ground against dueling. Amid very exciting circumstances a hostile meeting was about to occur between Colonel Bissell, of Illinois, and Jefferson Davis. Several members of the House were talking the matter over together when Colonel Baker denounced the practice of dueling as infamous, barbarous, inhuman. The entire party was struck with astonishment that one who had proved himself gallant, brave, and daring should condemn a practice so prevalent. The others endeavored at first to combat Colonel Baker's arguments, but they made such a deep impression that the friends of the principals in the quarrel determined to endeavor to adjust the matter peaceably, which they succeeded in doing.

Colonel Baker once said that he felt his greatest capacity was, not for eloquence or the law, but to command men. Possibly that conviction had something to do with an enterprise in which he engaged early in 1851, an enterprise "as wild as it was engaging." William H. Aspinwall, Henry Chauncey, and John L. Stevens entered into a contract with the Government of New Granada under which the individuals named were to construct a railroad across the Isthmus of Panama. It was a splendid, daring project, but it is unlikely that it would have drawn an Illinois lawyer away from his inland home unless there had been some peculiar reason to arouse his interest. That reason, I believe, was a connection between the families of Colonel Baker and Mr. Stevens. The capitalists wanted a man of integrity, of energy, and accustomed to command. Baker contracted to grade a section of the road. He gathered several hundred sturdy laborers in the West and sent them out to the Isthmus in charge of his brother Alfred, who was a skillful physician. The Colonel himself went down to superintend the work. In digging and constructing the Panama Canal the deadly influence of soil and climate has now been almost entirely overcome by the sanitary engineers of the United States Government. In 1851 sanitary science had scarcely been recognized; but even if it had been matured, the Illinois party could not have commanded such resources as have now made life safe and comfortable along the line of the Canal. Baker's party did energetic, effective work, but after many months their chief succumbed to the fierce malarial fever and was sent home to recover his health. That accomplished, Baker was receptive to the next magnificent adventure that should offer. California was the sensation of the time, — the land of unparalleled opportunity, the land of promise, of romance, of dreams, of vivid imagination. The very air was full of gold dust. The approaching years appeared full of hope and honors. While Baker had been toiling amid the luxuriant thickets of the Isthmus, many of his Illinois friends had gone to the Golden State — among them his professional friend McDougall. It was the most natural thing in the world for Baker to follow them, and in 1852, with his entire family, he migrated to California and settled in its chief city.

The Bar of San Francisco at that time comprised an unusual number of able men — men who would have been eminent in any city. There was Hall McAllister, "a commanding figure"; John B. Felton, unselfish and masterful; Henry Herbert Byrne, especially successful in bringing criminals to justice; Lorenzo Sawyer, a model, virtuous man, persistent in practice, afterward eminent on the Bench; Solomon Heydenfeldt, a man of mark as early as 1850, but later forced to discontinue practice because he would not take the oath of loyalty; Henry S. Foote, who had been Governor of Mississippi and United States Senator from that state; Alexander Anderson, who had been United States Senator from Tennessee [Anderson arrived in California two years after Baker]; Hugh C. Murray, whose talents earned him the chief justiceship of the state; Peter H. Burnett, the first governor of the state; General Charles H. S. Williams, one of the ablest lawyers who ever practiced on the coast; John T. Doyle, who left San Francisco for a time and became a partner of Mr. Rapallo, who was later a justice of the Court of Appeals of New York; Alexander Campbell, who had previously been district attorney of Kings County, New York, of lightning perceptions, courageous, and forcible; S. C. Hastings, who had sat in Congress from Iowa, and been chief justice of that territory before joining the Argonauts: — among his notable sayings was this: "I believe a state has the right to secede, and I believe the other states have a right to whip her back." Then, among the most interesting was Rufus A. Lockwood (an assumed name), who, when practicing in Indiana, was declared to have made "the best jury speech ever made on this continent — or any other"; a strange being, full of eccentricities, but at one time considered by many the leader of the San Francisco Bar. There were also Frank Tilford, from Kentucky, and his partner, Edmund Randolph, from Virginia, who was counsel for the Government in the suit over the ownership of the New Almaden quicksilver mine, his opponents being Reverdy Johnson, Judah P. Benjamin, and Archibald C. Peachy; Joseph G. Baldwin, who, while living in Alabama, had attained fame as the author of "The Flush Times of Alabama and Mississippi." S. S. Prentiss said of him, "A great man is Joe. He has no superior as writer and lawyer. He comes nearest to my idea of a universal genius." There was also Joseph P. Hoge, the Nestor of this remarkable company. Oscar L. Shafter and James McMillan Shafter, *par nobile fratrum*, came shortly after Baker and attained high distinction. Then, too, there were Edward Stanly, dignified and accomplished; Trenor W. Park, regarded as equal to any in the conduct of a case; John Currey, sturdy and exalted in character; and last, but far from least, James A. McDougall.

Baker's reputation had preceded him, and even in rivalry with such men as have been named he was soon enjoying a more lucrative practice than he ever had in Illinois. Mr. Shuck says, "His figure looms up as the most striking in our legal annals."[1] Mr. Stanly, in his oration at Baker's funeral said: "Time will not allow me to recount his many triumphs among eminent men at the Bar. The country well knows how preëminently great he was in cases of life and death, — how irresistible he was when he deprived men of their reason as he overwhelmed them in admiration of his transcendent genius. By universal consent he was regarded as having no rival in this branch of his profession."

Capital cases in which Baker was counsel aroused such interest that, instead of being regarded as merely trials, they became opportunities for the observation and enjoyment of the brilliant talents of an extraordinary advocate; so that old gentlemen

[1] *Bench and Bar*, p. 14. I am indebted to Mr. Shuck for most of these characterizations. — E. R. K.

who have indulged in the entertaining pastime of publishing reminiscences have exaggerated that feature of Colonel Baker's talents and practice and in some instances quite forgotten his success in civil cases. In the latter he had rivals; in the former he stood alone. It is said he never lost a capital case. It is true, as well, that his success in civil practice ranked him with the foremost. A contemporary said, "He practiced law here with distinguished brilliancy and success." [1] His first case outside San Francisco was in the matter of a promissory note, in Sacramento, and has already been referred to. He was counsel for the defense in a case where Major J. R. Snyder was charged with embezzlement. Major Snyder arrived in California several years before the Argonauts, and at various times held responsible offices. While he was superintendent of the San Francisco Mint he was tried on a charge of embezzlement, it being asserted that there was a continuous shrinkage in the precious metals brought to be minted. The defense claimed that the missing gold had gone up the chimney. Colonel Baker had the faculty of understanding mechanical principles. He spent several weeks in studying the chemical operations of the Mint, and on the trial showed that he knew more on that subject than anybody on either side. Judge Freelon declared that Baker's argument on that trial was the finest he ever heard him deliver. He heard Baker in the Cora case, and thought, while his

[1] *Bench and Bar*, p. 15.

speech was more brilliant, eloquent, and impassioned; yet, as a forensic effort, an argumentative display, a union of fact, argument, and expression, the speech on behalf of Major Snyder was more creditable to him as lawyer and advocate. In his argument he turned his knowledge to good account and displayed his best powers of oratory in illustration.[1] In 1856 Colonel Baker received a fee of $13,000 in a suit involving a supply of water for mining, which was tried at Downieville. Spectators declared that the Colonel won the case by a brilliant apostrophe to water. Everybody, including the jury, was carried away by the beauty of that passage in the closing of his argument. In a case arising out of a bank failure in San Francisco Baker's fee was $25,000, which was extraordinary if not unparalleled in those days.

The most celebrated and sensational of all Baker's jury trials was his defense of Charles Cora, in which General McDougall was associated with him. Cora, an Italian, was a gambler and a man of evil associations. On the eighteenth of November, 1855, Cora and United States Marshal Richardson met in a saloon. They were mutually presented, drank together several times, finally separating after a quarrel in which both were to blame. The following day they again encountered each other in the same place. Another dispute arose, they went outside, scuffled, and Cora shot Richardson through the heart. The killing of a Federal official so well

[1] *Bench and Bar*, p. 17.

known, following a large number of homicides and other deeds of violence, aroused the community to a degree of undiscriminating hysteria. The daily journals not only condemned Cora, — in advance of trial, — declaring it was a case of "assassination," of "cold-blooded murder," but they violently denounced the lawyers who consented to present his case to the court and jury. Eminent members of the bar quailed before the storm of obloquy. By the time Colonel Baker was called in it seemed as though the accused man was going to be unable to obtain the services of any lawyer competent to stand before the able prosecuting attorney and his aids. Mr. Oscar T. Shuck, of the San Francisco Bar, and one of the most popular authors of California, said of the jury that it "was a strong and worthy array." [1] In behalf of Cora it was claimed that he fired in self-defense. The jury disagreed.

A recent writer,[2] from whom I have taken some statements of details of the case, has gone out of his way to drag up base slanders upon Colonel Baker that have long lain "festering in the infamy of years." Mr. Lynch was writing the life of Senator Broderick, who admired Baker, and at whose funeral Baker pronounced one of the most beautiful memorial orations preserved in literature, an address which Mr. Lynch uses to enrich the pages of his book. After reprinting emanations of an orgy of detraction, Mr. Lynch asks, "What will not law-

[1] *Masterpieces of E. D. Baker*, p. 289.

[2] Jeremiah Lynch, in *A Senator of the Fifties*.

yers do for money?" Colonel Baker answered such questions when they were alive. Read a few words relative to this matter from his address to the jury: "The profession to which we belong is, of all others, fearless of public opinion. It has ever stood up against the tyranny of monarchs on the one hand and the tyranny of public opinion on the other. And if, as the humblest among them, it becomes me to instance myself, I may say with a bold heart, and I do say it with a bold heart, that there is not in all this world the wretch so humble, so guilty, so despairing, so torn with avenging furies, so pursued by the arm of the law, so hunted to cities of refuge, so fearful of life, so afraid of death, — there is no wretch so steeped in all the agonies of vice and crime, that I would not have a heart to listen to his cry and a tongue to speak in his defense, though round his head all the wrath of public opinion should gather and rage and roar and roll as the ocean rolls around the rock." [1]

It may fairly be assumed that Mr. Lynch is one of an unthinking multitude who would deny to an accused person whom the newspapers have convicted the right to have a lawyer present his case when he is put upon trial. Many appear to think that only an inferior lawyer should be allowed; or, if a superior lawyer, that he must not do his best for a client who has been convicted by the newspapers. Such things were sometimes said in Boston when Rufus Choate reigned at the Suffolk Bar.

[1] *Masterpieces of E. D. Baker*, p. 306.

When the memorial of Mr. Choate was presented to the Supreme Judicial Court the venerated Judge Benjamin R. Curtis remarked: "I desire, on this occasion, and in this presence, and in behalf of my brethren of this Bar, to declare our appreciation of the injustice which would be done to this great and eloquent advocate by attributing to him any want of loyalty to truth, or any deference to wrong, because he employed all his great powers and attainments, and used to the utmost his consummate skill and eloquence, in exhibiting and enforcing the comparative merits of one side of the cases in which he acted. In doing so he but did his duty. If other people did theirs the administration of justice was secured."[1]

It has been said that Colonel Baker's defense of Cora resulted in social ostracism for the advocate, boycott in his practice, and in his being "scared" or "banished" or "driven" from San Francisco; and such statements have gone so long without authoritative contradiction that some writers of honest purpose have accepted them as true. They are untrue. I have, I believe, read everything, or nearly everything, extant on this matter that is worth reading, and, unavoidably, much that is not. And not long ago I talked with a member of the jury in the Cora case. I have conversed, also, with men who were residing in San Francisco at the period when the events mentioned were current. I am thoroughly confirmed in the conclusion that if, in

[1] *Life and Works of Rufus Choate*, vol. I, p. 259.

accordance with American ideas of justice and American methods of dealing with all persons accused of crime, Charles Cora had a right to a trial, his lawyers cannot be blamed for faithfully and zealously representing him at that trial. It must, however, be admitted that Colonel Baker, who had been the idol of San Francisco, admired as much by political opponents as by political supporters, suffered a severe eclipse of popularity owing to his participation in the defense. That had little or nothing to do with his leaving San Francisco. Shortly after the Cora trial the Great Vigilance Committee assumed charge of the city. Most good citizens approved of its work. A considerable number, among whom were many lawyers, condemned it. Baker joined these, who were called the "Law and Order Party." Instead of being "scared," he made a speech to an outdoor meeting of the Law and Order Party so near to a meeting-place of Vigilantes that the noise of the latter interfered with the hearing of his remarks. However, as the Committee became the only government, and as Colonel Baker refused to practice law before the Committee, he went into other parts of the state where his services were in demand. When the committee dissolved and the regular courts resumed their functions, Colonel Baker returned to San Francisco. At first there was considerable feeling against him, but his popularity quickly returned and was soon as great as ever. By the year 1858, when, on the twenty-seventh of September, the city was aroused to great enthusiasm over the completion of the first Atlantic cable, Colonel Baker was with one accord chosen to voice the general jubilation, and his address on that occasion was at once adopted by the people of San Francisco as the finest oratorical treasure of the Pacific Coast.

The scope of this book precludes the incorporation of Colonel Baker's speeches, but some excerpts must be made from this address to illustrate one phase of his oratory. The symmetry is lost in condensing and much of the impression escapes, but the beauty may nevertheless be somewhat disclosed: —

"Amid the general joy that thrills throughout the civilized world we are here to bear our part. The great enterprise of the age has been accomplished. Thought has bridged the Atlantic and cleaves its unfettered path across the sea, winged by the lightning and guarded by the billow."

It was in the course of this speech that Colonel Baker uttered the apostrophe to Science that won such wide renown: —

"O Science! Thou thought-clad leader of the company of pure and great souls that toil for their race and love their kind! Measurer of the depths of earth and the recesses of heaven! Apostle of civilization, handmaid of religion, teacher of human equality and human right, perpetual witness for the Divine Wisdom, — be ever, as now, the great minister of peace! Let thy starry brow and benign front still gleam in the van of progress, brighter than the sword of the conqueror and welcome as the light of heaven!"

The following description is very fine: —

"The spectacle which marked the moment when the cable was first dropped in the deep sea was one of absorbing interest. Two stately ships of different and once hostile nations bore the precious freight. Meeting in mid-ocean, they exchanged the courtesies of their gallant profession. Each bore the flag of St. George; each carried the flowing Stripes and blazing Stars. On each deck that martial band bowed reverently in prayer to the Great Ruler of the tempest. Exact in order, perfect in discipline, they waited the auspicious moment to seek the distant shore. Well were those noble vessels named, — the one, Niagara, with a force resistless as our own cataract; the other, Agamemnon, 'the king of men,' as constant in purpose, as resolute in trial, as the great leader of the Trojan War. Right well, O gallant crews, have you fulfilled your trust! Favoring were the gales and smooth the seas that bore you to the land. And oh! if the wish and prayer of the good and wise of all the earth may avail, your high and peaceful mission shall remain forever perfect, and those triumphant standards, so long shadowing the earth with their glory, shall wave in united folds as long as the Homeric story shall be remembered among men or the thunders of Niagara reverberate above its arch of spray."

One of the most splendid passages is the allusion to the marvelous comet visible at that time: —

"But, even while we assemble to mark the deed and rejoice at its completion, the Almighty, as if to impress us with a becoming sense of our weakness as compared with his power, has set a new signal of his reign in heaven. If to-night, fellow citizens, you will look from the glare of your illuminated city into the northwestern heavens, you will perceive, low down on the edge of the horizon, a bright stranger pursuing its path across the sky. Amid the starry hosts that keep their watch, it shines attended by a brighter pomp and followed by a broader train. No living man has gazed upon its splendors before. No watchful votary of science has traced its course for nearly ten generations. It is more than three hundred years since its approach was visible from our planet. When last it came it startled an emperor on his throne, and while the superstition of his age taught him to perceive in its presence a herald and a doom, his pride saw in its flaming course and fiery train the announcement that his own light was about to be extinguished. In common with the lowest of his subjects, he read omens of destruction in the baleful heavens and prepared himself for a fate which alike awaits the mightiest and the meanest. Thanks to the present condition of scientific knowledge, we read the heavens with a far clearer perception. We see in the predicted return of the rushing, blazing comet through the sky, the march of a heavenly messenger along his appointed way and around his predestined orbit. For three hundred years he has traveled amid the regions of infinite space. 'Lone wandering, but not lost,' he has left behind him shining suns, blazing stars, and gleaming constellations — now nearer to the eternal throne and again on the confines of the universe. He returns with visage radiant and benign. He returns with unimpeded march and unobstructed way. He returns the majestic, swift, electric telegraph of the Almighty, bearing upon his flaming front the tidings that throughout the universe there is still peace and order; that amid the immeasurable dominions of the Great King his rule is still perfect; that suns and stars and systems tread their endless circle and obey the eternal law."

Colonel Baker naturally took part in politics directly he had settled in California. If he had been controlled by selfish considerations he would have joined the Democrats; the Democratic Party was in undisputed control. Baker's lifetime ambition was to be a senator. He was making a new start. But, no; he had been a Free-Soil Whig, and as a Free-Soiler he came out in San Francisco. In 1855 he was an unsuccessful candidate for election to the State Senate. With the dissolution of the Whig Party he appeared among the earliest advocates of the principles and candidates of the Republican Party, and in 1856 stumped the state for Frémont and Dayton, from San Diego to Yreka, cheerfully enduring the hardships of travel previous to the introduction of railroads. Several of his speeches were reported for the "Sacramento

Union," the leading news journal of the coast at that time, and some of them were adopted by the Republican State Committee and printed and distributed in large numbers. Of Baker's address at Forest Hill, Placer County, Henry Edgerton, himself one of the noblest orators of that epoch of oratory, declared that he never heard so grand a speech. Colonel Baker's address at Goodyear's Bar, three years before, was perhaps more dramatic. Goodyear's was a mining-camp, near Downieville, where there was a population of five hundred, all adults, nearly all men, and yet in the election of the previous year there was only one Republican vote. Colonel Baker declared that he would reënforce that one Republican. He arrived at Goodyear's toward the close of the day, found a carpenter's bench, engaged a man to help him drag it out in front of the chief saloon, mounted it, and began to speak. That one Republican came early and stood up beside Colonel Baker. At the start there were just twenty-one in the audience, but the Colonel took as much pains with his speech as if he had been addressing a thousand. Gradually the men came up, until nearly the entire population had collected. It was a tough-looking crowd, mostly Irish miners, but toned up by several saloon keepers and a number of gamblers and diversified by nearly a dozen Chinamen. For half an hour there was not a laugh, not a sign of applause, not even a look of interest, although Colonel Baker was doing his best, flashing his wit and pouring forth wave upon wave of eloquence. At times a sort of tremor ran through the obstinate throng. They squirmed, but they managed to repress any open display of feeling. At supper Colonel Baker had learned that several of the men had been in Riley's regiment in the Mexican War. He referred to his being with them in some of the battles. Pointing to a staff from which the Stars and Stripes had been lowered, he pronounced a glowing panegyric on the flag of our Union and the soldiers who had carried it to victory. They could not withstand that. First there came from one of the veterans a yell that was actually agonizing. That set off the rest and there arose a wild Irish howl. Everybody suddenly wanted to grasp the speaker's hand. Several leaped up on the bench and tried to embrace him. In the tumult the improvised platform was upset. But the crowd had packed together so close that none of those on the platform fell to the ground; they landed on the heads and shoulders of those nearest in the throng. It was, declares Calvin B. McDonald (from whose reminiscent letter in the Sacramento "Daily Bee" I have quoted), like the scene, described by D'Arcy Magee, of St. Patrick's conquest of the Irish on the Hill of Tara.

Those days were full of adventure. Colonel Baker was announced to speak in Marysville, in the Frémont campaign. As there were not yet enough Republicans to fill a hall, the advertisement announced that after Colonel Baker had concluded "any gentleman selected by the meeting" would be given the opportunity to reply. Although most of

Baker's listeners were Democrats, his lucid argument, his brilliant wit, his superb eloquence, and his abstention from abuse of adversaries had for the moment won the admiration and plaudits of his hearers. As soon as the applause ceased there were many demands for Montgomery — "Old Zach" he was familiarly called. Mr. Montgomery was a lawyer, an able man, a fluent speaker, but to an extreme degree the reverse of handsome or graceful, and was noted for bodily movements quite phenomenal. He had apparently expected the call, and he responded in a speech which lasted an hour, indulging his habit of denunciation (a habit of the period), and arousing most of those present to a high pitch of enthusiasm. When he sat down he was rewarded with vociferous cheers. Then Colonel Baker rose and advanced to the front of the platform. His face was serene. The hint of a humorous smile was lurking there. In a gentlemanly, winning tone — ah, what a voice was Baker's! There is none like it now on rostrum or in pulpit — with exquisite enunciation, he said, "In the advertisement of this meeting it was stated that after I was through speaking the audience would be asked to select some gentleman to reply. Will you take advantage of the offer?" This was so unlike the response Mr. Montgomery's speech might have provoked that the crowd was, for a moment, puzzled; but almost instantly came the consciousness that there had been a slight but peculiar emphasis on the word "gentleman," and a laugh began with those most alert to subtle impressions, which spread through the entire assemblage.[1] Much of Baker's success in speaking must be credited to the charm and fascination of his voice. Senator Sumner referred to it in his address in the memorial exercises of the Senate. Every one who has described Baker has mentioned it in glowing terms. It was a tenor. Without great effort Baker was able to make it carry to the limits of the largest assemblages. Before a jury its modulations worked a spell that bound his listeners to him. Once in a generation such a tenor voice is brought forward in Italian opera. Sometimes its possessor has no physical beauty, grace, or intellectual inspiration. Baker had all.

The quality and splendor of Baker's eloquence are not being exaggerated in this book, but, as Senator Latham said, after Baker's death, "The most brilliant mental efforts of his life are not upon record. The sudden bursts of his often matchless eloquence have passed away with the time and occasion of their utterance. Those preserved of his addresses on different occasions are cold and formal compared with others uttered without premeditation, when under the inspiration of the moment his mind glowed with the fire of genius and strength. His ease and grace of delivery, his felicity of expres-

[1] At the time of the outburst of loyalty evoked by the attack on Fort Sumter a newspaper office in San Francisco owned by Mr. Montgomery was destroyed by a loyal mob. During the first administration of President Cleveland Mr. Montgomery was honored with a high professional appointment — Solicitor of the Treasury, I think. — E. R. K.

sion, his wonderful flow of harmonious language, the musical intonations of his voice, can never be forgotten by those who have heard him in many of his happy efforts." [1] The Honorable George H. Williams, who was Attorney-General of the United States in the Cabinet of President Grant, was a few years ago giving his recollections of Colonel Baker: "I have heard many of the so-called greatest orators of the country, at the Bar, on the stump, and in the halls of legislation, but Edward D. Baker was the most eloquent man I ever heard speak. He had a rich, ringing, silvery voice, with an easy flow of beautiful language, and withal was an exceedingly handsome man. He had all that a man ought to have to be an ideal orator." [2]

After Colonel Baker's stumping tour in 1856 he was called the "Gray Eagle" or the "Gray Eagle of Republicanism," — his exquisitely fine hair, almost white, his lofty brow, his splendid, warm gray eye, his ample and perfectly proportioned nose, and the lofty flights of his eloquence, won him this distinguished and affectionate appellation, by which he was afterwards commonly known.

In 1859 he was a candidate for Congress, receiving the support of the Republicans and, as far as Broderick could control, of the Douglas Democrats; but the ticket of the Lecompton Democrats was successful. During this campaign he again spoke throughout the state and stood boldly for the anti-

[1] *Cong. Globe*, 37th Congress, part I, p. 55.

[2] Oregon newspaper.

slavery policy of the Republican Party. While the secession propaganda had not taken definite form enough to evoke public condemnation, Colonel Baker's speeches had much to do with inspiring and leading the minds of well-disposed men, for on all occasions he exalted the Union and inculcated the duty of loyalty.

Shortly after the election, which occurred in September, a delegation came down to San Francisco to invite Colonel Baker to migrate to Oregon. There were a number of citizens, and to give the movement a semi-official character there was a sub-committee of three of the Republican State Committee. Once before the Colonel had been urged to come to Oregon and take the lead in building up the Republican Party. There were a number of Illinoisians in this delegation, who now repeated and urged the invitation. They said to him, in substance: "We know what you used to do in Illinois. We know how you moved from one district that you had made Whig into another, always Democratic, until you turned it over to the Whigs, and we believe you can repeat such triumphs in Oregon. Our election comes next spring. Come to us. Take the lead. Speak in every legislative district. The state is now Democratic. You can make it Republican, and we will make you United States Senator." The sub-committee told him that they had not developed a popular and capable state leader. "There are many," they said, "in California capable of carrying forward the organization and the cause.

There are none in Oregon. We offer you the leadership. There will be no rival, no disappointment and envy. We will all follow and support you.'

It appealed to his chivalry, to his temperament for doing things impossible for others. Difficulties did not dismay him; they roused him to his best efforts. He believed in the principles of the Republican Party, and he believed in himself. In December he visited the state and looked the situation over. He was convinced that he was not only needed, but that he was wanted, and he determined to make the venture. He returned to San Francisco and closed up his affairs as expeditiously as possible. At that time the offices of Baker & Dwinelle were at 148 Clay Street, and the Colonel's home was far out in Pacific Street, near Larkin. At his home he was a bounteous provider and a hospitable entertainer. In his profession he was extremely prosperous. Others, therefore, looked on the Oregon project as wild and hopeless. Fred Low, afterwards Governor of California, bet Colonel Baker a suit of clothes that he would fail.[1] The Colonel laughingly accepted the hazard. On the 17th day of February, 1860, he sailed for Portland in the steamer Panama. Just before the steamer left her wharf at Folsom Street the Colonel was presented with a magnificent gold watch "from his friends." Merchants, bankers, artisans, judges, professional men, members of fraternal orders, clients, adversaries — the entire community — gave demonstrations of affec-

[1] *Bench and Bar*, p. 16.

tion and regard. The "Alta California," a journal which ranked very high, said:[1] "Colonel E. D. Baker takes his departure from California to-day for Oregon, to become a citizen of Salem in that state. He leaves behind him as large a circle of admiring friends as any man in California can boast, and the loss of his presence among us will be regarded with general regret."

[1] February 17, 1860.

CHAPTER IX

VENI, VIDI, VICI — BAKER RETURNS A SENATOR — SECESSION PROPAGANDA DEFEATED — EXTRAORDINARY MEETING IN SAN FRANCISCO — OREGON AND CALIFORNIA WON FOR LINCOLN

OREGON, which was admitted to the Union as a state on the fourteenth of February, 1859, was a "Democratic stronghold." Earlier it had been for a short time a pasture for Whigs. When General Taylor was President he tendered the appointment of governor of the territory to Abraham Lincoln; but during the administrations of Presidents Pierce and Buchanan, beginning in 1853, every Federal appointee had been a "reliable" Democrat. Under this influence the elective officials of the territory were equally "reliable." The first state legislature, which was almost entirely Democratic, elected General Joseph E. Lane and Delazon Smith United States Senators. There had never been a strenuous political campaign; matters were too much one way. One side felt that there was no use of their working hard and the other that there was no need.

It may almost be said that Oregon was a slave territory. Several families from the South brought slaves with them, not as freed servants but as property.[1] The gathering contest in the states appeared to most Oregonians as an array of the South against the North, and most of them sympathized with the South. At a Jackson Day banquet at the capital in January, 1857, one of the speakers, subsequently prominent in national affairs, — with amusing incongruity on the birthday of the man who stamped out nullification, — unreservedly indorsed the extreme Southern view of "state sovereignty," and all present supported him in that position. They were getting ready, poisoning minds.

In all the history of fallacies — divine right of rascally kings, supreme right of majorities to oppress minorities, right of factions to murder, as in the French Revolution — there has never one appeared more pestiferous and fatal to its dupes than the centrifugal doctrine of "state sovereignty." The world regards Robert E. Lee as an extraordinarily pure and lofty character. From his youth a ward, a pupil, a scholar of the National Government. By his own wish, his own choice, that Government, at the cost of citizens of Connecticut and Wisconsin as well as of citizens of Virginia, relieved his family of responsibility for his education, upon the explicit understanding that the Government, having trained him and made him an accomplished soldier, should be entitled to his services in its army. That was the contract. There were other Virginian youth who accepted the same benefits, —

[1] San Francisco *Chronicle*, July 24, 1881.

a technical education and rank in a noble profession; for instance, General George H. Thomas, commonly referred to as "the noblest Roman of them all," and General Winfield Scott. They kept the faith. "They rest from their labors, and *their* works do follow them." But Robert E. Lee, a pure and lofty character, poisoned by the virus of "state sovereignty," could find no obstacle to withdrawing from the national army and leading a hostile force in a desperate effort to destroy the Government. What a doctrine, that could work such ruin upon so noble a nature! This virus, this political bubonic plague, was being assiduously spread abroad in Oregon, as well as in California. The doctrine was inculcated with the purpose of weakening and loosening the ties that bound the people to the National Government.

The disloyal leaders did not stop there; they went the whole length of applying their doctrine. General Lane — "Joe" Lane — territorial governor, delegate to Congress, United States Senator, the most popular and influential man in the state — said in a public address, "Fellow citizens, I warn you that if you elect a Northern President that moment will see this Union dissolved." [1]

Lane was so satisfactory to the Southern leaders and so thoroughly trusted by them, and his influence in Oregon and on the Pacific Coast was estimated so highly, that they made him their candi-

[1] *Martin Monahan's Recollections*, Seattle newspaper, January 28, 1906.

date for Vice-President in 1860. Secretary Floyd wrote in his diary, under date November 8, 1860: "I had a long conversation to-day with General Lane, the candidate for Vice-President on the ticket with Mr. Breckinridge. He was grave and extremely earnest; said that resistance to the anti-slavery feeling of the North was hopeless, and that nothing was left to the South but 'resistance or disunion.' . . . He thought disunion inevitable, and said when the hour came if his services could be useful he would offer them unhesitatingly to the South." [1]

Though defeated in the national election, Lane adhered to the Southern cause and fully trusted that Oregon would follow him. Speaking in the Senate, on the 19th day of December, 1860, he said, in reply to a speech by Andrew Johnson: "I serve notice that when war is made upon that gallant South for withdrawing from a Union which refused them their rights, the Northern Democracy will not join in the crusade. The Republican Party will have war enough at home." [2]

And again: "When he [Andrew Johnson] or any other gentleman raises that banner [the flag of our Union] and attempts to subjugate that gallant people [South Carolina], instead of marching with him, we will meet him there, ready to repel him and his forces." [3]

[1] Quoted by Nicolay and Hay, vol. II, p. 316.

[2] *Cong. Globe,* 2d Session, 36th Congress, part I, p. 143.

[3] *Ibid.*

Two days before the expiration of his term as Senator, replying to Senator Baker, who had become his colleague, he said: "This I am warranted in asserting, — for I know long and well and intimately the gallant men of Oregon, — that they will not be found ready or inclined, at the Senator's or his master's beck, for a godless cause in fraternal gore."[1]

It was to this state, — Joe Lane's Oregon, — that vast expanse, where the silence of ages had not yet been broken by the sound of a locomotive whistle; to the Oregon of dark, deep forests, and rough roads, that Colonel Baker had come. He opened his law office in Salem and at the same time entered upon his especial task. On stage-coaches and on horseback he went everywhere, pouring out the floods of his inspiring oratory. The journals of that primitive period are marked with the traces of his travels and the evidences of his tremendous ardor. "Colonel Baker will address the citizens of Yamhill County Wednesday evening." "Colonel Baker made a lengthy, eloquent, argumentative speech." "In Colonel Baker's happiest vein, thrillingly eloquent; held his audience enchanted"; — these are expressions by which he may be tracked from place to place. It may be safely asserted of this serious, exhaustive campaign of speeches that for wit and eloquence, for convincing popular argument, inspiring passion, and captivating charm, they were never exceeded. They were not written,

[1] *Cong. Globe*, 2d Session, 36th Congress, part 2, p. 1344.

and alas! they were not reported. In one sense they are lost, — they are not available for present reading. But they accomplished their high and patriotic end. Even now there are some who heard the "Gray Eagle" in that adventurous contest. Occasionally one of the old men repeats the tale to some listening reporter; and it is plain that the memory of that early, that Homeric age, is cherished as a precious possession.

On the Fourth of July, 1860, Colonel Baker delivered an oration at Salem. One declaration shows how the dark cloud of disunion hung upon the horizon of that period, and discloses a sad prescience that would, in earlier days, have been regarded as prophetic. Referring to the threats of secession and civil war, the speaker said: "Whatever services I have rendered on the field of battle in other lands, in other days, I leave impartial history to record. But if it be reserved for me to lay my unworthy life upon the altar of my country in defending it from internal assailants, I declare here to-day that I aspire to no higher glory than that the sun of my life may go down beneath the shadow of freedom's temple and baptize the emblem of the nation's greatness, the Stars and Stripes, that float so proudly before us to-day, in my heart's warmest blood."

The voters of the state, like the voters of California in the election of the previous autumn, divided into three parties, — Republicans, Lecompton Democrats, who supported the Administration of President Buchanan, and Democrats opposed to the Administration, who, like Broderick's followers in California, were against secession, but were as yet unready to go over to the Republicans, and so accepted the title of Douglas Democrats. The election being over, when the legislature met these three parties were all represented. The Republicans, hitherto an insignificant group, now appeared strong and belligerent. Still, they had not a majority. There were two United States Senators to elect, but no party had votes enough for the purpose. The matter attracted wide attention. From Illinois came a letter from which the following is an excerpt: —

SPRINGFIELD, ILL., August, 1860.

FRIEND FRANCIS, — If you see Colonel Baker give him my respects. I do hope he may not be tricked out of what he has fairly earned. Yours forever,

As ever,

A. LINCOLN.

The Lecomptonites in the legislature desired to trade with the Douglas Democrats, but the latter, who were opposed to secession, and who had been deeply stirred by Colonel Baker's eloquence, chose to come to an arrangement with the Republicans. Then for the first time in Oregon the Republicans and loyal Democrats were called "Union men," a designation under which they coöperated for several years. When the Lecomptonites learned that they were to have no voice in the election of Senators they determined to prevent, if possible, any election whatever by depriving one branch of the legislature of a quorum; so many assemblymen withdrew. They went five miles outside the town and were hidden in a capacious barn, where, it was promised, they should be secreted and fed "until the Baker danger should be passed." But the sergeant-at-arms discovered their hiding-place and took in enough of them to make a quorum. Thus, while a number of seceders remained in the hospitable seclusion of "Uncle Nick" Schram's barn, still hoping they might thwart the purpose of the majority, their unwilling comrades were locked in their legislative chamber and the Republicans and Douglas Democrats elected Colonel Baker and James W. Nesmith to the Senate.[1]

Colonel Baker's first act was to pen a letter to his mother, who was in Illinois — a widow. At Salem, on the second of October, he wrote to his friend Colonel R. F. Maury: —

> MY DEAR SIR, — I am just elected Senator. Mr. Nesmith is my colleague. Will you please forward the inclosed [the letter to his mother] by special messenger to Yreka with instructions to be secret and tell nobody, and I will pay the expense when I see you, which will be soon, on my way down. Let the messenger start as soon as you get this.
>
> Very truly yours,
>
> E. D. BAKER.

In those days, as has been said, many letters were carried by Wells, Fargo & Company's Ex-

[1] *Martin Monahan's Recollections*, narrated by Edmond S. Meany in Seattle newspaper, January 28, 1906.

press, thus securing greater expedition than was practicable through the United States mails; but Colonel Baker was determined to beat both those instrumentalities by sending a special messenger to a point where his letter could be delivered to the pony express. In a few days he himself was on his way to San Francisco to take the steamer for Panama and the States. Among loyal men everywhere on the coast there was exultation over his election. When the news was received in San Francisco there was greater enthusiasm among the Republicans than they had ever had occasion to display. A salute of one hundred guns was fired from Stuart Street and another of two hundred guns from Telegraph Hill. Buildings were illuminated, fireworks set off, and the streets were thronged with cheering citizens. An impromptu procession was led by the "Wide-Awakes" and a meeting was held where speeches were made expressive of the greatest jubilation. The new Senator arrived in San Francisco on the morning of the nineteenth of October. As the steamer Brother Jonathan passed Fort Point a salute of one hundred guns was fired. The steamer reached her wharf at ten o'clock, where an immense throng awaited the victor.

It was a critical period in the presidential campaign of 1860. The regular Democrats, — the organization around the federal and state office-holders, — with abundant funds, great confidence, even arrogance, supported Breckinridge and Lane.

Their national leaders had not the slightest expectation or desire of electing Breckinridge. The time had come to secede; conditions favored; but they did hope to have California and Oregon vote for Breckinridge and Lane and thus identify themselves with the Southern cause. Broderick's party, without his leadership, was animated by revenge for his death, imbued by devotion to the principle of allowing each state, when admitted to the Union, to decide whether it would have slavery or not, and ardent for Douglas.

The Republicans had expected and desired the nomination of William H. Seward. His preëminence in the party was conceded. The Californians wanted no "dark horse" or inferior as a candidate. They were disappointed at the nomination of Abraham Lincoln. It was not long, however, before they were actively enlisted in the campaign, but not with the enthusiasm they would have displayed in support of Seward. Little was said of Lincoln; little was known. Some documents were, I believe, sent from New York, and a brilliant stump speaker known as "Tom" Fitch came from the East, dashed into the arena, and adorned the sober arguments of the campaign books with flowers from the opulent garden of his brain. I remember hearing him at an outdoor meeting in Marysville, when, pointing to the sublime spectacle of the California sky, he pronounced the stars "the auger-holes of Heaven," — which figure, I suppose, he may have brought from Milwaukee, where he had married the daughter of a well-to-do carpenter. But I do not mean to disparage Mr. Fitch or depreciate his work for Lincoln, which was indeed earnest and effective.[1] The regular speakers, too, came around, — some of them deeply impressed with the unusual momentousness of the campaign; but there was no inspiring leader, unless it was Mr. Fitch. Where they got the money for the expenses I never knew. They had no office-holders to assess; and the prospects of victory were at first not sufficient to justify those expectant of office in contributing very liberally.

In long campaigns there come stages of discouragement; perhaps they are due to fatigue, exhaustion. There was such a stage in the first McKinley campaign, about three weeks preceding the day of election. Everybody was tired, everybody was scared, everybody had to subscribe over again. Such a stage was reached in California at one time in the campaign of 1860. There had been hard, uphill work. There were twenty-two newspapers pouring forth or repeating the arguments and the confident boasts of the Breckinridge Party; twenty-four supporting Douglas; and only seven for Lincoln. In the East the Republicans were cheered and encouraged by the result of the October elections in Pennsylvania, Ohio, and Indiana.

For weeks after these encouragements the Republicans of California were still ignorant of

[1] Since then Mr. Fitch has held high rank as an orator.

them.[1] There were no reserves, no resources. The Republicans never had won anything in the state, — save a few local officers and some members of the legislature, — and it looked as though their record of adversity was to continue. They were accustomed to disappointment. They had small hope of the sweet rewards of victory to encourage them — none of the coherences of public plunder.

At such a moment Colonel Baker arrived from Oregon. He had been gone so short a time — not much longer than many took for a visit to the States — that the general public scarcely realized he had been gone at all. Here was an oratorical Cæsar who might, as truly as the great Julius, declare, "Veni, vidi, vici," — "I came, I saw, I conquered." It was amazing — Oregon — Joe Lane's own state — and he a candidate for Vice-President! Yet here was the man, with the commission of United States Senator in his possession. Curiosity to see him was great — to hear him greater. A writer describes his appearance and manner at this time: "Baker's delivery was rapid, his voice melodious, his diction polished, his gesture free and full of grace. He had a splendid person, an eye of fire, a noble forehead, and nose and mouth and chin were finely chiseled. His hair had long been gray. On the platform his manner was marked by perpetual animation. He loved all arts, all sciences. His imagi-

[1] The results in the "October States" were first made known to Californians in the San Francisco *Evening Bulletin* on Wednesday, the thirty-first of October.

nation was rich, his reading wide, his memory extraordinary. His countenance and bearing and his gray locks recalled the picture of Thorwaldsen, of whom it was said that when he moved in the midst of a crowd it would separate as if it felt the presence of a superior being. His disposition was the perfection of amiability. In his most heated forensic and political contests he was never betrayed into saying an unmanly thing of an adversary."[1] In his Oregon campaign Colonel Baker frankly avowed his candidacy for the Senate, but after the nomination of Lincoln and Hamlin became known he put that forward as being of the greatest importance; and I have been told that Baker's speeches did more than any other instrumentality to secure the electoral vote of Oregon for the Republican candidates.[2] The Republican Committee of California persuaded him to speak in the commercial metropolis of the coast. The place chosen was the old American Theatre (where later stood the Halleck block), a vast auditorium, and the date Friday, the twenty-sixth of October. It is to me unaccountable that Bancroft could describe Colonel Baker's brilliant and unparalleled and victorious canvass for the Senate as giving Oregon "the benefit of his rhetoric," and, although admitting that Baker "aided in arousing Union sentiment,"[3] could refer

[1] *Bench and Bar*, pp. 19, 20.

[2] Lincoln's plurality was less than three hundred. It is easy to believe that Baker's speeches won over more than that number. — E. R. K.

[3] Bancroft, vol. XIX, p. 276.

to his San Francisco speech with a sneer. By frequent iteration and reiteration the veteran campaigner had developed to their utmost the salient issues of the contest, had clad them in the most gorgeous imagery, and arranged them in the most captivating and convincing order. He had attained that perfection which comes of practice. Then, besides the inspiration of noble principles, he was speaking for Abraham Lincoln, the friend of his lifetime. The circumstances surrounding the occasion could not fail to arouse his utmost powers — and he had powers. Of Baker at this meeting Mr. Shuck said, "Perhaps on that occasion he excited his audience to a pitch of enthusiasm and delight beyond all his other triumphs."[1] Hittell, a historian, not merely an employer of compilers, says: "It was in this campaign that Edward D. Baker pronounced, in favor of Freedom and the Republican Party, what was supposed to be the greatest speech ever delivered in California."[2]

Many people from other parts of the state went to San Francisco to hear the "Gray Eagle." I journeyed from Marysville, — a trip that took twenty-four hours. All day the thought of the meeting obsessed the city. Not Republicans only were filled with expectancy; Democrats were conscious of something that boded ill for their cause, something like a calamity they were unable to avert. They appeared to realize sullenly that they were as pow-

[1] *Bench and Bar*, p. 18.

[2] Hittell (San Francisco, 1897), vol. IV, p. 272.

erless as they would have been to arrest the rising tide of the ocean. Stores and offices closed earlier than usual. People began collecting about the doors of the theatre in the afternoon. By six o'clock the customary directions of pedestrian movement at that hour were reversed and the tide was setting strongly toward the corner of Halleck and Sansome streets. Little was said. People acted as though some great event was portending from which they must not be diverted. The sidewalks and streets rapidly filled, throngs extending in every direction. It was estimated that by seven o'clock there were twelve thousand persons present. The theatre would hold four thousand. When the doors were opened the place was filled almost in an instant. So dense and tightly packed was the crowd in the aisles and standing places that persons who fainted were passed out over the heads of others. In composition and character, in spirit and influence, it was much the most important meeting ever held by any political party on the Pacific Coast. At eight o'clock B. W. Hathaway, Chairman of the Republican State Committee, came forward and said: "Ladies and Gentlemen, — We have met here to listen to the first Republican who has ever been elected to a distinguished position on the Pacific Coast . . . . Our guest is one of the champions of freedom, the orator of the Pacific Coast."

As soon as the president and other officers of the meeting were chosen, cries of "Baker," "Baker," resounded from all parts of the hall. Soon the gallant "Gray Eagle" was seen coming up from the rear of the stage, and as the assembly caught sight of his silvery locks, the multitude sprang to their feet and cheer rose upon cheer in indescribable enthusiasm. When the presiding officer, the Honorable E. L. Sullivan, was able to make himself heard, he spoke briefly and introduced "the Honorable Edward D. Baker, United States Senator from the State of Oregon." At this the tumult broke out afresh. The entire audience again sprang to their feet, shouting, cheering, waving hands, arms, hats, handkerchiefs, — waving themselves, indeed, — while before them stood that joyous, serene man; and thus the thousands roared and demonstrated until they were exhausted. Then Colonel Baker spoke. The first tones of that splendid voice that had so often charmed the people of San Francisco electrified the immense throng. It is often said that the speech was not reported. Even Mr. Hay, in his brilliant article about Colonel Baker in "Harper's Magazine,"[1] falls into this error. The speech was "reported by Sumner and Cutter," which expression I quote from a copy of "Campaign Document No. 15, Printed by the Republican State Central Committee of California," in my possession.

Baker's opening sentence was greeted with applause — and laughter. The people present considered Colonel Baker a Californian and a San Franciscan. He had gone in and out among them

[1] December, 1861.

for years. Here he was, in an unexpected and a distinguished capacity. How had it happened? It had been understood that General Lane had a life lease of the Oregon senatorship for himself and any colleague he might designate; yet here was Colonel Baker — of San Francisco, as they all understood it — on his way to Washington as United States Senator from the neighboring state. The people present looked on Colonel Baker as their own hero, who had gone up to Oregon, wrested a splendid prize from all contestants, and brought it back, not so much for service in Washington as for their delight and pride. He was like an eagle that had gone out and seized great spoil and returned with it to his eyrie; so when the speaker, after the magnificent welcome, began, "I owe more thanks than my life can repay — and I wish all Oregon were here to-night," they applauded, and, as they were struck with the incongruity of Oregon's having anything to do with it, they laughed. The idea seemed pleasing to Colonel Baker, too, for he continued: "We are a quiet, earnest, pastoral people; but by the banks of the Willamette there are many hearts that would beat as high as yours if they could see what I see at this moment. [Applause.] People of San Francisco and of California, I owe you very much. But I owe Oregon more."

The notion of Colonel Baker as one of the quiet, pastoral people dwelling by the banks of the Willamette was amusing enough, and, emphasized as it was by a sly, subtle suggestion of drollness in the orator's face, and a peculiar quip in his voice, the effect was comical and the listeners exploded in laughter and cheers. Then, too, they remembered that California defeated Baker for Congress, while Oregon had elected him to the Senate, and it seemed as though they proposed making amends, on this night of triumph, by the heartiness of their acclaims.

A few minutes later Colonel Baker again referred to "my country, Oregon," when he was again interrupted by laughter; but he continued, "where the hospitality of the people is a great deal broader than their convenience. In my country" — and another interruption by laughter; so that the Colonel changed his expression and said, " Well, in Oregon," whereupon there was "great laughter," as the report says. Then Colonel Baker added, "As a friend here, whose country it is, reminds me, if it is n't mine it is n't Joe Lane's," and then there was more laughter.

Colonel Baker referred felicitously to the fact that John C. Frémont, who had been their candidate four years before, was present, but he was soon over with preliminaries and in the midst of his subject. First, taking up some of the charges against the principles and character of his party, he refuted them with argument, with wit, and with eloquence. "They used to say that we were sectional," said he, "because we were not represented in the Electoral College, or in the national convention which met in Philadelphia, by delegates from all the states in the Union. I saw a letter last week from a very honest and a very good man by the name of Abraham Lincoln [tremendous applause], and he, in thus communicating with a friend,[1] said that it was very queer he should be called sectional by certain politicians when it was a fact that he got more votes from the South in the Chicago Convention than Judge Douglas did in the Baltimore Convention. 'Yet the party to which I belong is said to be sectional while that of Judge Douglas claims to be national.'... Whose fault is it? You won't let us go down South and make Republicans or we would soon have a host of converts in that latitude. [Applause.] I believe that my friend Judge Douglas intimates that Lincoln can't go South to see his mother. [Laughter.] Surely this is no cause for your complaint against us if you won't allow us the liberty of speech in order to express our opinions or even to record our votes in your states. That is not sectionalism in us, is it? If so the fault is yours and not ours."

Colonel Baker next argued the secession project and made this significant statement: "I am told that here in California your stump speakers boldly proclaim the doctrine of Senator Lane, from Oregon, that if the South does n't stand up for her rights she doesn't deserve any. . . . What do disunionists propose to dissolve the Union for? They say, with the grammar and sense of Van Buren, 'Our sufferings is intolerable' [laughter],

[1] It is easy to surmise who that friend was.

and they propose in alleviation to dissolve the Union. Speaker Orr does it; Yancey does it; thousands do it. They echo it and reëcho it here." Mentioning the Fugitive Slave Law, Colonel Baker said: "When a black man runs away from Kentucky into Ohio, or any other free state, he shall not have a jury trial. When a question arises as to the personal liberty of a human being he is denied the privilege of judge or jury trial in the ordinary forms of law. But a black horse cannot be transferred from one man to another, where there is a dispute about the ownership, without the matter being fully determined by twelve men. Again, they repeat, all this talk will do very well for a white man, but it don't do for a nigger. If you don't allow us to have a fugitive slave law, in order to facilitate our operations in catching negroes without any interference by jurors, we will dissolve the Union. Oh, very well, we say, if you are going to dissolve the Union, why take your nigger [laughter]; we won't break up the Union for such a reason as that. So the Fugitive Slave Law was passed in 1850."

The speaker then discussed the question of slavery in the territories. Replying to the Southern contention that men must be allowed to take slaves into territories, as well as any other kind of property, he said: "Some property is good, other property is bad; some is productive, other unproductive; some is safe, other dangerous. Indeed, if a man wanted to take a pet jackass [laughter], instead of a pet lapdog, into a parlor, would it be right for him to do it?" He concluded this branch of his speech as follows: "The normal condition of a territory is freedom. [Applause.] Stand upon the ridge of the Sierra Nevada, or upon some mountain height that overlooks the eastern and western valleys beyond you, and what do you behold? The savage may be there; the beasts of the forest may be there; the pestilence may be there; but slavery is NOT there [applause], and if it goes there, you take it with you by your force, your fraud, or your laws."

The Colonel asked, "Is there one land which sympathizes with the attempt to govern this country for the purpose of slavery? Do you? Does England? Does Russia? Does Germany? Does Spain? Does Mexico? Why, one of the most affecting incidents I know of in connection with the war with Mexico occurred when the Mexican Commissioners met the American Commissioners, near Mexico, to determine the treaty of peace. They said, in effect, to Mr. Trist: 'Sir, we are a conquered people. You can prescribe your own terms. But we implore you, in the name of humanity and liberty, that you do not force slavery upon an unwilling people.'"

Colonel Baker showed how, during the Democratic control of Congress and the Executive, every effort to promote the building of Pacific railroads had failed, and reminded them that it was the pledge of the Republican Party that if it prevailed the trans-continental railroads should receive government assistance.

Up to this point Colonel Baker, according to his habit, had spoken rapidly, sweeping all before the resistless phalanx of his words. As he approached the most splendid part of his address his voice became unusually effective and he paused at the conclusion of many sentences. There were some — they did not know the man — who questioned whether the aid of Democratic votes in his election might moderate his passion for the cause of liberty. He would leave no doubt concerning that. "We live," said he, "in a day of light. We live in an advancing generation. We live in the presence of the whole world. We are like a city set on a hill, that cannot be hid. The prayers and tears and hopes and sighs of all good men are with us, of us, for us. [Applause.] As for me, I dare not, I will not, be false to freedom. [Applause.] Here, many years long gone, I took my stand; and where in youth my feet were planted, there my manhood and my age shall march. I am not ashamed of Freedom. I know her power. I glory in her strength. I rejoice in her majesty. I will walk beneath her banner. I have seen her again and again struck down on a hundred chosen fields of battle. I have seen her friends fly from her. I have seen her foes gather around her. I have seen them bind her to the stake. I have seen them give her ashes to the winds, regathering them that they might scatter them yet more widely. But when they turned to exult, I have seen her again meet them face to face, clad in complete steel, and brandishing in her strong right hand a flaming sword red with insufferable light."

During the utterance of these sentences the listeners were finding it difficult to repress their feelings. When Colonel Baker, always as graceful in gesture as in speech, came to the mention of the sword, he — a veteran officer of two wars — appeared to draw his own weapon, so that the last words were spoken with his arm uplifted. The excited thousands again sprang to their feet, the pent-up enthusiasm broke loose, and such a wild tumult as greeted the hero on his introduction was repeated with wilder power. Cheer after cheer rolled from side to side, from pit to dome. Even the reporters were swept away in the frenzy and left their desks and tables to fall in with the shouting multitude. A young fellow just come of age — afterwards famous as Bret Harte — leaped upon the stage and frantically waved an American flag. In this era of prearranged demonstrations that would excite little attention, but no such scene had ever been witnessed at a political meeting in California; none, I think, has ever occurred since; and it may well be doubted whether — excepting in national conventions — the equal of it was ever witnessed in the United States. It was nearly a quarter of an hour before the uproar ceased. Meantime Colonel Baker stood motionless, intent, transfixed. When, at last, there was perfect silence, he spoke as if he had not been interrupted, and in a golden, throbbing tone that thrilled like an electric current said: "And I take courage. The genius of America will at last lead her sons to freedom." [Great applause].

This was the conclusion, so far as the speech related to the issues of the political campaign; but Colonel Baker, meeting a host of friends for the first time since his departure for Oregon, and for the last time before he should sail for the East, had a personal statement to make, a statement which, even after the brilliant close of his superb speech, aroused new emotions in his hearers: —

"It is but a year ago, a few days past, since I was beaten in this fair state for the office of Representative in Congress. With my heart bruised, my ambition somewhat wounded, my hopes crushed and destroyed, it was my fortune one week later to stand by the bedside of my slaughtered friend Broderick, who fell in your cause and on your behalf [sensation], and I cried, 'How long, oh, how long, shall the hopes of Freedom and her champion be thus crushed!'

"The tide has turned. I regret my little faith. I renew my hopes. I see better omens. The warrior rests. It is true he is in the embrace of that sleep that knows no earthly waking. Nor word, nor wish, nor prayer, nor triumph can call him from that lone abode [sensation], but his example lives among us. In San Francisco, I know, I speak to hundreds of men to-night — perhaps to thousands — who loved him in his life and who will be true to his memory always. And if I were not before a vast assemblage of the people I would say that in a higher arena it may be my privilege to speak of him and for him — as I will [tremendous applause and cheering]. I hope, I believe, that I shall be able to say that his ashes repose among a people who loved him well; who are not and never will be forgetful of the manner of his life nor of the method of his death [profound sensation].

"People of San Francisco, I thank you for the honor of your presence here to-night. You make me very happy and very proud. . . . And expressing to you, again and again, my thanks, I bid you a cordial, heartfelt, affectionate farewell."

The report from which these quoted passages are taken adds, "Senator Baker retired amid a wild storm of applause and cheering." The scene defies description. The excited multitude were disinclined to leave the place. Long they continued cheering and shouting and singing. Deeper even than this manifestation was the feeling of many, who, touched by their hero's words of farewell and the pathos in his voice, wept, and even sobbed aloud. When, at last, the thousands had departed, they went out in a mood quite different from that in which they entered the hall. Then they were expectant; now they were full of courage and confidence, which spread abroad with the speed of thought. From time to time some reminiscent veteran recalls the "oratorical drama" of that fateful night, always with the feeling that he was present when history was made.[1] The people had not reached their homes before the shorthand notes were being written out and set up in type. The morrow's sun had not risen when copies of the pamphlet containing the speech were ready for the outgoing steamboats and stage-coaches that were to convey them to the uttermost parts of the state. In many places crowds assembled to hear the speech. I myself read it aloud in a public hall in Marysville. It was like the effect of mountain air. Republicans everywhere took heart.

A few days later the presidential election occurred; Abraham Lincoln had a plurality of six hundred and fourteen in the State of California. Colonel Baker had won the state for the party of Freedom.

[1] I have refreshed my recollection by reference to some of the daily journals, and am especially indebted to an article by Calvin B. McDonald, which appeared in the Sacramento *Bee* on the ninth of June, 1894. — E. R. K.

CHAPTER X

BAKER IN THE SENATE — HIS REPLY TO BENJAMIN

DURING the next few days there were many conferences between Senator Baker and leading Republicans of the state. If Mr. Lincoln had been elected President, as they hoped, there would be justification — nay, more, owing to the disloyalty of the Federal office-holders there was an imperative necessity — for a "clean sweep" and the appointment of men who could be trusted to sustain the Government; and it was regarded as certain that Senator Baker would have great influence in selecting the new officials. On his last day in the city Senator Baker received the most magnificent set of silver plate that had ever been made or seen on the Coast. It had been on exhibition and was known as the "Railroad Set," as the decorative work was emblematical of railroad articles, — locomotives, cars, bridges, and the like. It cost its donors about five thousand dollars, and every piece bore this inscription: "Presented to E. D. Baker by the Merchants of San Francisco as a token of their esteem and confidence." "No man considered a politician was invited to contribute toward this superb gift, but there were men of all parties among the merchants who gave it." [1]

[1] *Alta*, November 10, 1860; also *Union*, same date.

Senator Baker sailed for Panama on the steamship Sonora, on the tenth of November, 1861. A great throng was at the wharf to bid him farewell. I am sure there were many, that day, who could have applied to the "Gray Eagle" Longfellow's apostrophe to the "Ship of State": —

> "Our hearts, our hopes, are all with thee;
> Our hearts, our hopes, our prayers, our tears,
> Our faith triumphant o'er our fears,
> Are all with thee, — are all with thee!"

The voyage was uneventful. Doctor Gwin kept in his room much of the time. Senator Benjamin and Reverdy Johnson were companionable, especially the latter; but Baker's intimate talk was with the gallant Colonel Lander. Baker, however, was not in a talkative mood. He was in a hurry, — impatient and eager to be at the capital. Those who knew Colonel Baker will understand how he walked the deck, "rapidly pacing back and forth, climbing into the rigging, passing out on the bowsprit to view the phosphorescent sea as the ship ploughed her onward way." [1]

Colonel Baker arrived in Washington on the fifth of December, after Congress had begun its sessions. When he was sworn in, his colleague, Senator Lane, did not present his credentials and escort him forward to take the oath. That courteous service was performed by Senator Latham, a political oppo-

[1] Letter of L. Holmes, Portland, Oregon, November 20, 1885. This phosphorescence is much more brilliant in the Pacific than in the North Atlantic. — E. R. K.

nent. The dream of Baker's boyhood, the determination of his youth, the passion of his manhood, and the ambition of his later years, the inspiration that had sustained him in adversity and cheered him in success, were realized and gratified. As he had been at one time the only Whig in Congress from the State of Illinois, he was now the only Republican in either house from the whole Pacific Coast, — the only member of a party that was so soon to assume the responsibility of carrying on the Government; the only member of either house with whom Sumner and Fessenden and Wade and Trumbull and Dixon and the others of that company of great men could counsel when the affairs of that remote and imperiled section of our country were considered. It was a position such as no senator had ever occupied or ever has. The circumstances of his election were not well known. Mystery, that has such power to excite interest, surrounded his coming. Legend and romance were fruitful upon his past. Then it was known that he was the lifetime friend and the confidant of the strange new man who was soon to come out of the West and grasp the reins of government. The conditions surrounding Baker's advent in the Senate, as also his earlier appearance in the House, excited so much interest that discussions by friend and foe were often charged with personal allusions, and these required replies from the personal point of view. Baker's unique position in the Senate was at once appreciated; it took but a short time for him to obtain the recognition of his talents. Senator Sumner declared that "Oregon first became truly known to us on this floor by his eloquent lips." Senator Breckinridge, in debate, spoke of him as "the Senator from California." Senator Baker interrupted with merely the word "Oregon"; to which Mr. Breckinridge replied, "The Senator seems to have charge of the whole Pacific Coast."[1] After the inauguration of Mr. Lincoln, Senator Powell referred to Baker as "the personal and confidential friend of the President, — and I think I can say, without reflecting upon any gentleman on the other side of the chamber, one of the most distinguished and able Senators on this floor."[2]

Senator Baker's appearance at this time is fairly shown by the frontispiece of this book — his appearance in repose. No portrait is capable of suggesting the divine fire that irradiated from his countenance when his mind was aroused. Mr. Wallace describes him as follows: "He was now verging close on fifty, and about his bodily presence there was that air of blended grace and dignity which betokened something more than an ordinary man. Of medium height, his figure was still erect, and roundly and compactly built. His head (which might have formed a model for a sculptor) was partially bald and his hair and small side whiskers almost white. His complexion was florid; his nose, large and long, was of the Roman type; his eyes of a grayish tint, and capable of

[1] *Cong. Globe*, 1st Session, 37th Congress, p. 379. [2] *Ibid.*, p. 69.

expressing every varying emotion of the soul. His manners were easy and urbane, whilst his voice was penetrating and finely modulated as in the days of yore."[1]

Mr. Blaine says: "From the far-off Pacific came Edward Dickinson Baker, the Senator from Oregon, a man of extraordinary gifts of eloquence; lawyer, soldier, frontiersman, leader of popular assemblies, tribune of the people. In personal appearance he was commanding, in manner most attractive, in speech irresistibly charming. Perhaps in the history of the Senate no man ever left so brilliant a reputation from so short a service. He was born in England, and the earliest recollection of his life was the splendid pageant attending the funeral of Lord Nelson."[2]

Congressman W. D. Kelley, of Pennsylvania, said: "He was a fascinating companion; and I know not which most to admire, the heartiness, ease, and grace of his social intercourse, or his power as a thinker, orator, and leader of men. Who that has seen his eye flash, as his voice swayed the Senate or the assembled multitude of eager listeners, shall forget its fire? Or who that has heard him quietly relate some mirth-moving incident will forget the genial light with which it illuminated his sweet smile?"[3]

Upon the invitation of the President-elect Sena-

[1] Wallace, pp. 63, 64.

[2] *Twenty Years of Congress*, vol. I, p. 321.

[3] *Cong. Globe*, 37th Congress, 2d Session, p. 66.

tor Baker visited Mr. Lincoln in Springfield. Wallace, who was noted for his care and accuracy, errs in saying that "this visit was paid while en route to Washington." Baker stopped but a day in New York, upon his return from California, and was present in the Senate on the fifth of December. The visit to Illinois took place in the latter part of the month, Senator Baker being all day Christmas in the train, one of his fellow travelers being David Wilmot, whose name recalls the famous proviso. Senator Baker had washed off the dust of travel and was lying down for a brief rest, conversing with his stepdaughter, Mrs. Judge Matheny, when he saw out of a window a great, gaunt man put one leg over the front gate, lift the other leg after, and in another moment the long-legged man came unannounced into the room. It was the first meeting of the two men since Baker had left Illinois, more than a decade before. "Hello, Baker," was Mr. Lincoln's salutation; "I am glad to see you. I'd rather have had you elected Senator than any man alive." Senator Baker, with mischief in his eye, responded in mock formality, "I was coming soon to call on you, Mr. President"; whereupon Lincoln interrupted him with "None of that between us, Baker."[1]

There is, naturally, no record of what occurred in the conferences between the President-elect and the Senator. That Mr. Lincoln sent for the only Republican Representative from the Pacific Coast

[1] Newspaper correspondent at Springfield.

creates the inevitable conclusion that, whatever else they talked about, the affairs of the Pacific Coast received consideration. When he returned to Washington Baker bore a message from the President-elect to General Scott.[1] Secrecy was essential at the time, but we must suppose the message was encouraging to the venerable and faithful chief, who had been baffled in his arrangements to preserve government property and defend the capital when not ignored by the traitors in President Buchanan's Cabinet.

People in Illinois who remembered the delight afforded by Baker's speeches when he resided in that state, and were deeply concerned with the perilous state of affairs, urged him to speak. At first he declined, but he finally yielded to the insistency of old friends and spoke in two towns of his former congressional district. One of them was chosen because his mother was still living there and wished to hear her son with all his added dignity and responsibilities.

It was an era of oratory. Wood pulp had not ousted the human voice from its ascendency. Every state had its men whose utterances were heard by the Nation. Massachusetts alone contained such oratorical dynamos as Wendell Phillips, Edward Everett, Charles Sumner, Ralph Waldo Emerson, John A. Andrew, and Nathaniel P. Banks. Little Connecticut had "Joe" Hawley, Colonel Henry C. Deming, Richard D. Hubbard,

[1] Nicolay and Hay, vol. IV, p. 250.

and the immortal Governor Buckingham. In New York were William H. Seward, Daniel S. Dickinson, James W. Nye, William M. Evarts, Roscoe Conkling, George William Curtis, and numerous others.

Beecher —*facile princeps* — and Storrs and Chapin and Simpson and Starr King, from the pulpit, flooded the land with splendors of eloquence that fused love of country with the principles of religion and the love of God. Bryant, Stedman, Boker, Whitman, Longfellow, Whittier, Lowell, and Holmes breathed forth the sublime inspirations of patriotism in undying verse. Minor poets occasionally flashed up in brilliant nationalism. Congress contained numerous men who would at any time have been regarded as able speakers, whom the profound interests of liberty and union at this epoch raised to greatness. Of such a crisis as had now been reached in national affairs it might truly be said, —

> "Kings it makes gods, and meaner creatures kings."

In such a time Baker came to the National Capital from the little-known Pacific Coast. Sumner said, "In the Senate he at once took the place of orator." On the second of January, 1861, — less than a month after his credentials had been presented, — the new Senator rose to speak. Lane and Gwin interposed other matters, apparently for the purpose of throwing Baker off the track. Baker offered to give way to the Pacific Railroad Bill if that could be taken up. Trumbull, of Illinois, insisted on Baker's right to the floor, and the Oregon Senator began. Senator Judah P. Benjamin, of Louisiana, had, a few days before, made a speech which his admirers pronounced unanswerable. Nevertheless, Baker answered it. Charles Sumner said of Baker's reply, "Perhaps the argument against the sophism of secession was never better arranged and combined, or more simply popularized for the general apprehension." Mr. Sumner added, "That speech passed at once into the permanent literature of the country, while it gave to its author an assured position in this body" [the United States Senate]. The late Senator Dolliver once told me he had read every word of the debates in the Senate and the House of that remarkable session of Congress, and that he considered "the high-water mark was reached in the speech of Mr. Benjamin on the Southern side and the speech of Senator Baker on the side of the Union."

The exordium was brief. After a generous tribute to the high plane and courteous tone of Mr. Benjamin's speech, Mr. Baker entered at once upon the discussion. "I propose," he remarked, "in opposition to all that has been said, to show that the Government of the United States is in very deed a real, substantial Power; ordained by the people, not dependent upon states; sovereign in its sphere; a Union, and not a compact between sovereign states; that according to its true theory it has the inherent capacity of self-protection; that its Constitution is a perpetuity, beneficent, unfailing,

THOMAS STARR KING

grand; and that its powers are equally capable of exercise against domestic treason and foreign foes"; — no longer disputed propositions, but, in 1860, the very points upon the denial of which Southern advocates based the claim of a right of their states to secede without hindrance. "I deny," said Mr. Baker, "that this Union is a compact between sovereign states at all. . . . There is but one sovereign, and that sovereign is the People. The State Government is its creation; the Federal Government is its creation; each supreme in its sphere; each sovereign for its purpose; but each limited in its authority, and each dependent upon delegated power. . . . Mr. Webster has well observed that there can be in this country no sovereignty in the European sense of sovereignty. . . . Therefore all assumption and presumption arising out of the proposition of sovereignty — supremacy on the part of the state — is a fallacy from beginning to end." Mr. Baker went on to show that "the Constitution . . . is the work of one People; that the Constitution declares itself to have been made by the People — not by sovereign states ; . . . not a compact, not a league; . . . but it declares that the People of the United States do ordain and establish a government."

A question to Mr. Benjamin led to a long and interesting colloquy. The Louisiana Senator apparently realized that he had been driven from the ground first taken, — that secession was a right inherent in the Constitution, — for he finally asked

Mr. Baker "if the State of South Carolina were refused more than one Senator on this floor, whether she would have a right to withdraw from this Union, and if so, whether it would arise out of the Constitution or not." After considerable fencing on both sides to distinctly fix the point, Mr. Baker showed that as the Senate was "the judge of the qualifications of its own members" it might at some time decide that a senator sent up from South Carolina was unfit, but he declared that "would not be cause of withdrawal or secession or revolution or war." He added, "I will meet the question in the full spirit in which, I suppose, it is intended to put it." After considerable more discussion between the two, Mr. Baker said, "The right of South Carolina to withdraw, because the fundamental right of representation is denied her, is the right of revolution, of rebellion. It does not depend upon constitutional guarantees at all."

From this position Mr. Baker resumed his attack. He mentioned the Puritan Revolution led by Cromwell, the revolution that resulted in the Dutch Republic, and the revolt of the American Colonies, in each of which cases the grounds for revolt enlisted the sympathies of the world. Referring to the American Declaration of Independence, he said, "I ask the honorable Senator to bring his reasons for revolution, bloodshed, and war here to-day and compare them with that document."

After squirming under question and assertion, the Louisiana Senator, said Mr. Baker, had fallen back upon the declaration that the "wrongs" under which South Carolina "groans," and the injuries which justify and demand revolution, are to be found "chiefly in a difference of our construction of the Constitution." Mr. Benjamin seemed surprised to perceive the point to which he had been driven. He started another colloquy, but failed to shake Mr. Baker off. The Oregon Senator asked the Southern champion if he remembered that, although they might differ in construction, "there is between us a supreme arbiter, and that upon every conceivable clause about which we may differ, or have differed, that arbiter has decided always upon one side." He declared that the "defective construction," of which the North was alleged to be guilty, "is to be found upon two subjects: one in relation to the fugitive slave question, and the other the government of the territories." As to the first, "We did in argument give a construction. . . . We were overruled. We have obeyed that decision loyally ever since." As to the second, Mr. Baker argued at length. The Southern contention was that slaves were property, and therefore might be taken into the territories, where owners must be protected in their possessions as were the owners of other property. Mr. Baker contended that slaves were property only where made so by local law, and he declared he would never vote to extend slavery into new territory.

Mr. Baker continued: "Passing from that, the Senator from Louisiana, in the second item of the 'dreary catalogue' which he recounts in his speech, says, in substance, that we attack slavery generally. Now, I am going to reply at some little length to that count in the indictment. I begin thus: If the gentleman means that, in violation of the Constitution of the United States, we of the North or West, by any bill, resolution, or act, do in any wise interfere with the state and condition of slavery where it exists within the states of this Union or any of them by virtue of local law, . . . we deny it. We have offered no such interference; we claim no such power." Mr. Benjamin interrupted to say "the charge is not that Congress does it, but the states do it." Mr. Baker replied, "Again we deny it. The fact is not so. The proof cannot be made. Why, sir, I might ask, in the first place, how can the states so interfere?" Upon this Mr. Benjamin burst out in a violent and surprising description of John Brown's raid and denounced the people of Massachusetts as having approved of that foray. He went on: "The people of Massachusetts in their collective capacity have done more. They have sent Senators upon this floor *whose only business* has been, year after year, to insult the people of the South. . . . They have done that, *and nothing else,*[1] ever since I have been in the Senate!"

Senator Wilson, of Massachusetts, rose to reply, but Mr. Baker said, "Oh, never mind. Mr. President, I asked the gentleman from Louisiana to point out to me and to the Senate how if the

[1] The italics are mine. — E. R. K.

State of Illinois were desirous to interfere with the existence of slavery in Virginia, it could be done. I leave to his cooler temper and better taste to examine how he has answered me. . . . I hold that his answer is an acknowledgment that a free state cannot, as a state, interfere in any considerable way with slavery in a slave state; and that being so, we advance another step. We agree now that Congress never have interfered and that states never can."

Mr. Baker then discussed Mr. Benjamin's charge that individuals in the Northern States have interfered with slavery in the Southern States, and conceded that to be true. He added that individuals in the Northern States had sometimes also interfered with the possession of property in horses, and that he presumed that had been so in Louisiana, and that the distinguished Senator from that state might have been sometimes called on to defend men against whom such charges had been made. He asked, "Will you plunge us into civil war for that?"

Mr. Benjamin again interrupted in the endeavor to take up a position upon which he could firmly rest, and asserted that "it is the desire of the whole Republican Party to close up the Southern States with a cordon of free states for the avowed purpose of forcing the South to emancipate the slaves." Mr. Baker replied, "Very well, sir. See how gloriously we advance step by step. . . . The great ground of complaint has narrowed itself down to this. . . . Why, if I read history and observe geography rightly it is so girdled now. . . . Which way can slavery extend itself that it does not encroach upon the soil of freedom? . . . Being so hedged, circled, girded, encompassed, it will some day, — it may be infinitely far distant, so far as mortal eye can see, — but it will be some day lost and absorbed in the superior blaze of freedom. And, sir, that would be the case just as much as it is now if there were no Northern free states. . . . Therefore it appears to me idle — and I had almost said wicked — to attempt to plunge this country into civil war upon the pretense that we are endeavoring to circle your institution, when, if we had no such wish or desire in the world, it is circled by destiny, by Providence, and by human opinion everywhere."

Mr. Baker then examined the Southern complaint that the press in the free states was offensive. "As for destroying the liberty of our press, as for abolishing societies formed to promote the abolition of slavery, or for any other purpose in the world, do Senators think, when they ask us to do that? Sir, I ask them how? . . . I inquire, how do they expect us to abolish the right of free speech and free discussion?" After further remarks on this point, Mr. Baker flashed forth one of those extraordinary passages which illumined so many of his speeches — a few words of which may be presented here. "Sir, the liberty of the press is the highest safeguard to all free government. Ours could not exist without it. It is with us, nay, with all men, like a great, exulting, and abounding river. . . . On its broad bosom it bears a thousand barks. There Genius spreads its purpling sail. There Poetry dips its silver oar. There Art, Invention, Discovery, Science, Morality, Religion, may safely and securely float. . . . Without it civilization, humanity, government, all that makes society itself, would disappear, and the world would return to its ancient barbarism. . . . Sir, we will not risk these consequences — even for slavery. We will not risk these consequences — even for Union. We will not risk these consequences to avoid that civil war with which you threaten us; that war which you announce as deadly, and which you declare to be inevitable." Mr. Baker added: "I will never yield to the idea that the great Government of this country shall protect slavery in any territory now ours, or hereafter to be acquired. It is, in my opinion, a principle of free government, not to be surrendered. It is, in my judgment, the object of the great battle which we have fought and which we have won."

The Oregon Senator then discussed the suggestions of compromise. "Do you mean that I am to give up my conviction of right? Armies cannot compel that in the breast of a free people. Do you mean that I am to concede the benefits of the political struggle through which we have passed, considered politically only? You are too just and too generous to ask that. Do you mean that we are to deny the great principle upon which our political action has been based? You know we cannot." He declared that if the proper courts should declare any of the Northern laws unconstitutional, "we will repeal them," and that the North would show a generous disposition. He continued, "I will not yield one inch to secession; but there are things I will yield, and there are things to which I will yield. It is somewhere told — and the fine reading of my friend from Louisiana will enable him to tell me where — that when Harold of England received a messenger from a brother with whom he was at variance, to inquire on what terms reconciliation and peace could be effected between them, he replied, in a gallant and generous spirit, in a few words: 'The terms I offer are the affection of a brother and the Earldom of Northumberland'; 'and,' said the envoy, as he marched up the hall amid the warriors that graced the state of the king, 'if Tosti, thy brother, agree to this, what terms will you allow to his ally and friend Hadrada the giant?' 'We will allow,' said Harold, 'to Hadrada, the giant, seven feet of English ground, and if he be, as they say, a giant, some few inches more'; and as he spake the hall rang with acclamation. Sir, in that spirit I speak. . . . I will yield no inch, no word, to the threat of secession — unconstitutional, revolutionary, dangerous, unwise, at variance with the heart and the hope of all mankind save themselves"; but he went on to show how far the North would be willing to go to relieve the South of apprehension that their institution was to be disturbed where it was already protected by its local laws.

He then took up another of Mr. Benjamin's "wrongs": "What if a Northern President, just elected, should come in and give all the offices to Northern men, eating out the substance of us of the South; what then? Well, I answer to that, Wait, and do not dissolve the Union upon a hypothesis. I might tell my friend from Louisiana that, after all, this thing of not having office is not so very hard to bear. We Whigs tried it a long time; we Republicans have experienced it very often." Mr. Baker continued: "Sir, as I approach a close I am reminded that the honorable Senator from Louisiana has said, in a tone which I by no means admired, 'Now, gentlemen of the North, a state has seceded; you must either acknowledge her independence or you must make war.' To that we reply, we will take no counsel of our opponents; we will not acknowledge her independence. They say we cannot make war against a state; and the gentleman undertakes to ridicule the difference which we make between a state and individuals. . . . Now, sir, let us examine for a minute this idea that we cannot make war. First, we do not propose to do it. . . . It would not be very strange if a Government, and hitherto a great Government, were to coerce obedience to her law upon the part of those who were subject to her jurisdiction." Mr. Baker then riddled the assertion that the Federal Government could not continue to collect revenue, and showed how thoroughly

President Jackson had arranged to do that very thing in the harbor of Charleston if South Carolina persisted in its threat to nullify the Federal laws. He added, "If, from that, collision come, let him bear the danger who provokes it. . . . If in consequence of an attempt to violate the revenue laws some persons should be hurt, I do not know that it will better their condition at all that South Carolina will stand as a stake to their back." Mr. Baker's close was serious and eloquent: "At whatever cost, by whatever constitutional process, through whatever of darkness and danger there may be, let us proceed in the broad, luminous path of duty, 'till danger's troubled night be past and the star of peace return.'"

Senator Baker, observant of the custom of members in their first year, refrained from debate on most subjects, but in measures for the support of the Government in suppressing the rebellion, and when bills especially concerning the Pacific Coast were discussed, he was alert and ready. After more than two years of discussion on a certain measure, — and many more years of wasted talk over the subject, — the House had passed a bill for government support in constructing a Pacific railroad. In the Senate there was, on the part of the secessionists, a strong effort to defeat the bill. Several times when it was up Senator Baker spoke in its favor. He encountered, among others, Senator Benjamin, who was shrewd but courteous, and Jeff Davis, who was insolent. Senator Bragg, of North

Carolina, wanted to amend the bill, thus making it necessary to send it back to the House, and possibly, since the session was late, lose it altogether. Mr. Bragg said: "Whenever I or any other gentleman offers [*sic*] an amendment here, he is held up as an enemy of the bill, and his purpose is said to be to defeat it."

Senator Baker at this point remarked: "We desire to know — and I think it is proper and respectful that we should know — if the gentlemen will vote for the bill at last if we put in their amendments. Will the honorable Senator from North Carolina himself?" — to which Senator Bragg replied that he would not![1]

General Lane, Senator Baker's colleague, opposed the bill, ostensibly because it provided that the western terminus should be San Francisco instead of some place further north. Senator Baker, as to that reason, remarked: "I am going to vote for the bill as it is, as nearly as I can, without any amendments or alterations; and I am going to do so while, as I believe, I represent a constituency further north than any other gentleman upon this floor. I am going to vote against any material amendment, or, indeed, any at all, although I am told that the northern road proposed will benefit the immediate people whom I represent, very greatly. . . . Quite alive to the interests of my constituents; quite sure that my conduct may be the subject of misapprehension or misrepresenta-

[1] *Cong. Globe*, 2d Session, 36th Congress, part 1, p. 386.

tion; quite sure that all that strong feeling of locality for our state, our road, may be brought to bear upon me in the future; yet, risking my justification upon the idea that I believe I am doing the best I can to promote the connection between the Atlantic and the Pacific *now*, I shall vote for these roads. And if hereafter, here or elsewhere, my vote may ever be brought in question, I have but this to say: no man who can observe the conditions in which this bill is to-day in the Senate can do otherwise than know — and I say, with emphasis, *know* — that unless we do, within a very few days, pass the measure substantially as it is, we cannot pass it at this session, and we risk it forever. Hereafter, whether here or at home, I shall say this in my defense and make no other."[1] For the railroad, for the bill giving it government support, Senator Baker spoke earnestly and repeatedly.

It was in 1860, and it is to-day, the custom of some Senators and Representatives to seek for liberal appropriations to be expended in their states or districts — often for unworthy objects — and then to go home and expect popular approval of their conscienceless conduct. Senator Baker did not belong to this log-rolling crowd. He was as desirous as any man of having a daily overland mail, to be conveyed in coaches, but when appealed to by Senator Doolittle as to whether the amount proposed for the work in a pending bill was too large, Senator Baker frankly declared he believed it was.[2]

[1] *Cong. Globe*, 2d Session, 36th Congress, part 1, pp. 383, 384.

[2] *Ibid.*, part 2, p. 1277.

When the Army Appropriation Bill was under consideration, Senator Lane offered amendments to provide sums to be expended at the entrance to the Straits De Fuca and at the mouth of the Columbia River — points within his state. Senator Fessenden, chairman of the Finance Committee, in opposing General Lane's propositions, remarked: "Every body knows that at the present time our ability is exceedingly small. We are borrowing money at a loss every day to live upon, to continue this Government; and when we are doing that, with no sort of prospect of any foreign difficulties, the idea which the Committee on Finance had was to do as little as possible. . . . Under these circumstances I appeal to the Senators upon the Pacific Coast not to urge upon the Treasury at this time what it cannot bear." Senator Baker instantly expressed his concurrence in the sentiments of Mr. Fessenden.[1] Later Senator Baker said: "I believe I have troubled the Senate with no motion and no resolution this winter. I have felt it my duty to vote against most of the appropriations presented for argument. I have just done so, reluctantly, on a fortification bill. I did so upon the Coast Survey Bill. I have done so upon many measures which come very much home to my people, because I did not think the condition of the Treasury justified them." [2]

Senator Baker also opposed an attempt of Senator Lane to secure an appropriation for paying

[1] *Cong. Globe*, 2d Session, 36th Congress, part 2, p. 1213.

[2] *Ibid.*, p. 1217.

the Nez Percés Indians for a portion of their reservation and for "holding a treaty with them." [1]

However, Senator Baker himself offered an amendment to the bill, to appropriate $50,000 for the protection of emigrants on the overland routes between the Atlantic Slope and the Oregon and Washington frontier. This excited an animated debate. Mr. Mason, of Virginia (who did all he could to destroy the Constitution and the Government), opposed Senator Baker's proposal because he considered it unconstitutional! The venerable Senator Crittenden joined in the opposition, but Senator Baker prevailed. His motion was adopted by twenty-three votes in its favor, there being seventeen against it.[2] On a bill to improve the navigation of Red River, strongly urged by several Southern Senators, to which the hackneyed constitutional objection was raised, Senator Baker stated his position as follows: ". . . I am very glad that there is a measure of this kind to which I can give my assent; and I do it now, expressing the reason why I do it, as an evidence that I am disposed to do so not only in this case, but in all others where I can, in my poor way, wield the Constitution as a beneficent, broad instrument of good, stimulating the energy and enterprise of our people in every section of the country." [3]

On the twenty-second of January, when the withdrawal of Senators from seceding states was

[1] *Cong. Globe*, 2d Session, 36th Congress, part 2, pp. 1145, 1146.

[2] *Ibid.*, part 1, pp. 1217, 1221.

[3] *Ibid.*, p. 539.

absorbing the attention of the Senate, Senator Baker very clearly defined his view of the proper attitude for the Senate to take on the subject.

The tariff bill being under discussion, Senator Baker made the following statement: "I shall take this occasion, Mr. President, in very few words to explain the principle by which I shall be governed in voting upon this measure. Iron, sugar, tea, and coffee are the articles which, in Oregon, we consume most of, and upon which the heaviest duty is laid, so far as our interests are concerned. The sentiment of the people there, and I apprehend upon the Pacific Coast, is not in favor of the principle of the tariff. They incline in their opinions towards what is called free trade; and the duty which we agree to have levied is, in our judgment, in pursuance of the highest obligation to the Government of the whole country. We have looked for a Pacific railroad; I believe we shall not get it. We have looked for an overland mail. We are taxing the country heavily for what we have received in that particular, and we are looking for a system which will yet tax it heavily. I have hoped, and shall hope until after Thursday [the day of adjournment], that the debt contracted by the State of Oregon for the reduction of the savage foe upon her frontier will be paid; and in return, actuated by that expectation, still hoping that, if not to-day, or next year, some time before long that great highway of nations will be made, and that debt will be paid, I propose at this session, loyally, — in consideration of the difficulties under which the country is laboring in point of finance and because we are in a state of revolution, — I propose, living distant as I do, to vote for measures oppressive upon all our interests, for the maintenance of the Government, and to afford revenue for that Government. . . . I trust gentlemen upon all sides of the Senate will remember, who desire to look at the interests of all sections of the confederacy, an obligation not to regard the measures which we propose, lightly, nor to support them doubtfully or unwillingly."[1]

Senator Baker predicted that the product of wine in California would grow to be of great importance, and he supported a forty per cent duty on imported wines "of all kinds." He pleaded for a duty — a very small duty, one cent a pound, equal to about five per cent *ad valorem* — on wool.[2] Since every state was striving for tariff provisions to benefit its own people, Senator Baker declared he felt justified in trying to get something for Oregon. At one time he said: "Mr. President, I once heard a great judge say that, next to doing justice, the best thing was to appear to do it. Now, I do not know that a duty of one cent a pound on wool will kill the manufacturers, or will make the farmers of the West or of Oregon rich, but it will let some of them know that we are here thinking about it; and I earnestly hope we may be considered, and that Senators will

[1] *Cong. Globe*, 2d Session, 36th Congress, part 2, p. 994.

[2] The special session of Congress in 1911 proposed to *reduce* the tariff on wool to twenty-nine per cent!

give us a duty of five per cent. I do not think it will ruin Massachusetts. I have better faith in her." [1]

Replying to Senator Henry Wilson, of Massachusetts, Senator Baker said, "I, as a Whig, in old times, understanding a little of the principles of a tariff and very little of the details, used to argue with the distinguished Senator from Illinois (Mr. Douglas) in the presence of a great many people, to make them believe that the way to have things that they wanted to eat, to drink, and to wear, very cheap, was to put a very high duty on them [laughter]. Well, I reasonably believed that then and I reasonably believe it now; that is, I believe that in the infancy of a manufacture you may really help the country by laying a protective tariff in its favor. I believe, moreover, that protection is sufficient when you give the revenue duty upon the proposed article. I am content with that; and I am trying to protect the manufacturers of the country by raising revenue by a tariff, discriminating as I do. That being so, it would be very hard for me to go home and tell my people that Senator Wilson convinced me that, in the case of wool, the only thing we raise and care much about, the way to get the better price for it is to have no duty at all." [2]

Senator Baker had an animated and somewhat amusing passage with Senator Sumner on the wis-

[1] *Cong. Globe*, 2d Session, 36th Congress, part 2, p. 1026.
[2] *Ibid.*, p. 1026.

dom of laying a duty on old books. Mr. Sumner declared it would be "a tax on knowledge." Mr. Baker thought old books, rare editions, were but little used for imparting knowledge. He would treat them as luxuries, and, while the Government was seeking in all directions subjects of taxation, he would place a revenue duty on Mr. Sumner's old editions. The Senate concurred in Senator Baker's view by a vote of twenty-four to twelve.

On the twenty-sixth of February Senator Baker made an important statement of his position on a question of great moment at that time. He said: "I hold myself bound by the events of the last two years on the Pacific Coast to vote in favor of what is called 'popular sovereignty,' so far as it may be regarded as a measure, not a principle; and therefore if, in any territorial bill, the direct question comes up, Shall Congress delegate to the people of a territory the power to determine the question of slavery as of other subjects, I shall feel myself bound to vote in favor of that delegation, saying at the same time that I believe Congress has the undoubted power of prohibiting slavery in any territory of the United States."[1]

It is very certain that Senator Baker felt complete confidence that "Popular Sovereignty" as a method would never fasten slavery upon any new state.

On the twenty-second of February a bill for the payment of expenses incurred by the State of Cali-

[1] *Cong. Globe*, 2d Session, 36th Congress, part 2, p. 1206.

fornia some years before, in the suppression of Indian hostilities, was before the Senate. Senator King, of New York, opposed it, using some tart expressions, and concluding his remarks, "For these general reasons,—not because I know much about these particular claims, but because I do not know that they are due and ought to be paid,—I shall vote against the bill." There were but a few moments for reply, then another matter would become the special order, and Senator Baker in speaking was very pointed and less gracefully courteous than usual.[1]

When the venerable Senator John J. Crittenden, of Kentucky, fathered in the Senate and advocated constitutional amendments approved by a convention of delegates from many states,—proposals designed for the purpose of conciliating the Border States and holding them to their allegiance, and, some hoped, even to recover some of the states that had seceded,—Senator Baker stood almost alone among the Republicans in favor of submitting the proposed amendments to the people of the country.

Speaking of the convention that had just been held, he said:—

"Twenty states assembled in what is called the 'Peace Convention.' They recommend to us, in times of great trial and difficulty, the passage of these resolutions. They are eminent men; they are able men; they are—very many of them, at least—great men; they have been selected by the states

[1] *Cong. Globe*, 2d Session, 36th Congress, part 2, pp. 1213, 1214.

which they respectively represent because of their purity of character and ability. The country is in great trouble. Six states have seceded; and I am told by very many men in whom I have great confidence that their states are to-day trembling in the balance. I believe it. I am told — and upon that subject I have not yet made up my mind — that the adoption of this measure by the people will heal the differences with the Border States. I do not believe that I can do wrong, therefore, in giving the people of the whole Union a chance to determine these questions.

"Mr. President, we sometimes mistake our opinions for our principles. I am appealed to often; it is said to me, 'You believed in the Chicago Platform.' Suppose I did? 'Well, this varies from the Chicago Platform.' Suppose it does? I stand today, as I believe, in the presence of greater events than those which attend the making of a President. I stand, as I believe at least, in the presence of peace and war; and if it were true that I violate the Chicago Platform, the Chicago Platform is not a Constitution of the United States to me. If events, if circumstances, change, I will violate it, appealing to my conscience, to my country, and to my God, to justify me according to the motive." [Applause in the galleries.]

Mr. Baker then explained his understanding of the effects of the compromise propositions: —

"Mr. President, I should have been exceedingly pleased, as a partisan and a man, if the inauguration of Mr. Lincoln could have been one at which all the states would attend with the old good feeling and with the old good humor. I have seen six states separate themselves, as they say, from us, and form a new Confederacy, — with great pain and greater surprise. I cannot shut my eyes, if I would, to the existing state of things. I listen to the warning of my friend from Kentucky.[1] I listen to the warning of my friend from Tennessee.[2] I have been in both states. I know something of their people. I believe that there, even there, the Union is in danger; and I believe if we break up here without some attempt to reconcile them to us, and us to them, many of the predictions of friends and foes as to the danger will be accomplished.

"I said in the earlier period of the session — I repeat it — I would yield nothing to secession. . . . But to-day the case is altered. Virginia, Kentucky, Tennessee reiterate their love for the Union. . . . It is from them I would take counsel and advice; and now they tell me, 'Pass these resolutions.' . . . I agree; with all my heart I will do it. . . .

"Besides, sir, what else can I do? As I sit down, let me ask Senators upon every side, what else can any of us do? Shall we sit here for three months when petition, resolution, public meeting, speech, acclamation, tumult, is heard, seen, and felt on every side, and do nothing? Shall state after state go out and not warn us of danger? Shall Sen-

[1] Mr. Crittenden. [2] Mr. Johnson.

ators and Representatives, patriotic, eloquent, venerable, tell us, again and again, of danger in their states, and we condescend to make no reply?"

Mr. Baker spoke on the following day, and yet again, with the deepest earnestness, urging that the constitutional amendments proposed should be submitted to the people of the entire country. His position was attacked by Senator Trumbull and Senator Baker vigorously responded.

On the fourth of March, 1861, when James Buchanan retired from the Presidency and Abraham Lincoln appeared to take the oath of office, there were circumstances of remarkable interest associated with the formal exercises. Mr. Lincoln entered the Senate Chamber on the arm of President Buchanan, escorted by Senators Foot, Pearce, and Baker. The procession of Senators and other dignitaries moved to the central portico of the Capitol, where a vast concourse awaited the event. Mr. Lincoln was wearing a silk hat. As he removed it, preparatory to addressing the people, he looked for a place to put it. On the instant Senator Douglas, his antagonist in many hard-fought political battles, his rival in the national contest that resulted in his election to the Presidency, relieved Mr. Lincoln of the hat and held it during the delivery of the inaugural address. "To Senator Baker was awarded the chief honor of the occasion, — after Mr. Lincoln, — and stepping quickly to the front, his silvery voice rang out over the multitude with these simple words: 'Fellow citizens, I introduce to you Abraham Lincoln, the President of the United States of America.'"[1]

[1] The sentences in quotation marks are from L. E. Chittenden's *Recollections.*

CHAPTER XI

SILENCE AND ERRORS OF HISTORIANS — THE SECESSION PERIL IN CALIFORNIA — SENATOR BAKER'S INFLUENCE AT WASHINGTON — GENERAL SUMNER SUPERSEDES GENERAL JOHNSTON — THE CRISIS PASSED

THE perilous state of affairs on the Pacific Slope in 1861 has been partly set forth in earlier chapters. Further evidence shall presently appear. It will be interesting to note how little the "history books" have to say on the subject and how incorrect much of that little is.

Von Holst's "Constitutional History of the United States" does not comprehend the secession movement in its scope: it drops California at the year 1848. George Ticknor Curtis's work, with a title similar to the German Professor's, contains nothing. "American History Told by Contemporaries," edited by Albert Bushnell Hart, has not a word. "The American Nation, A History," of which Professor Hart is the editor, is equally silent, if the index may be relied on. In the same writer's work, "National Ideas Historically Traced," no idea is traced to or from California or Oregon. McMaster's "History of the People of the United States," so far as the people on the Western Coast are concerned, stops twelve years short of the critical period. Woodrow Wilson, although his "History of the American People" undertakes to narrate the events of the Civil War, is oblivious of the Pacific States as having borne any relation to that mighty conflict. "The History of the United States," by William Cullen Bryant and Sydney Howard Gay, purports to describe "the long period from the first discovery of the Western Hemisphere by the Northmen to the end of the Civil War," but it contains no mention of California and Oregon as concerned with the struggle. In his spirited "History of the American Conflict" Horace Greeley makes no mention of California and Oregon as participants in the conflict, although Mr. Greeley knew that there was such a section, for he had visited it. "American Political History," by Alexander Johnson, excludes the Pacific Coast from all part in that history. However, the author is aware of the existence of Senator Baker, whom he quotes on the subject of reconstruction, Baker having, before his death in 1861, outlined the policy initiated by President Lincoln after the Government armies had expelled the rebel forces from some of the Southern States. "The United States, A History," by Edwin Earle Sparks, comes up to the year 1900, but says nothing relative to the Pacific Slope during the secession period or in the Civil War. In Benson J. Lossing's "Illustrated History of the Civil War," also, there is nothing; but the author contrives to refer to Senator Baker as "a prominent Democrat." "The History of the United States," by James Schouler, disposes of the period of agitation with the remark that "a rising man here in politics was Broderick, who had bossed a fire-engine in New York City, and whose father, a stone-cutter at Washington, had, it was said, dressed some of those stony pillars in the Chamber where his son was destined to sit as a senator."[1] Mr. Schouler comprehends the war-time in the statement that "the Pacific Coast States of California and Oregon were so utterly beyond the range of military operations that filial love furnished the only pledge of abiding loyalty to the Union through the four years of trial."[2] General Sumner's testimony was different. Then there is a book in several volumes called "History of the United States," by one Henry William Elson. It narrates some occurrences as recent as President Roosevelt's time, but its author appears to have been ignorant of affairs in California subsequent to the state's admission to the Union. His one mention of Colonel Baker, describing the circumstances of that noble patriot's death, is a coarse and heartless libel. The Latin proverb that it is sweet and honorable to die for one's country has for centuries expressed the sentiment of civilized men. Mr. Elson is the exponent of a contrary view.

The writers who have made California and the Pacific Coast their especial theme have known something about the situation in the years of dan-

[1] Vol. V, p. 266. [2] Vol. VI, p. 90.

ger. Hittell, referring to the governor whose term began in 1860, remarks, "Downey's unionism was not of the kind by which the Union could be preserved."[1] The same writer quotes from a speech by John B. Weller, who had been governor and a Representative at Washington, this significant declaration: "I do not know whether Lincoln will be elected or not. But I do know that if he is elected, and if he attempts to carry out his doctrines, the South will surely withdraw from the Union, and I should consider them less than men if they did not."[2] The historian states that Union resolutions were adopted by the legislature in 1861 "by an almost unanimous vote," but he informs us that in the same legislature Mr. Weller received twenty-seven votes for United States Senator, and John Nugent, who was of the same school of politics, received nine. Hubert Howe Bancroft's "History of the Pacific States" is recognized as an invaluable compilation. Some of the volumes devoted to California contain many facts relating to the secession movement, — many, though by no means all or nearly all; but they are so distributed, and so associated with various contexts, as to be deprived of their convincingness. Instead of being marshaled in orderly array, they are unorganized, and many of them are relegated to the unsuitable obscurity of footnotes. Mr. Blaine evidently knew something about the case. He says, "Jefferson Davis had expected, with a confidence amounting

[1] Hittell, vol. IV, p. 271. [2] *Ibid.*, p. 274.

to certainty, and based, it is believed, on personal pledges, that the Pacific Coast, if it did not actually join the South, would be disloyal to the Union."[1]

Professor Royce has given us an excellent short history of California in the decade from 1846 to 1856. He remarks that "the prevalence of disunion sentiments among certain classes of the pioneers in the years before the war would form an interesting topic for a special research."[2] It is regrettable that one so eminently fitted for the task has not undertaken it. It is, perhaps, more to be regretted — certainly unfortunate — that Professor Royce should, without research, have projected five years beyond the period allotted to his book a declaration that "California seemed at the outset [of the rebellion] a trifle in danger," but that the state "really could not have been led out of the Union by the most skillful of party leaders."[3] The Professor tells us that California "gained, by the consent of the Government, an exemption from the direct burdens of the war," and adds that many of the citizens of the state "did indeed take personal part on one side or the other. But they left the state to do so, and at home all remained tranquil."[4] James Ford Rhodes, whose copious "History of the United States" (1904) is otherwise barren of information on this subject, says, — almost superfluously referring to Royce as his authority, — "At the

[1] *Twenty Years of Congress*, vol. I, p. 308.

[2] Royce, p. 456. [3] *Ibid.*, pp. 498, 499. [4] *Ibid.*, p. 499.

outbreak of the war it had seemed that she [California] was in danger of joining the South, but she speedily espoused the Union cause, although for reasons satisfactory to the Washington Government she did not furnish any troops for the Northern Army." [1] Now, as I myself helped to raise a company of volunteers in Marysville, California, responsive to President Lincoln's call, I knew these statements of two historians to be incorrect. The slighting reference to the peril of 1861 is, I trust, disposed of on other pages. The statements that California was exempt from "the direct burdens of the war" and that the state "did not furnish any troops" for the Union Army are blunders I will correct right here.[2] The Adjutant-General of the United States, on the seventh of June, 1911, wrote me as follows: "From this statement

[1] Rhodes, vol. v, pp. 255, 256. Why "Washington Government" instead of "the Government"? And why "Northern Army" instead of "Union Army"? — E. R. K.

[2] I have been shocked at the mistakes in histories and works of reference. There is scarcely a biographical encyclopædia in the Public Library of New York City that does not err in some particular relative to General Baker. The *Political Register and Congressional Directory* (1878), by Ben: Perley Poore, states that General Baker "removed to Oregon in 1861 and was elected United States Senator from that State, taking his seat Dec. 5, 1860!" The new edition of the *Encyclopædia Britannica*, article, "California," disposes of the secession project in half a sentence: "On the eve of the Civil War it [the Gwin party] considered the scheme of a Pacific republic." The *Britannica* also states that Senator Broderick "declared in 1860 for the policy of the Republican Party." Broderick died Friday morning, September 16, 1859, never having declared for the policy of the Republican Party. — E. R. K.

[a printed compilation that accompanied the Adjutant-General's letter] it appears that the number of men furnished by California during that war was 15,725. It should be borne in mind, however, that this number represents enlistments (credits) and not the actual number of individuals in service, which latter has never been officially determined, no compilation of enlistments having been made. It is estimated by this office, however, that the number of individuals from California in service in the Union Army, Navy, and Marine Corps during that war was 12,528." For the year 1861 California's share of the Federal War Tax was $254,538, which was promptly paid in one sum by vote of the legislature. The state also paid $200,000 as the cost of military encampments.[1] Nor were these all the burdens the state cheerfully bore after the loyal revival; but they are enough for the present purpose.

Now, let us return to the matter of the secession movement, conspiracy, project, plot, or what you will. There have always been facts enough; it was requisite only for historians to trace them to their resting-places. Mr. McDougall was speaking in the United States Senate in January, 1862, the question being on the expulsion of Senator Bright, of Indiana, for treason. Mr. Bright had given a man who had superior weapons for sale a letter of introduction to Jeff Davis, head of a government at war with ours. The California Senator said the letter

[1] Bancroft, vol. VII, pp. 294, 295.

"was written at a time when we were at war. Yes, I was at war in California in January last. In the maintenance of opinions that I am now maintaining I had to go armed to protect myself from violence. The country, wherever there was controversy, was agitated to its deepest foundations. That is known; perhaps not to gentlemen who live up in Maine or Massachusetts, or where you are foreign to all this agitation; but known to all people where disturbances might have been effective in consequence. I felt it, and had to carry my life in my hands by the month, as did my friends surrounding me. I saw that all through last winter war had been inaugurated in all these parts of the country where disturbed elements could have efficient result." [1]

The Honorable James W. Nesmith, United States Senator from Oregon, writing to a leading Californian on the twenty-fifth of August, 1861, relative to the approaching state election in California, said: "I am only speaking what I *know* when I say that an effort is being made by the McConnell party [2] to revolutionize the state. . . . The disunionists, for the most part, are the most desperate men in the state, and are banding together in secret societies. They want to make California what Missouri is at this moment. . . . If California swerves from her allegiance, the defection will doubtless

[1] *Cong. Globe,* 2d Session, 37th Congress, part 1, pp. 583, 584, 585.

[2] McConnell was the Lecompton-Gwin candidate for governor.

extend throughout this entire Western section of our country."[1]

Justice Field, from whose reminiscences quotations have been made, in closing his narrative briefly refers to a number of subjects, personal and public, which under other circumstances he might have described, and makes the following significant statement: "I could have recounted the efforts made in 1860 and 1861 to keep the state in the Union against the movements of the secessionists, and the communications had with President Lincoln by relays of riders over the Plains."[2]

There were, undoubtedly, others than Judge Field who were more or less aware of the operations of the secessionists and who communicated their fears to the loyal authorities in Washington. Fortunately there was one man fully alert to the imminent gravity of the situation and in position to make his knowledge serve. Directly Mr. Lincoln had taken up the duties of the Presidency, Senator Baker called at the White House, where he was always treated almost as a member of the houshold, and explained the importance of sending a loyal man of high military rank to relieve General Johnston in the command of the Department of the Pacific. Seven states had already seceded, and energetic efforts were being made to persuade others to follow. Baker knew that such efforts would include — did already include — in their baleful influence

[1] San Francisco *Herald*, August 26, 1861.

[2] *Early Days in California*, p. 124.

the states and territories of the Pacific Slope. General Scott, loyal to the last drop of his blood, was at the head of the Army, but he still believed in the fidelity of General Johnston. Later, Scott issued orders for Johnston's arrest. But in the crucial moment there was apprehension that General Scott's confidence in General Johnston might enable the secessionists to effect their desperate designs. Senator Baker realized the responsibility resting upon him and undertook his task promptly and earnestly.

The personal friendship existing between Lincoln and Baker has been described. Incidents that occurred about this time show the close official relations between the Senator and the President. On the thirtieth of March the President, who was to receive a delegation of Californians respecting certain appointments in their state, invited Senator Baker to breakfast with him. The invitation was accepted, and after breakfast the President asked the Senator to walk with him to his reception room, where the delegation of Californians was to have its hearing. Baker accordingly accompanied the President, and a large number of Californians representing different factions were soon in the presence of the President and the Oregon Senator. Mr. James W. Simonton, one of the editors of the San Francisco "Bulletin," representing an Anti-Baker faction, presented to the President a protest against the right of Senator Baker to be heard in regard to the appointments in California. Mr. Simonton then read an address to the President, said to have been couched in disrespectful language. It was exceedingly severe upon several citizens of California who were known friends of Colonel Baker and were in favor of Mr. Birdseye for Collector of the Port of San Francisco. After Mr. Simonton had concluded his reading, the President took his manuscript, and, crushing it in his hand, threw it into the fire, and then, turning to the Californians, said, "I will destroy this in the presence of the parties who bore it. The protest is more respectful, and that I will file for consideration. Colonel Baker I have known for twenty-five years. He is my friend. This attack upon him is unjust, and not borne out by the facts." He then intimated to the protestants that they could go. A large number of the friends of Colonel Baker, mistrusting what was going to happen, took occasion to be on hand. Of course, they were indignant, and some of them denounced the protestants one by one as they passed out of the Executive Mansion. Bancroft, who seldom mentions Baker without some disparaging remark, entirely misrepresents the Senator's presence, calling it an "intrusion," and says that "Lincoln, with his usual good sense, put an end to the quarrel by giving the Californians their choice." [1]

The fact is that Senator Baker and Messrs. Leland Stanford, John Satterlee, C. Wattrous, and Judge Mott had a second and protracted interview with the President in the afternoon, when a com-

[1] Bancroft, vol. VII, p. 292.

promise was effected according to which Senator Baker and Messrs. Stanford and Satterlee were constituted a committee upon whose recommendation the California appointments were made.[1]

During the autumn an unusual if not an unparalleled order issued from the Headquarters of the Army at the National Capital. Adjutant-General Thomas, ignoring the Governor of Oregon, wrote to three loyal citizens of the state, — Colonel Thomas R. Cornelius, Hon. B. F. Harding, and R. F. Maury, Esq., authorizing them "to raise for the service of the United States one regiment of mounted troops," and, after instructions as to officers and equipments, added, "Unless otherwise ordered, you will be governed by any directions sent to you by Colonel E. D. Baker." [2]

Could there be more convincing evidence of the absolute and implicit confidence in Senator Baker at the capital? Such an order would not have been likely to originate with an officer of the Regular Army. Evidently it came from some one not afraid to do an unprecedented act; some one who knew Colonel Baker well enough to delegate such authority to him. That one could have been none other than Abraham Lincoln. The project must have arisen in the mind of some person acquainted with conditions in Oregon, aware of the needs of the loyalists, and able to name safe and true men. We

[1] These facts are summarized from a dispatch in the New York *Herald*, March 31, 1861.

[2] *Rebellion Records*, series I, vol. I, part 1, p. 622.

are not left to conjecture. Adjutant-General Thomas, communicating with the three men appointed, wrote, "Acting upon the strong recommendation of the Honorable E. D Baker, Senator from Oregon, the Department relies confidently upon the prudence, patriotism, and economy with which you will execute this trust." [1]

It was this faithful Senator who had undertaken to defeat the secession conspiracy to dislodge California and Oregon. Day after day he urged immediate action. There are men still living who knew Baker — knew how impatient he became when affairs did not move with the celerity he desired. This was the most grave and important matter in which he had ever been concerned, and he grew insistent. The President had absorbing demands on his time and thoughts from other states and from many other men. For Baker there was one supreme demand, — that Johnston should be removed and the army forces on the Pacific Coast be subject to the orders of a loyal man. Finally, a fortnight after the inauguration, General Scott wrote to Brigadier-General E. V. Sumner to prepare to sail for California, "to be gone some time." [2] The following day a formal order was confidentially issued to General Sumner directing him to "without delay repair to San Francisco and relieve Brevet-Brigadier-General Johnston in command of the Department of the Pacific." [3] General Sumner was in-

[1] *Rebellion Records*, series L, vol. L, part 1, p. 633.

[2] *Ibid.*, p. 455.

[3] *Ibid.*, p. 456.

structed to leave his orders sealed until he should have crossed the Isthmus of Panama and got fairly out on the Pacific, and the remarkable precaution was taken of having the General rowed out to the Aspinwall steamer after she had gone down the Bay of New York, and there were no reporters about to spread the story of his embarkation. It was hoped thus to conceal the enterprise from the volunteer spies who infested the departments in Washington, and of whom there were also many in New York. Sumner arrived at his destination on the twenty-fourth of April, 1861. Notwithstanding the pains taken to keep the matter secret, tidings of his appointment were ahead of him. Disloyalists at the capital, speeding their communications by rail as far as St. Joseph, Missouri, thence by stage-coach and pony express across the plains and over the mountains, and down through California valleys, got word to General Johnston and to the leading secessionists in San Francisco the evening before General Sumner's steamer sailed in through the Golden Gate.

But the secessionists failed to act. Did their courage desert them? Did they lack a leader? Was the time too short? General Johnston's resignation from the Army had been forwarded by mail to Washington a fortnight before. Did the secessionists, perhaps, learn too late — for there is evidence that he was approached — that Johnston would not betray his command? Too late, because Buchanan was out and Lincoln was in. Possibly if they could have had time to use the machinery of the State Government to call a convention and have the convention declare Calfornia out of the Union, with that decorous respect for constitutional proprieties which their Southern friends observed in tearing the Government to pieces, the disunionists would have been enabled to fulfill their promises of coöperation with the Southern leaders. Possibly if Senator Baker had been less insistent with President Lincoln, and General Sumner had taken the next steamer after that in which he sailed, the relation of the Pacific Coast to the Government might have been different during the War for the Union. But when General Sumner, — name honored and revered by every loyal man who remembers those exciting days, — when General Sumner called on General Johnston, gave him the President's orders and General Scott's, and remarked, "I am now in command of the Department," the crisis was past.

So, by his representations of the peril and his eager insistence on the relief; through his influence with Abraham Lincoln, who trusted this man as he trusted few others, — few or none, — Edward D. Baker had saved the Pacific Coast to the Union.

CHAPTER XII

CONDITIONS ON THE COAST — SEDITIOUS DEMONSTRATIONS — GENERAL SUMNER'S ENERGETIC MEASURES — THE GENERAL RETURNS TO THE EAST

General Sumner arrived on the twenty-fourth of April, toward the close of the day, — "not a day too early," declares the historian Tuthill.[1] That same evening the "Bulletin" and the "Alta" in their late editions published the news that the South had begun hostilities by firing on Fort Sumter.[2] Two days after came the tidings that Sumter had fallen, — tidings that thrilled the people of the cotton belt; that converted laggards into determined rebels; that precipitated the secession of doubtful, hesitating states; and that were calculated to "fire the Southern hearts" that beat so sympathetically in the breasts of the Pacific Coast disloyalists, and spur them to action. But, one day before, on the 25th, the telegraph had apprised the people of the Pacific Coast that General Johnston had been relieved, and every officer and soldier of the

[1] Frank Tuthill, *History of California*, p. 584.

[2] "Per telegraph to St. Louis; thence by telegraph to Fort Kearney; thence by pony express to Fort Churchill; thence by telegraph to San Francisco." San Francisco *Evening Bulletin*, April 24, 1861.

Regular Army was subject to the orders of General Sumner. The crisis, it is true, was past, but the danger was not ended. The secessionists continued defiant, and seditious demonstrations occurred in many places, a common feature being the hoisting of the Bear Flag accompanied by military ceremonies. In his first report to Washington General Sumner said: "There is a strong Union feeling with the majority of the people of this state, but the secessionists are much the most active and zealous party, which gives them more influence than they ought to have from their numbers. I have no doubt there is some deep scheming to draw California into the secession movement, — in the first place as the 'Republic of the Pacific,' expecting afterwards to induce her to join the Southern Confederacy."[1] The General at once called in troops that were widely scattered, and disposed his forces so as to safeguard important cities, forts, and army posts. The day he assumed command he telegraphed to Vancouver and summoned "the Light Battery of the Third Artillery, guns, horses, and men, by the first steamer to this place."[2] The following day he summoned Companies G and M, Third Artillery, from Oregon. That day — the same on which the news of the rebel success in Charleston Harbor became known — a detachment of troops under Lieutenant Casey was ordered to Fort

[1] *Rebellion Records*, series I, vol. L, part 1, p. 462. Other references to this same volume in this chapter will give only the pages.

[2] Page 469.

Alcatraz, in San Francisco Harbor, "to-day."[1] On the 30th the General wrote to Assistant Adjutant-General Townsend, Washington: "I have found it necessary to withdraw the troops from Fort Mojave and place them at Los Angeles. There is more danger of disaffection at this place than any other in the state."[2] On the seventh of May Captain Winfield Scott Hancock, commanding at Los Angeles, reported: "The Bear Flag was raised at El Monte, twelve miles distant, on the 4th instant. The escort was, say, forty horsemen. I have, I believe, reliable evidence that it will be raised here on Sunday, the 12th instant, — that is, that flag will be paraded through our streets under a strong escort."[3] Sumner had not been dilatory. On the third of the month he had ordered Company K, First Dragoons, from Fort Tejon to Los Angeles.[4] Captain Hancock wrote to the Headquarters of the Department: "There is here, belonging to the state, a new bronze field-piece and carriage (I think a 6-pounder gun), which in case of difficulty is not likely at first to be in the hands of persons supporting the Federal Government. I would respectfully suggest, therefore, that it might be wise to send here a gun of equal or greater calibre."[5] At another time Captain Hancock wrote: "When once a revolution commences the masses of the native population will act, and they are worthy of a good deal of consideration. If they act it will be most likely

[1] Page 469. [2] Page 474. [3] Page 480.
[4] Page 475. [5] Page 476.

against the Government."[1] The vigorous measures of General Sumner and the presence of the troops, efficiently commanded by Captain Hancock, rendered the secessionists cautious and emboldened Union men, so that before the Captain relinquished command of the post he declared there was "but little fear of the future."[2]

On the eighteenth of May the following order was sent to Captain Adams at Fort Crook: "Send Company E, Sixth Infantry, to Benicia Barracks immediately."[3] On the twentieth of the month General Sumner reported to Washington that he had "found it necessary to withdraw the greater portion of the garrison from Fort Umpqua and one company of infantry from Fort Crook for the purpose of reinforcing the commands at Benicia and the Presidio" [San Francisco].[4] On the 27th, ordnance men were sent from the arsenal at Benicia to Fort Point (San Francisco) "for temporary service, to assist in mounting guns."[5] On the fifth of the following month the ordnance men were ordered to return to the Benicia Arsenal "without delay."[6] Captain Lendrum's Company I, Third Artillery, was ordered in from Honey Lake to "join the company at Alcatraz Island, bringing with it the movable public property."[7] On the sixth of June General Sumner wrote to the Collector of the Port of San Francisco, saying that he thought "a cutter of some kind for the use of the custom-house and the Marshal is very

[1] Page 480. [2] Page 483. [3] Page 486. [4] Page 486.
[5] Page 491. [6] Page 499. [7] Page 491.

MAJOR-GENERAL EDWIN V. SUMNER

necessary at this particular time," and suggesting that the Collector should charter a vessel for the purpose.[1] The following day Colonel Wright, commanding the District of Oregon, was directed to "send to this place [San Francisco] with the greatest possible dispatch seven of the infantry companies which can best be spared from his command."[2] Three days later, Company F, Fourth Infantry, was ordered from Fort Vancouver, Washington Territory, "to embark on the next steamer for San Francisco."[3] The same day Captain Wallen was ordered from Fort Vancouver to "proceed with his company by first steamer to San Francisco and report to the General commanding the Department."[4] On the 11th Captain Augur was ordered from Fort Vancouver to "embark on the first steamer for San Francisco." Captain Russell, Company K, Fourth Infantry, received the same order. Company D, Ninth Infantry, Captain Pickett, and Company C, Fourth Infantry, Captain Hunt, were also ordered to San Francisco by the first steamer. Company A of the Fourth received a similar order.[5]

General Sumner reported to Adjutant-General Thomas, in Washington, that he had "found it necessary to withdraw from Oregon a considerable part of the force stationed there to reinforce the troops in California and Nevada Territory." The General at this time underestimated the secession

[1] Page 501. [2] Page 503. [3] Page 509.
[4] Page 509. [5] Page 512.

element in Oregon, for he said there was "nothing to apprehend there but the possibility of some Indian disturbances, which seems to me of little consequence in comparison with preserving the integrity of the Union." Respecting California he remarked, "I believe there is a large majority of Union men in this state, but they are supine from confidence, while there is an active and zealous party of secessionists who will make all the mischief they can." [1] The latter part of August General Sumner wrote to the Colonel commanding at Benicia Barracks, "I wish you to encamp a company close to the new Ordnance Building and put a strong guard at the Magazine." [2]

San Bernardino was another troublesome centre. A company of cavalry was organized among the Mormons, who were numerous there, and commanded by a man who had resigned from the Regular Army. They pretended to be loyal, but they cheered the name of Jeff Davis.[3] Major Ketchum ordered two companies of dragoons to the place. The Major reported that he was expecting an attack from the secessionists, and he adds, "As we were here much sooner than expected, the secessionists were not prepared." [4]

A number of loyal men at Santa Barbara wrote to the Commanding General that the secessionists were armed and active, and that Government troops ought to be sent to the place. The General replied "that the more pressing necessity for the

[1] Page 506. [2] Page 593. [3] Page 622. [4] Page 594.

presence of troops at other points will render the establishment of a post at Santa Barbara at this time impracticable."[1] On the second of June, "guns, carriages, and ammunition for San Diego" were shipped from the Benicia Arsenal.[2] On the twenty-first of June, Lieutenant Carr wrote from Fort Tejon that the disloyal whites were giving the Indians whiskey and inciting them to trouble. Major Carleton promptly sent reinforcements.[3] Later two companies of infantry were ordered to proceed immediately to reinforce the troops at Fort Yuma, who were apprehensive of an attack from a rebel force.[4]

On the seventeenth of September, General Sumner wrote to Assistant Adjutant-General Townsend: "The disaffection in the southern part of the state is increasing and becoming dangerous, and it is indispensably necessary to throw reinforcements into that section immediately. The rebels are organizing, collecting supplies, and evidently preparing to receive a force from Texas, and the worst feature of the affair is this: they have managed to seduce the native Californians by telling them they will be ruined by taxes to maintain the war." The General then explains his disposition of forces to overcome the danger.[5]

Early in June General Scott directed General Sumner, "in concert with the naval commander on the Pacific Station," to prevent the carrying

[1] Page 492. [2] Page 496. [3] Page 520.
[4] Page 600. [5] Page 623.

out of rebel plans for "annexing Lower California to the so-called Southern Confederacy."[1] The information that necessitated this measure came from Secretary Seward and was undoubtedly well grounded.[2] Later, when the project of a rebel force to come from Texas seemed to have taken definite shape, and the secessionists were counting on such a force to appear in California and begin operations, General Scott contemplated a counter-expedition to be led by General Sumner from California to Texas. Concerning this General Sumner wrote to Assistant Adjutant-General Townsend (August 30): "I feel it to be a duty to the General to let him know precisely the state of things on this coast. Up to the time of the reverse in Virginia [at Bull Run] everything was perfectly safe here. There has always been a strong secession party in this state, but it was overawed and kept quiet. Since that news was received these people have been getting much bolder, and I have found it necessary to take strong measures to repress any attempt on their part to thwart the government. I think I can do it, but if they succeed in electing their candidate for Governor, of which they are very confident, I shall not be able to do it without the most stringent measures."[3] On the seventh of September, General Sumner wrote again, in a more confident vein: "The Union party has triumphed in the election, which makes things much safer here. There are about 20,000 secession voters in

[1] Page 498. [2] Page 504. [3] Pages 593, 594.

this state,[1] and the dissolute and loose portion of this party are congregating in some force in the southern counties in the hope of receiving support from Texas. I am reinforcing the regular troops in that quarter as speedily as possible, in order to check this movement. The great and unaccountable success in Arizona and New Mexico will no doubt embolden them, and it is by no means certain that they will not make some attempt in this direction, and if they should ever get an organized force into this state as a rallying-point for all the secession element it would inevitably inaugurate a civil war here immediately."[2]

The project of an expedition of California troops to Texas excited alarm among Union men, and evoked one of the most impressive statements of the dangerous conditions existing in California as late as the close of the summer of 1861. A communication, dated the twenty-eighth of August, was addressed to the Honorable Simon Cameron, Secretary of War, remonstrating against the withdrawal of so many loyal troops as would be required for the Texas enterprise. This communication, which was signed by many of the foremost men of San Francisco, — merchants, bankers, lawyers, and

[1] Later General Sumner corrected himself and stated that "the secession party in this state numbers about 32,000 men and they are very restless and zealous, which gives them great influence. They are congregating in the southern part of the state, and it is there they expect to commence their operations against the Government." Page 643.

[2] Page 610.

other business and professional men, — stated that it was understood that five thousand additional men were to be enlisted in California and that then a force would be sent across the country under command of General Sumner.

"This report," they say, "has caused the most lively apprehensions of danger in our midst, and so deeply are we impressed that your Department is not sensible of the true condition of affairs on this coast that we most respectfully ask the rescinding of so much of the order as calls for the withdrawal of the troops to be raised and that transfers General Sumner to another field of operations; and thereto we present the following reasons: —

"A majority of our present state officials are avowed secessionists, and the balance, being bitterly hostile to the Administration, are advocates of a peace policy at any sacrifice upon terms that would not be rejected even by South Carolina.

"Every appointment made by our governor within the past three months indicates his entire sympathy and coöperation with those plotting to sever California from her allegiance to the Union, and that, too, at the hazard of civil war.

"About three eighths of our citizens are natives of slave-holding states and are almost a unit in this crisis. The hatred, manifested so pointedly in the South, and so strongly evinced on the field of battle, is no more intense there than here. . . .

"Our advices, obtained with great prudence and care, show us that there are about sixteen thousand

Knights of the Golden Circle [1] in this state, and that they are still organizing, even in our most loyal districts." [2]

The communication further states that through gross misrepresentations the powerful native Mexican element of the population has been won over to the secession side, and ends by protesting against moving the California troops out of the state and against returning General Sumner to the East. It is a tradition of that time that Senator Baker's intercession was asked in support of the memorial. It would be hard to believe that the anxious San Franciscans overlooked that powerful influence. Certainly the projected expedition to Texas was for the time abandoned.

It is essential, both for proving the reality of a secession peril and for showing General Sumner's realization of it, to mention briefly more of the conditions on the coast, the activities of the secessionists, and the measures adopted for their repression. We have seen how promptly the forces in San Francisco and vicinity were augmented. A close watch had to be maintained over every section of the coast. In addition to the Knights of the Golden Circle, many disloyal men associated for hostile action in numerous places. A company of two hundred, organized at Oroville ostensibly to join the Union Volunteers, their arms and equipment having been paid for in part by Union men, was found

[1] The secret semi-military organization of the secessionists.

[2] Pages 589, 590, 591.

to be intended for the rebel army.[1] On the eighth of June General Sumner ordered a "special observation" to be maintained over the steamer Diana, which certain persons contemplated fitting up "with an armament," — certainly not for use by the government authorities.[2]

Bancroft [3] describes several subsequent attempts of the same sort. The speedy clipper ship J. W. Chapman was loaded with arms, powder, etc., and it was pretended they were for the Mexicans, who were then engaged in their conflict with Maximilian and his French soldiers; but the naval authorities seized the Chapman as she was about to sail. It was ascertained that the parties in control of the vessel planned to capture a steamer along the coast, and, using her, then capture other steamers that should be conveying the gold of California to the East. Bancroft continues: "In connection with this piratical scheme was a plan to form secret associations of men favorable to the Confederacy in every community, who were to be secretly armed, and, when their numbers were deemed sufficient, to meet at Sacramento, cut the telegraph wires, seize a steamboat, run down to Benicia, secure the arsenal, take by surprise Fort Point and Alcatraz, which three objects being accomplished they would declare California out of the Union and one of the Confederate States." The chief conspirators were convicted and sentenced to imprisonment and to

[1] Page 827.
[2] Page 505.
[3] Bancroft, vol. VII, pp. 287, 288.

pay heavy fines. "A plot to take Mare Island and the navy yard was discovered only a little later than the Chapman affair. The steamboat Guadalupe, in Napa Creek, was to be taken by a force of two hundred men, who were to cross over to Vallejo, take the works and government shipping by surprise, and, with the vessels and arms obtained, the plotters were to make an assault on San Francisco. The discovery of the conspiracy was its defeat, but it was of sufficient importance to detain the United States steamer Saginaw from leaving the harbor." [1] By the middle of June General Sumner reported to the Government that he had checked the secession movement in the southern part of California, which, however, revived at a later date and became acute.

At this time the General reported that the disloyal element had organized and become active in the Territory of Nevada. Citizens wrote from Virginia City to Captain Hendrickson, commandant at Fort Churchill, that the secessionists had completed an organization under a certain Dr. McMeans. It was stated that the general impression was that the rebels expected "to seize the fort and get possession of the territory." [2] Later a citizen wrote to General Sumner that "we are eleven twelfths Union men, but we are without arms or organization, while the rebels have control of all

[1] Bancroft, vol. VII, p. 288. These marine plots were hatched after General Sumner had gone East.

[2] Page 490.

the public or private arms here." [1] General Sumner reported, early in June, that he was "informed of the organization and partial armament of a body of men in Carson Valley for the purpose of overawing the Union portion of the population there and involving the territory in the cause of secession." [2] A company of the Sixth Infantry was immediately dispatched to report to the commanding officer at Fort Churchill. Captain T. Moore was sent to Carson with a detachment of dragoons under the command of Lieutenant Baker, and they succeeded in disarming several parties of secessionists. Captain Moore reported: "I was informed from the most reliable residents of the place [Virginia City] that there was beyond doubt an organization to subvert the authority of the Federal Government in the territory and declare in favor of the Confederate States." [3] This expedition arranged for enrolling nearly five hundred loyal men, who were furnished with arms by order of General Sumner. The general wrote that "the seizure of the arms as reported had the effect to check at once the action of the secessionists in Nevada Territory." [4]

The situation in Oregon was — or rather would have been — grave if the Government had not been so strongly represented. On the twenty-first of June, A. G. Henry, a practicing physician, an old Illinois friend of Abraham Lincoln, wrote from his home at

[1] Page 499.
[2] Page 502.
[3] Page 510.
[4] Page 511.

Lafayette, Oregon, to the President: "There is a much stronger secession feeling in Oregon than is generally believed. In my opinion the election of Baker and Nesmith to the Senate, and the consequent defeat of Breckinridge and Lane in Oregon and California in November, is all that saved this coast from going with the South. As it was, the timely appearance of General Sumner at San Francisco saved the public property of California from falling into the hands of secessionists. I think all is now safe, notwithstanding the Governors of both California and Oregon openly avow their hostility to your policy of putting down the rebellion." [1]

In August Justice Stratton, of the Supreme Court of Oregon, wrote to General Sumner: "It is not to be doubted that the Governor of this state strongly sympathizes with the rebels, and there are many who believe that under the influence of General Lane he would seize any opportunity to give Union men trouble. It is understood and believed that the withdrawal of United States forces from this and other posts would offer an occasion of which the Governor would have availed himself to call out troops to occupy them. It would be an easy matter to obtain such only as he could rely upon. A few men of desperate fortunes, with arms in their hands, might give us infinite trouble. Oregon has a large faction of her population who are as devoted to the rebels as any men to be found

[1] From a copy in the possession of Miss Hopkins.

in the South."[1] General Sumner replied that he had felt compelled to withdraw many of the United States troops from Oregon, because the need for their services has been greater elsewhere, but he assured Justice Stratton that no more of the force in that state should be taken, and he added that Colonel George Wright, commanding the Regular Army forces in Oregon, had been authorized to muster volunteers into service without consulting the state officials.[2] Still, the activity of the disloyalists continued. Lieutenant Campbell, writing from Fort Hoskins as late as November, stated that "the disaffected seem to be again about to give us trouble" and "the late commander aided the inhabitants in their nefarious designs on the Government." Lieutenant Campbell then tells of the distribution of arms to the Indians by secessionists, with promise of further favors if they would "fight for Jeff Davis." The Lieutenant stated that "rebels" proposed to set fire to a block-house occupied by government troops "and shoot the officers as they come out."[3]

In the Territory of Washington the secession peril also lifted its front, but the acting governor, a presidential appointment, was loyal and his promptness and zeal in organizing the militia of the territory discouraged acts of open hostility.[4] The presence of a number of Regular troops was also effective, but at one time this effectiveness

[1] Page 571.
[2] Page 578.
[3] Pages, 739, 740.
[4] Pages 488, 489.

was neutralized by the disloyalty of several officers.

The secessionists were as audacious in Arizona as in any section of the department commanded by General Sumner. In June several of them wrote to a man who had resigned from the Regular Army and urged him to intercede with the Confederate authorities for a territorial organization under that government. They asked for arms and equipment for a regiment, declaring that such an organization "would strengthen and perpetuate that sympathy with the South which is now unanimous." [1]

General Sumner, as the result of his long experience in army operations, appreciated the importance of knowing what the enemy was planning and hoping to do; so the General kept thoroughly informed concerning affairs in every section of his extensive department. His orders, issued from time to time as occasion required, fairly stung the disloyal, while they inspired Union men and incited them to preparation and organization. At a time when the small force in the southern part of California was expecting an incursion from Texas, General Sumner issued the following laconic order: —

No Federal troops in the Department of the Pacific will ever surrender to rebels.

E. V. Sumner,
Brigadier-General commanding.[2]

[1] Pages 501, 502.

[2] Page 603.

Another order declared that "No public property will ever be surrendered in this department." [1]

Another, instructing commanders everywhere: "Any citizen in the employment of the Army in this department who is opposed to the Union will be instantly discharged." [2]

At a time when the secessionists had purchased a vessel and secretly fitted it up to serve as a privateer General Sumner promulgated the following: "Any vessel sailing under the secession flag, so-called, which shall enter, or attempt to enter, any of the waters of the United States on this coast will be immediately captured by the troops stationed there. Any such vessel which shall fail to come to or surrender on being duly warned, or which shall attempt to escape, will be fired into and sunk if necessary." [3]

Much additional testimony to prove my opening proposition could be introduced. It would, however, be cumulative, which in law tends merely "to prove the same point to which other evidence has been offered." [4] It seems strange that so many historians have ignored it.

It is less unaccountable that the career and services of Senator Baker are so little known. His untimely death deprived him of opportunities to share the harvest of glory gathered in field and forum by those who served through the War for the Union. But there were those who knew of Baker's ardor and efficiency. The Honorable Timothy J.

[1] Page 486. [2] Page 486. [3] Page 494.

[4] *Webster's Dictionary.*

Phelps, who had become a member of Congress from California, in his tribute to Baker in the House of Representatives, declared that "the whole country is indebted to him in no small degree that California is to-day in the Union."[1]

Congressman Aaron A. Sargent, afterwards Senator from California, on the same occasion said: "I do but strict justice to his memory when I say that California is largely indebted to Edward D. Baker that she is not to-day within the grasp of secessionists."[2]

The time came when General Sumner's great talents and experience made his presence indispensable in the field of military operations in the East, and on the twenty-first of October he sailed for Panama on the steamship Orizaba. He was succeeded in the command of the Department of the Pacific by Colonel Wright; but it was stated that Colonel Wright would remain but a short time and would himself then go East and be succeeded by a volunteer officer of such dubious loyalty and unsatisfactory antecedents that the announcement aroused strong remonstrance. General Sumner, writing to Washington a few days before his departure, said, "Colonel Wright ought to remain here in command. The safety of the whole coast may depend upon it."[3]

Bancroft gives the following interesting state-

[1] *Cong. Globe*, 2d Session, 37th Congress, part 1, p. 63. Mr. Phelps was speaking in December, 1861.

[2] *Cong. Globe*, 2d Session, 37th Congress, part 1, p. 64.

[3] *Rebellion Records*, series L, vol. L, part 1, p. 658.

ment in a footnote: "Either by accident or design General Sumner and staff sailed on the same steamer with Senator Gwin and Calhoun Benham. Gwin had returned to California in June and remained until October, but found no opportunity to carry out any of the Confederate designs against the public property, and was now departing on the Orizaba to prosecute them elsewhere. Just before reaching Panama, on learning that some of his officers had been approached, Sumner arrested Gwin, Benham, and J. L. Brent on a charge of treason, compelling them to accompany him to New York and Washington. On the evidence it appeared that Gwin expected to meet Slidell and Mason, the Confederate emissaries to Europe, at Havana, and proceed abroad with them. Had not his plans been frustrated, he must have been arrested in their company and confined in Fort Warren. As it was, he and his companions had a brief residence in Fort Lafayette, and were released. Benham and Brent joined the Confederate Army at the first opportunity, and Gwin spent some time in Mississippi before going to France to labor for the recognition of the Confederacy.

" Sumner did not seem to realize that he had it in his power to discover all the plans of the conspirators on the Orizaba. He simply sent for them to come to the Captain's office, when he placed them under arrest, but not in confinement. They returned to their rooms and threw overboard a quantity of maps and papers, a fact unknown for half an hour afterwards. At this point Gwin disappears from the political history of California. Like Lane, of Oregon, to whom his example was fatal, he betrayed his state and his country." [1]

How different the last words concerning General Sumner may be. His splendid service in the Eastern armies is beyond the purpose of this book to recount. It is the proud possession of the American Nation. I will, however, with the warmest approval, quote a few lines concerning the General from the "History of Abraham Lincoln." "He died at Syracuse, New York, on the twenty-first of March, 1863, universally respected and beloved by all who were able to appreciate his noble qualities, his valor, and his patriotism. He was the finest type the Army possessed of the old-fashioned soldier; the quick eye, the strong arm, the unquestioning spirit of loyal obedience; the simple heart that knew not a pulse of fear or of hesitation; that beat only for his friends, his flag, and his God." [2]

Bancroft refers to Colonel Wright, "whose conscientious discharge of duty in his whole department was of the greatest value to the Government and the state. Nothing escaped his observation, and at every point the disaffected were met with stern reproof." [3] As long as the war lasted the secession element on the coast continued in its readiness for revolt and occasionally indulged in malignant but futile demonstrations.

[1] Bancroft, vol. VII, p. 284. [2] Nicolay and Hay, vol. VI, p. 222.
[3] Bancroft, vol. VII, p. 284.

CHAPTER XIII

BAKER IN THE THIRTY-SEVENTH CONGRESS — HIS FORESIGHT — DEFEATS A CONFERENCE COMMITTEE REPORT — THE REPLY TO BRECKINRIDGE — ANNOUNCES HIS DECLINATION OF APPOINTMENT AS BRIGADIER-GENERAL

PURSUANT to the call of the President a special session of Congress began on the fourth of July, 1861. Notwithstanding Colonel Baker's hard work with his brigade, he took a lively interest in the proceedings of the Senate. On the tenth of July, speaking upon a bill reported from the Military Committee, Senator Baker said: —

"I approve, as a personal and political friend of the President, of every measure of his Administration in relation to the rebellion at present raging in this country. I propose to ratify whatever needs ratification. I propose to render my clear and distinct approval not only of the measure, but of the motive which prompted it. I propose to lend the whole power of the country — arms, men, money — and place them in his hands, with authority almost unlimited, until the conclusion of this struggle. He has asked for four hundred million dollars; we propose to give him five hundred million. He has asked for four hundred thousand men; we propose to give him half a million; and for my part, if, as I do not apprehend, the emergency should be still greater, I will cheerfully add a cipher to either of these figures.

"But, sir, while I do that, I desire by my word and my vote to have it clearly understood that I do that as a measure of war. As I had occasion to say in a very early discussion of this question, I want sudden, bold, forward, determined war; and I do not think anybody can conduct war of that kind as well as a dictator. But, as a senator, I deem it my duty to look forward to returning peace. . . . Whether that peace shall be conquered at Richmond, or Montgomery, or New Orleans, or in the wilds of Texas, I do not presume to say; but I do know, if I may use so bold a word, that the determined, aggregated power of the whole people of this country, of its treasure, of its arms, of its blood, of its enthusiasm, kindled, concentrated, poured out in one mass of living valor upon any foe, will conquer.

"Here, as a senator, looking beyond the immediate contingency, I still desire to show by my conduct and my vote that I venerate the principles of the Constitution of the United States. I believe that a standing army is always dangerous to liberty; and I believe that the ambition of men, and the interests of men, and the tendency of power to the lust of power, always seek and find excuses for the increase and continuance of standing armies in all public emergencies. No standing army ever was raised, even in a despotic government, except under some pretense of maintaining good order or putting down resistance to good government. Therefore, while I cheerfully add to the standing army, — though I confess that would not have been the policy I should have preferred, — while I cheerfully yield my acquiescence in the measures of the Administration which work a large increase of the standing army for purposes of war, I propose to limit it to the time when that war exists." [1]

In the same speech Senator Baker recurred to his support of the Crittenden compromise propositions at the previous session, and remarked: —

"My honored friend from Maine [Mr. Fessenden] will bear me witness that I was perhaps the last man in the Senate to give up the hope that something might be done by conciliation and compromise — words I propose never to use again. I hoped, I sympathized, I struggled to the last. Now I hope to be among the last of all men willing to lay down arms at all. I will never vote to do it till, without treaty, the flag of the United States waves over every portion of its territory, and over a population either enthusiastically rallying beneath its shadow or else abjectly subject to its sway. Till then, give the President a million men. Till then, give him not only the whole revenue of the Government, but the whole property of the people. Do not refuse a single regiment; do not furl a single sail; do not abate a single jot of all your embattled

[1] *Cong. Globe*, 1st Session, 37th Congress, p. 44.

vigor till that hour shall come; but when peace returns, resume the condition and the arts of peace. Do not make peace until the glory of the American flag shall be its own defense."

Senator Baker also evinced a sad prescience. He continued: —

"I am one of those who believe there may be reverses. I am not quite confident we shall overrun the Southern States, as we shall have to overrun them, without severe trials of our courage and our patience. They are a brave, determined people, filled with their enthusiasm; false in its purpose, as I think, but still one which animates almost all classes of the population." [1]

The reading of still other of his remarks impresses one with his extraordinary foresight. When you consider President Lincoln's letters to General Grant and Secretary Stanton's communications to General Sherman, as the rebellious armies were surrendering, you observe that the Government insisted on precisely the conditions which Senator Baker in 1861 declared must be those upon which the Government would end the war.

The following day Senator Powell, of Kentucky, was expending his intellect in explaining how impossible, how unlawful, how unconstitutional, it would be for the Government to use the means requisite to suppress the rebellion. Replying to the remarks of Senator Baker on the preceding day, Mr. Powell said: —

[1] *Cong. Globe*, 1st Session, 37th Congress, p. 45.

"The Constitution of the Senator's country and of my country declares that 'the United States shall guarantee to every state in this Union a republican form of government'; and yet the Senator in his speech proclaims that he is willing to reduce the South to conquered provinces, and give them governors from Massachusetts and Illinois; and in the very same speech he expresses his reverence for the Constitution. Would these states have republican governments when you had put the iron heel of your military power on them, when you had overthrown their liberty, when you had deprived them of the right to elect governors, and sent a Massachusetts governor to Louisiana, or Texas, or any state South?"

At this point Senator Baker interrupted and remarked, "The Senator from Kentucky is catechizing me, and I will reply."

Mr. Powell: "Not catechizing."

Mr. Baker: "It was very courteously done, and I will reply to it. He accuses me of want of reverence for the Constitution, because I said that, in some circumstances, I would govern those states as territories. He tells me that the Constitution guarantees to those states a republican form of government. I tell him that a territorial form of government is a republican form of government, and I told him so when I was going to vote to admit Kansas as a state, and he would not. It is true that a territorial form of government may be a republican form of government as well as a state government may be. That is the answer to that. . . . If they will not come here as states, we will not let them out of the Union for that reason. If they will not govern themselves in Congress, we will govern them. Rather than separate from them, and lose them, we will govern them as territories, and govern them a great deal better than they will govern themselves."[1]

On the seventeenth of July Senator Baker briefly but forcibly expressed his disapproval of the proposition to create an Army Retiring Board. On the 29th the Senator discussed the army ration, and said, "I confess to a profound astonishment at the report of the Committee of Conference. Sir, I will not vote for it in any part. Two thirds of the time I have spent with the troops during the last month has been to rectify the difficulties about the Commissary Department — provisions. There is not a day that there are not one hundred men in every regiment in this army who go to bed hungry. I introduced, and was able to carry through this body, a provision increasing the article of bread, adding a little beans, and giving the men a pound of potatoes a day three times a week if practicable. To my great astonishment I found that stricken out by the Committee of Conference and a poor, emasculated substitute, that the Commissary-General may change the character of the ration, provided the expense is not increased. . . . The proposition stricken out of this report gives the private soldier twenty-two ounces of dry bread."

[1] *Cong. Globe*, 1st Session, 37th Congress, p. 69.

The senator then went on, as only one familiar with the subject could, referring to other details, and added: "That, with a little sugar and coffee, and three quarters of a pound of salt meat, practically constitutes his rations. Now consider, again, what three quarters of a pound of salt meat is. In the first place, three fifths of the time it is issued to us it is salt pork, that fat [the honorable Senator illustrated by showing the length of his hand], and nearly as old as I am [laughter]. In the next place, it is issued to us by the barrel — two hundred pounds to the barrel, whether it is one year old or three. Every merchant knows, you, sir [Mr. Chandler], know, the difference between real weight and the weight we buy. In the next place, if sometimes we get hams — such hams! You eat a piece of broiled ham for breakfast. If you buy three quarters of a pound and take the fat and that which is not fit to eat, the bone, the spoiled part, you do not on the average get six ounces or seven ounces at the most of what is fit to go into a man's stomach."

Senator Baker further explained the sufferings under which many of the volunteers were laboring, and, being supported by Mr. Sherman, of Ohio, and others, was successful in having the report of the Conference Committee rejected and a new conference called for.[1]

On the third of August Mr. Baker contended with both the Senators from Kentucky, first, in favor of

[1] *Cong. Globe*, 1st Session, 37th Congress, pp. 309, 310.

putting out of office a disloyal United States Judge whom both the Kentucky Senators strongly supported, and second, creating a new United States District Court for Kentucky and Missouri.[1]

The occurrence of greatest interest to us during the session was Senator Baker's reply to Senator Breckinridge. Mr. Breckinridge was not one of the most astute or able statesmen in the Southern interest, but he possessed superior powers of oratory and his prestige at this time was great. He had been Vice-President of the United States. The day he ceased to hold that exalted office he took his place in the Senate as one of the two representatives from the State of Kentucky. His family, too, was honorably distinguished. As many of the best people in Kentucky remained faithful to the Union, under trials of their fidelity that residents in the Northern States probably never appreciated, it had been hoped that Mr. Breckinridge would see it his duty to continue true to his oath of office. It became, alas, early evident that his sympathies were entirely with the secessionists, and with them he finally cast in his lot — leaving his state fast anchored to the Union.

It was known that Mr. Breckinridge had been preparing to speak upon a bill "to suppress insurrection and sedition and for other purposes." On Thursday, the first of August, the Senate had an unusually busy day. On that day the bill mentioned was a special order. It was evident to Senators

[1] *Cong. Globe*, 1st Session, 37th Congress, p. 423.

that Mr. Breckinridge was now about to deliver the speech which he had been preparing. Mr. Blaine describes the scene when Senator Baker replied to Mr. Breckinridge: "On the first of August, while performing the double and somewhat anomalous duty of commanding his regiment and representing Oregon in the Senate, Mr. Baker entered the Chamber in the full uniform of a colonel of the United States Army. He laid his sword upon his desk and sat for some time listening to the debate. He was evidently impressed by the scene of which he was himself a conspicuous feature. Breckinridge took the floor shortly after Baker appeared, and made a speech of which it is fair criticism to say that it reflected in all respects the views held by the members of the Confederate Congress then in session at Richmond. Colonel Baker evidently grew restless under the words of Mr. Breckinridge. His face was aglow with excitement, and he sprang to the floor when the Senator from Kentucky took his seat. . . . It is impossible to realize the effect of the words so eloquently pronounced by the Oregon Senator. In the history of the Senate no more thrilling speech was ever delivered. The striking appearance of the speaker in the uniform of a soldier, his superb voice, his graceful manner, all united to give to the occasion an extraordinary interest and attraction."[1]

Mr. Blaine was evidently unaware of some of the circumstances under which Colonel Baker spoke. As the hour when the Kentucky Senator was ex-

[1] Blaine, vol. I, p. 344.

pected to take the floor drew near, several Republican Senators were conferring about the debate. They felt it important that a reply to the expected address should go out with the same dispatches that should spread the speech abroad. As one Senator said, "The antidote must go with the poison." When it was asked who should be selected to make the reply, instantly to put before the country the case for loyalty and the Government, the answer was Baker, and the wisdom of the choice was at once recognized. "Well," it was asked, "where is Baker?" Messengers were sent in haste to discover the Oregon Senator. He was found drilling his regiment and was told he was wanted in the Senate. He sprang into his saddle and rode to the Capitol. He was met on his arrival at the Senate Chamber by some of his colleagues, who explained the situation. There was no time to change his apparel, so he sat down at his desk. And that is how Colonel Baker chanced to speak in his colonel's uniform in the Senate, and to be, I believe, the only man who ever spoke in military uniform in both houses of Congress.[1] Directly the speech was concluded. Colonel Baker remounted his horse and rode back to his regiment at the foot of Meridian Hill, about a mile from the Capitol.

Senator Latham in his remarks in the memorial

[1] The circumstances relating to Senator Baker's reply to Senator Breckinridge were narrated to me by a senator who was one of those who sent for the Colonel. Colonel Baker's speech in the House of Representatives is described on pages 102 and 103 of this book.

session for Baker, in the Senate, said, "In my judgment his impromptu reply to Senator Breckinridge, during our session in July, was his best in the Senate." [1]

The last appearance of Colonel Baker in the Senate was on the sixth of August, 1861, which is noted in the "Globe" as follows: "Mr. Baker stated that he had declined to accept the office of brigadier-general tendered to him by the President of the United States. He considered it his duty to make this statement, as the matter had been spoken of." [2]

[1] *Cong. Globe*, 2d Session, 37th Congress, part 1, p. 55.

[2] *Ibid.*, 1st Session, 37th Congress, p. 455.

CHAPTER XIV

THE LOYAL REVIVAL IN CALIFORNIA — T. STARR KING — SECESSIONISTS DEPART FOR THE SOUTH — EFFICIENCY OF THE VOLUNTEERS — MUNIFICENT GIFTS TO THE SANITARY COMMISSION

In one of his reports, referred to in a preceding chapter, General Sumner declared that he found the Union men of California supine. This is susceptible of explanation entirely creditable to their citizenship. At first they were unaware of the extent and virulence of the disunion movement in the South. In this respect they were no more ignorant than the people of the North, the generality of whom, we understood, long cherished the hope that war would be averted. Then, as most of the scheming and contriving of the secessionists on the coast was carried on in secret, Union men were incredulous as to rumors and stories of disloyal plots near home. With the assumption of the command of the forces of the Regular Army by General Johnston there was a shock and a realization of being at a disadvantage. Perhaps a feeling of helplessness, more or less warranted. Again, the Republicans had never exercised any authority in affairs. They were unaccustomed to responsibility. How could they be expected to act against the combined power of the National and State Governments?

General Sumner was writing in June; but on the twenty-second of February a Union meeting was held in San Francisco at which, it was estimated, there were fully fourteen thousand people present. As an expression of sentiment this was imposing, but the power still lodged in the other party. Union men, however, began to organize clubs. One of the first steps was taken in San Francisco. Sheriff Doane, in conjunction with David Scannell, chief of the volunteer fire department, where Broderick's influence still survived, collected nearly a thousand loyal men into companies. Similar work was done in other towns. The firing on Fort Sumter aroused the loyalists and the arrival of General Sumner inspired them with confidence. Among the earliest organized associations to feel the impulse were the churches. There were, to be sure, disloyal clergymen, pastors of disloyal churches. But throughout the state, generally, Jews and Christians, Catholics and Protestants, were merged in one fervid mass of determined loyalists, and the Stars and Stripes were flung to the breeze from many steeples. The Catholic Archbishop Alemany, owing to the influence of his character and his powerful ecclesiastical position, was especially serviceable in the cause.

The leader of loyal sentiment, the prophet, the Voice of patriotism, was the Reverend Thomas Starr King. Called from Boston to the pastorate of an influential church in San Francisco, Mr. King hoped to repair his delicate health in the genial climate of California. He sailed from New York on the fifth of April, 1860, by the wooden side-wheel steamer Northern Light, and arrived in San Francisco about the first of May. He soon carried the popularity of his church beyond all previous heights, and when the occasion offered he flung himself into the advocacy of the Union with remarkable fervor and power.

Errors relating to Mr. King's work have grown up in the East. A New York daily paper recently stated that Mr. King's speeches did much to give the electoral vote of California to Lincoln. In point of fact, Mr. King did little or nothing to that end. An illustrated weekly paper published in New York declared not long ago that Mr. King saved California from secession. Now, no California loyalist would allow himself to be driven into a position where he must seem to depreciate the services and influence of "Starr King," as he was called. The history that shall preserve the knowledge of the ardor of Henry Ward Beecher in supplying heart and spirit and faith and fervor and conquering determination to the Union cause in the East, during the trying days and years of the Civil War, — so that President Lincoln, when sending the Brooklyn pastor to celebrate the hoisting of the Union flag over Fort Sumter after that famous ruin was retaken by the government forces, could say that if it had not been for Mr. Beecher there might not have been any Union flag to hoist, — that history must ever bear upon its glowing page the name of T. Starr King for similar service in the imperiled West beyond the Sierra Nevada. Sumner had guns, and men to use them. Starr King revived and led the irresistible force of public sentiment. Sumner overawed the secession conspirators. Starr King aroused Union men to enthusiasm, organization, coöperation, action. The command of the soldier was, "No surrender to rebels." The orator chanted in inspiring tones, —

> "We are coming, Father Abraham,
> Three hundred thousand more."

Or, if there were not quite so many, there were enough.

On the evening of Memorial Day, 1899, the American Unitarian Association held a service in Tremont Temple, Boston, "to commemorate the patriotic services of some of its great leaders during the Civil War." Mr. Horace Davis, speaking for Starr King, made these remarks: —

"When in the spring of 1861 the cotton states resolved to secede, he determined at once to throw himself, with all his heart and all his strength, into the fight against secession. California was in a peculiar position; a large part of her citizens, powerful in wealth and social position, favored the South; another portion was loyal to the Union; while between the two opposing forces stood the lukewarm and timid — no inconsiderable number — and doubted the wisdom or prudence of using force against the rebels. To stimulate the patriotism of the loyal, to convince the doubters and bring them into the Union lines, was the task Mr. King set for himself. In the blaze of the intense feeling of that period he wrote the fine lectures on 'Washington, Father of his Country,' 'Lexington and Concord,' and 'Webster, Defender of the Constitution,' in the hope that, by reviving the traditions of the fathers and the memory of their heroic struggles and sufferings, he might bring very vividly to their minds the treason and wickedness of destroying the Republic. And after the war actually began he followed with still more intense appeals to the patriotism of the people. Armed with these he went through the length and breadth of the state, fighting for California to save her to the Union. His power and influence were soon felt, and strong measures were used to force him out of the field. He received anonymous letters hinting at assassination. He was openly threatened with personal violence. Pistols were actually drawn on him in rude interior camps; but no persuasion either of love or fear could turn him from what he deemed his high privilege of defending his country. He never ceased his labors till the verdict of the ballot in September confirmed his appeals and our state became unalterably loyal.[1] Then came a lull, but the tide of feeling was running too high for any permanent repose. Men began to ask: 'Why are we doing nothing? The fight is going on. Our brethren of the East are sustaining the country in her time of trial with men and with money and we are doing nothing. If the Government thinks it best not to call on us for

[1] In 1861.

men,[1] we can at least send our money for the wounded, the sick, and the suffering.' Mr. King entered into this movement with intense energy, for it appealed to his whole nature. Patriotism, humanity, and religion all beckoned him into the field again. He traversed the state in its length and breadth, appealing to their love of country and their pity for the sick and wounded soldiers, organizing committees everywhere to carry on the work, over the Siskiyou Mountains by stage to Oregon, and on north to Puget Sound. You know the result, the inestimable mercies and comforts that came to our men from these gifts. The Pacific Coast gave nearly a million and a half dollars; and its gifts came at the most critical period, when they could do the greatest good."

Here is no exaggeration. Indeed, the fame of Mr. King would have justified a panegyric even more glowing. "One star differeth from another star in glory." There is enough for King and Sumner and Baker.

So little of a permanent character is written about one who deserves so much renown that I am sure I shall be pardoned for incorporating here some things relative to Mr. King that are not essential to the main purpose of this book, although they portray conditions in the states we are concerned with. Mr. R. B. Swain, at a meeting of Mr.

[1] Mr. Davis is slightly inexact. California was — somewhat tardily — responding to the first requisition for volunteers months before the election of 1861. — E. R. K.

King's religious society in San Francisco after the death of their pastor, read many familiar letters which he had received during the tours which have been mentioned. In a communication from Yreka, on the twenty-ninth of May, 1861, Mr. King wrote:

"Here I am, perched on the top of the state, where I can almost toss a copper or 'five-cent piece' over to the Yankees in Oregon — but I don't try it, for fear of corrupting their Union principles. My health is very good. The journey has been quite fatiguing. From Shasta to Yreka we were twenty-seven hours on the road, and I had an outside seat day and night, without a shawl. But I am all right, and my brain has settled again right side up, I believe. . . . To-night I am to speak in a village with the sweet name of 'Dead-Wood,' and to-morrow I shall dine and sleep at your brother's in Scott Valley, and speak in the evening at the very important and cultivated settlement of 'Rough and Ready.' 'Scott's Bar' honors me. 'Horse Town' is after me. 'Mugginsville' bids high. 'Oro Fino' applies with a long petition of names. 'Mad Mule' has not yet sent in a request, nor 'Piety Hill' nor 'Modesty Gulch,' but doubtless they will be heard from in due time. The Union sentiment is strong, but the secessionists are watchful and not in despair." [1]

In 1862 Mr. King made another tour. Writing again from Yreka, in July, he said: —

"We rode all night of Saturday through from

[1] *Representative Men*, p. 196.

Shasta here, making the trip in twenty-four hours. The journey from here will be trebly hard, and I almost regret that I made the overland trial. From Jacksonville, where we go to-morrow, to Salem, will be as tough as it can be — it will take three or four days.[1] I doubt if I shall have time to see all I wish to at Oregon and Puget Sound. It will take me another week to reach Portland, and I begin to fear that I shall have to abandon the Puget Sound and Victoria expedition. And the expenses are simply frightful. It cost me over $80 for passage from Marysville to Shasta Town, and if I travel through part of Oregon by extras, as I must, $60 a day will be the lowest I can do it for, and I have purchased through tickets besides." [2]

The effects produced in California by the news of war in South Carolina were, among the faithful, much the same as the effects in the loyal states in the East. There were public demonstrations in many places. A Union meeting in San Francisco, early in May, was so vast that the entire business of the city was suspended, as if it were a legal holiday. The feeling among the disloyal was different from the silent gloating of Northern Copperheads. The Southern element in California, irrespective of numbers, was the dominant element. It had governed so long, and filled all the offices, federal and state, so many years, that it felt a sense

[1] Over these same mountain roads Colonel Baker journeyed when he captured the State of Oregon.

[2] *Representative Men*, p. 197.

of proprietorship in the Government. The tidings that had evoked these Union demonstrations were tidings of a Southern victory; to the disloyal an auspicious opening of the premeditated conflict. What should hinder their redeeming the pledges of Gwin and Company to line their state up with the South? Nothing but General Sumner. If the forts could have been "acquired," as they were in Texas through the perfidy of the infamous Twiggs; if an officer capable of surrendering the government forts at the demand of a state had been in command of the military department that extended from Vancouver to San Diego; if the detachment of the Nation's Regular Army which had been sent out to guard that distant field could have been rendered useless and impotent; the Pacific Republic would have been proclaimed. But Sumner was in command — and in control.

I do not intimate that General Johnston would, even under the malign power of his cherished theory of state sovereignty, have developed into another Twiggs. He might have surprised everybody and disappointed those who placed him in command — Gwin, Floyd, et al. — by refusing to play the part for which he had been cast. It is useless to conjecture what might then have happened; the secession ranks were full of desperate men. General Sumner said in his first report to Washington: "It gives me pleasure to state that the command was turned over to me in good order. General Johnston had forwarded his resignation before I arrived, but he continued to hold the command and was carrying out the orders of the Government."[1] General Johnston's resignation from the Army was dated the ninth of April. It was accepted by the Secretary of War on the third of May.[2] The Army Regulations of that time, having all the force of law, provided: "No officer will be considered out of service on the tender of his resignation, until it shall have been duly accepted by the proper authority. In time of war . . . resignations shall take effect within thirty days from the date of the order of acceptance." I have been unable to learn the precise date when General Johnston was thus released from his obligations to the Army. The letter notifying him of the acceptance of his resignation was dated the sixth of May[3] and was doubtless in his hands early in June. He appears to have remained decorously quiescent in the mean time. Shortly after receiving his release General Johnston started overland in a company of about two-score, of whom several had tendered their resignations from the Army. They crossed the Colorado River at Fort Yuma on the first of July. The notorious Judge Terry was in another party, the members of which are said to have stolen the horses on which they rode to the Confederacy. A party of eighteen, led by a rabid secessionist named Dan

[1] *Rebellion Records*, series L, vol. L, part 1, pp. 471, 472.

[2] *Ibid.*, pp. 463, 464.

[3] Letter of the Adjutant-General to me August 28, 1911. — E. R. K.

Showalter, was captured by a detachment of the First California Volunteer Infantry, on the border of the desert, on the twenty-ninth of November,[1] pursuant to Colonel Wright's determination to prevent further reinforcements of the rebel armies by Californians.[2] The disloyalists who remained abated none of their ardor and occasionally some hot-head committed an overt act. But the strength of the military was too great and too manifest for them. And Union men, inspired by the eloquence of Starr King, Thomas Fitch, Henry Edgerton, Edward Stanly, and others, were organized, alert, and determined. When Leland Stanford became governor, in January, 1862, the State Government at last assumed the attitude of hearty support of President Lincoln's Administration.

To those historians who have slighted California and asserted that the state bore none of the burdens of the War for the Union I commend a reading of the following: —

HEADQUARTERS DEPARTMENT OF THE PACIFIC,
SAN FRANCISCO, October 1, 1861.

Lieut.-Col. George A. H. Blake,
First Cavalry, U. S. Army,
Comdg. Fort Churchill, Nevada Territory.

SIR: The general commanding the department directs me to inform you that all the Regular infantry and cavalry on this coast have been ordered to New York.

[1] *Rebellion Records*, series L, vol. L, part 1, p. 30.

[2] My friend Mr. James R. Morse has kindly written an account of meeting such a party, who had got tired of waiting for action in California. Mr. Morse's narrative appears on page 340.

The general desires you to have your command in readiness to be relieved by volunteer troops. . . .

Very respectfully, your obedient servant,

RICHD C. DRUM,
Assistant Adjutant-General.[1]

And this should be read also: —

SAN FRANCISCO, October 1, 1861 — 3 P.M.

Col. B. L. Beall,
First Cavalry, U. S. Army, Comdg. Dist. of Oregon,
Fort Vancouver, Wash. Ter.:

Notify the regular troops in the District of Oregon to be in readiness to be relieved by volunteers. . . . All the Regulars go to New York.

RICHD C. DRUM,
Assistant Adjutant-General.[2]

This was effective service on the part of the volunteers of the Pacific States, garrisoning the forts and army posts and thus supplying the Eastern armies with educated, skillful officers and disciplined and seasoned soldiers, in the early months of the war, when the qualities possessed by the experienced Regulars were needed but lacking in the Union armies. The volunteers had also much to do besides garrison duty. There were Indian raids on established settlements and savage attacks on emigrants crossing the Plains, a kind of war calling for the greatest sagacity on the part of officers and the greatest bravery and steadiness on the part of the men. Then, the relay stations on the overland stage route had to be guarded to prevent the rebels from getting possession of rich silver mines. And

[1] *Rebellion Records*, series I, vol. L, part 1, p. 644.

[2] *Ibid.*, p. 644.

all the time a close watch had to be kept on the disloyal; otherwise a smouldering fire might easily have burst into flame. If the nature of their tasks afforded the Pacific Coast volunteers less opportunity for winning military glory than their comrades had under Grant, Sherman, Thomas, Sheridan, and the rest, nevertheless their alacrity, their zeal, their unwavering fidelity under depressing conditions, and the indispensable service they rendered, entitle them to the gratitude of the Nation and the recognition of history.

Nor should annalists ignore the munificent gifts of the Pacific Slope to the merciful work of the Sanitary Commission in the Eastern armies. During the war the people of California contributed $1,234,257.31 to the Commission, and Oregon, Nevada, and the rest of the coast gave $234,506.25 more.[1]

The sympathy of that isolated but faithful section was touchingly expressed in a short poem by Bret Harte: —

OUR PRIVILEGE

Not ours, where battle smoke upcurls,
And battle dews lie wet,
To meet the charge that treason hurls
By sword and bayonet.

Not ours to guide the fatal scythe
The fleshless reaper wields;
The harvest moon looks calmly down
Upon our peaceful fields.

[1] Bancroft, vol. VII, p. 295.

The long grass dimples on the hill,
The pines sing by the sea,
And Plenty, from her golden horn,
Is pouring far and free.

O brothers by the farther sea!
Think still our faith is warm;
The same bright flag above us waves
That swathed our baby form.

The same red blood that dyes your fields
Here throbs in patriot pride; —
The blood that flowed when Lander fell,
And Baker's crimson tide.

And thus apart our hearts keep time
With every pulse ye feel,
And Mercy's ringing gold shall chime
With Valor's clashing steel.

CHAPTER XV

BEGINNING OF HOSTILITIES — COLONEL BAKER SPEAKS AT THE UNION SQUARE MEETING — A BRIGADE RAISED FOR HIM — EXPERIENCES IN CAMP AND FIELD

When Mr. Lincoln assumed the duties of the Presidency several states had already seceded and prepared for war against the Government. Actual hostilities began on the twelfth of April, 1861, when South Carolina troops fired on Fort Sumter, in Charleston Harbor. With a traitor as Secretary of War and the President an imbecile, reinforcements, supplies, and munitions had been withheld until the rebels had erected batteries that made it impossible for a government ship to reach the fort. The defense was at first vigorous; but, their ammunition all used up and their supply of food exhausted, the little garrison finally evacuated the fort, marching out with colors flying.

Throughout the North, and among the faithful in the Border States, the response to this attack was the most tremendous and overpowering outburst of loyalty the world has ever seen. One week after the government troops left Fort Sumter they appeared with their commander, Major Robert Anderson, at a meeting in Union Square, New York

City.[1] Several stands had been erected from which eminent men spoke — among them the Senator from Oregon. Unknown in the East, an unheralded stranger, Colonel Baker on being introduced instantly arrested attention. His handsome figure, beautiful, spiritual face, prematurely white hair, marvelous gray eyes, and his grace and distinction of movement "gave the world assurance of a man." He waited, silent, a moment, — a habit of his, practiced to obtain attention, — and then the splendid tones of that incomparable voice carried clear and far to thousands. His first words rose to the height of the occasion: "The majesty of the people is here to-day to sustain the majesty of the Constitution [cheers], and I come, a wanderer from the far Pacific, to record my oath along with yours of the great Empire State." Shout after shout of wild enthusiasm followed almost every sentence. George D. Prentice was quoted as declaring Colonel Baker's ad-

[1] The late William M. Evarts said in a speech at Cooper Institute, November 1, 1876: "I was one of five men that on Tuesday after the firing on Fort Sumter met in a private office in Pine Street to feel the pulse of this people, to arouse them and call a public meeting, and we did not know whether we dared do it, lest the fewness of the numbers should be counted and the game should be lost; and we did not dare to take the Academy of Music for fear our shrunken columns would display the poorness of the patriotism of New York. But by Saturday, the 19th, we determined there was no place that could hold the loyal people —the organized loyal people — and on the 19th day of April we had 100,000 men there, and there would have been 100,001 if Governor Tilden had been there [laughter and applause]. There were 99,999 without Fernando Wood, and he was there." I am indebted to Allen W. Evarts, Esquire, for obtaining for me this excerpt from his father's speech. — E. R. K.

dress the most eloquent delivered by an American since Patrick Henry's speech concluding with "Give me liberty or give me death." The closing was worthy the beginning:—

"And if from the far Pacific a voice feebler than the feeblest murmur upon its shore may be heard, to give you courage and hope in the contest, that voice is yours to-day. And if a man whose hair is gray, who is well-nigh worn out in the battle and toil of life, may pledge himself on such an occasion and in such an audience, let me say, as my last word, that when amid sheeted fire and flame I saw and led the hosts of New York as they charged in contest on a foreign soil for the honor of the flag, so again, if Providence shall will it, this feeble hand shall draw a sword never yet dishonored, not to fight for honor on a foreign soil, but for country, for home, for law, for Government, for Constitution, for right, for freedom, for humanity — and in the hope that the banner of my country may advance, and wheresoever that banner waves there glory may pursue and freedom be established." [Tremendous and prolonged cheering.]

On the fifteenth of the month President Lincoln called for volunteers. On the 21st, a meeting of citizens and former citizens of California and Oregon was held at the Metropolitan Hotel in New York City, nearly three hundred being present. It was there resolved "to raise and offer to the Government a regiment, to be composed as far as possible of persons at some time residents of California."

The chairman of the meeting, the Honorable J. C. Birdseye, wrote to Senator Baker that it was unanimously resolved that he be requested to accept the colonelcy of the regiment. It was stated that already "about six hundred men have been enrolled and are now under drill by competent instructors, and we hope within the next forty-eight hours to be able to apprise you that the full complement of men is enrolled and ready to be mustered into service." Senator Baker at once wrote to the Honorable Simon Cameron, Secretary of War, inclosing a copy of Judge Birdseye's letter and offering the regiment for service. On Colonel Baker's letter was the following indorsement: —

> I most cordially concur in raising the regiment suggested by Senator Baker, and I hope this patriotic movement will be authorized.
>
> JOHN E. WOOL, Major-General.[1]

From a veteran major-general of the Regular Army who had seen Baker in service in Mexico, this was very high approval. Secretary Cameron immediately authorized the Colonel to raise a regiment of infantry, "to be taken as a portion of any troops that may be called from the State of California by the United States, and to be known as the California Regiment."[2] Recruiting began also in Pennsylvania, under Isaac J. Wistar, "who had commanded Indian Rangers in California and Oregon in 1850, and who had had considerable experience in the

[1] *Rebellion Records*, series L, vol. L, part I, p. 470.

[2] *Ibid.*, p. 480.

warfare incidental to the early settlements of the Pacific Coast."[1] The ranks were soon filled, but it was found impracticable to credit the regiment to California. Nor was it entirely a New York or a Pennsylvania regiment. Having been raised by authority of the President of the United States it was for a time regarded as if it belonged to the Regular Army, but not being actually thus enrolled it was at some disadvantage. Finally it was credited to the Keystone State and designated the Seventy-first Pennsylvania Infantry, Baker being colonel, Wistar lieutenant-colonel, and R. A. Parrish, major; but it continued to be known as the "California Regiment." The New York contingent was encamped near Fort Schuyler and was drilled every day. Here the Philadelphia recruits joined, making the membership sixteen hundred, said to be the largest regiment mustered into the service during the war.

Recruiting was begun on the third of August for the Philadelphia Fire Zouaves, and so great was the enthusiasm that the ranks were filled in one week. The regiment was mustered in as the Seventy-second Pennsylvania and attached to "Baker's Brigade."[2] The Sixty-ninth Pennsylvania, composed mainly of men of Irish birth or extraction, was also placed in the brigade.[3] The One Hundred and Sixth Pennsylvania was also recruited for Baker's "California Brigade."[4] Thus Baker was in fact a brigade commander from the outset.

[1] Banes, p. 9. [2] *Ibid.*, p. 10. [3] *Ibid.*, p. 14. [4] Ward, p. 1.

On the first of July the California Regiment was ordered to Fortress Monroe.[1] The Sacramento "Union" reprinted [2] from the Cincinnati "Commercial" the following statement: —

"The writer met Colonel Baker on the steamer going from Baltimore to Fortress Monroe. He said he did not expect to survive the war; that in his judgment he never should see the shores of the Pacific again. This was hardly so much a presentiment on his part as a calculation. He said the troops were green, and it would be necessary for the officers to expose themselves. He had seen service and would feel it a duty to lead his regiment. The enemy had plenty of sharpshooters and he presumed they would pick him off. He said he believed it would be his fate to die at the head of his regiment. It may illustrate the temper and character of the man to mention that after saying, with as perfect calmness as he could have named the most trivial circumstance, that he believed it would be his fate to fall in battle and that he should never see his home on the Pacific again, he retired from the guard-rail, where he had engaged in conversation, to the cabin, and seating himself at the piano played, with grace and skill remarkable for a gentleman amateur on that instrument, several touching airs, among them that favorite of the English soldiers before Sebastopol — sweet and mournful 'Annie Laurie.'"

This beautiful ballad has received an added leaf

[1] Banes, p. 10. [2] November 18, 1861.

of laurel from the genius of Bayard Taylor, a few of whose stanzas may appropriately be quoted here: —

SONG OF THE CAMP

"Give us a song!" the soldiers cried,
The outer trenches guarding,
When the heated guns of the camp allied
Grew weary of bombarding.

The dark Redan, in silent scoff,
Lay grim and threatening under;
And the tawny mound of the Malakoff
No longer belched its thunder.

There was a pause; a guardsman said,
"We storm the forts to-morrow;
Sing while we may, another day
Will bring enough of sorrow."

They lay along the battery's side,
Below the smoking cannon,
Brave hearts from Severn and from Clyde,
And from the banks of Shannon.

They sang of love, and not of fame;
Forgot was Britain's glory;
Each heart recalled a different name,
But all sang "Annie Laurie."

Colonel Baker showed thoroughly soldierly qualities in camp. He was strict but patient in discipline; he personally looked after the rations and clothing and sanitary arrangements and health of his entire command; and he shared the work of drilling the officers and men.[1] While the regiment was encamped at the little village of Hampton,

[1] Banes, p. 25.

near the Fortress, an officer from the Regular Army was detailed to assist in the drill. He was an excellent drillmaster, but given to swearing violently at men and officers alike, much to their disgust. Colonel Baker concluded that he must rebuke him, which he did effectively

Right here I may introduce a few words of testimony communicated to me in a letter of the tenth of April, 1905, from John W. Frazier, Registrar in the Department of Public Works, Philadelphia, who was a member of the Seventy-first: "Colonel Baker was our hero, our idol, and never was hero-worship more fitly sanctioned." And although this commander was but a few months more than fifty years of age, his white hair and his paternal care for his men led them commonly to speak of him as "Father Baker." [1]

Another side of Baker's character was referred to at a recent reunion of surviving members of his regiment. A speaker said: "I remember the day when a comrade from Vermont was led out to be shot for sleeping at his post. General Baker was there, and I saw tears trickling down his face. There was the tender heart that wept over our boys when they suffered."

On the fourth of September General McClellan ordered Baker to march with his brigade "immediately" and take position in advance of the Chain Bridge, near Washington. Colonel Baker was directed to bring two days' cooked rations and to have

[1] Banes, p. 29.

the men bring their overcoats or blankets, detailing as small a force as necessary to guard the camp and baggage left at their position near the Fortress.[1] This order was received after seven o'clock in the evening. It indicated urgency, so the brigade broke camp, arranged for the guard ordered, and marched at three o'clock the next morning.

Unusual curiosity was attracted to the brigade because a United States Senator was in command, and because that Senator, unknown in the East a few months before, had aroused uncommon interest. "On one occasion Senator Breckinridge, accompanied by Senator McDougall, visited the camp and went out with Colonel Baker to witness dress parade, which was then forming. As they walked along the line the men recognized Breckinridge. Suddenly there was a low murmur, as of an approaching wind. It gradually increased in volume until it deepened into an unmistakable groan from the throats of sixteen hundred men. As soon as the Colonel realized its import he sprang forward, and said, with flashing eye and in a commanding tone, 'Men of the California Regiment, I hope you will remember the courtesy that is due to your commander's guest.' Then, turning to the Senator, he said, 'I trust you will pardon the rudeness of the men.'" [2]

At another time President Lincoln, accompanied by Secretary Seward, visited the camp. The men

[1] *Rebellion Records*, series I, vol. v, p. 584.

[2] Edward B. Jerome, in *California Magazine*, May, 1880.

had not been paid for nearly three months. They had erected a stuffed image near the entrance to the camp and labeled it "The Defunct Paymaster." As the carriage containing the distinguished visitors rolled up the avenue of tents toward Headquarters some of the men recognized the President, and thinking, probably, to give him a hint of the Government's delinquency, dragged the "defunct paymaster" from his elevation and formed an impromptu procession with the effigy at their head, marching behind the carriage. As the guests, followed by this boisterous crowd, arrived at Headquarters, the Colonel came down to greet his friends. When he caught sight of the procession a little way in the rear his eye twinkled and he remarked, "Mr. President, allow me to congratulate you on the fine appearance of your bodyguard." Mr. Lincoln turned and for the first time saw the effigy of the "defunct paymaster." A broad smile spread over his genial countenance, and he said, "Men, I take the hint. Your case shall be attended to." The men gave three cheers for "Uncle Abe" and broke ranks. The next day a live paymaster came and paid the troops in shining gold—the last of that metal the regiment saw during the war.[1]

On the twenty-fifth of September, Brigadier-General William F. Smith ("Baldy") made a reconnoissance in force from his position near Chain Bridge, Washington, toward Lewinsville. Among the troops was the first battalion of the "First California" and

[1] Edward B. Jerome, in *California Magazine*, May, 1880.

two companies of the Philadelphia Fire Zouaves.[1] One of the Zouaves wrote an account of this reconnoissance that contained details not comprised in General Smith's official report. I condense from the letter, which was printed in the Sacramento "Union" on the twenty-fifth of October, 1861: —

"We made an advance yesterday with fifteen thousand men,[2] for what object I do not know. I had the honor to command a detachment of ten men from our company, who, in conjunction with ten men from each company of our regiment, formed the advance skirmishers for the army. We were thrown out, and with the Seventy-ninth Highlanders and Berdan's Sharpshooters, who took the left, we advanced about eight miles, driving in the rebel pickets. We finally came in sight of one of their batteries, without being discovered. Generals Smith and Baker came up and signaled our battery, which took a very good position under the command of Captain Mott. Our skirmishers were sent out again, and in scouting through the woods we came upon a number of their pickets, but having orders not to fire on them we contented ourselves by taking their captain prisoner, who, by the way, was an aide-de-camp to General Stuart. Their battery soon commenced shelling the woods. But most of our men were to the right, behind the hill. There

[1] *Rebellion Records*, series I, pp. 215, 216. I trust I may be pardoned a personal note of great interest to me, namely, that a brother of mine in the Fifth Wisconsin Infantry was in this movement and slight engagement with Colonel Baker. — E. R. K.

[2] General Smith states the number as much less.

were four wounded, however, when our guns opened on them and completely annihilated their batteries. They had got our range pretty accurately and their balls were coming uncomfortably near, when Mott got his eye on them. When he fired he knocked their battery all to pieces, killing some men. We could see their guns turning a complete somerset, when General Baker, who was laughing, said, 'Now, you devils, give three cheers,' which we did emphatically, I tell you. Some of their balls must have come within two feet of his head, but he never flinched, never retired, but stood on top of the hill in full view, telling us every shot that told. I tell you what, when they burst over your head, within five or six feet of you, it makes you feel queer! Then Colonel Baker would sing out, 'Down, men; don't you see that fellow coming?' and I tell you he would be quickly obeyed."

Three days later, on the 28th, at ten o'clock at night, two of Baker's regiments, the Sixty-ninth Pennsylvania and the California Regiment, were started on another of General Smith's demonstrations, this time to Munson's Hill, Virginia. The Irish Regiment lost one man killed and had two wounded. The California Regiment had four killed and fourteen wounded.[1] I quote, now, from the history of this brigade by Brevet-Lieutenant-Colonel Banes: —

"September 30th, the brigade recrossed the

[1] *Rebellion Records*, series I, vol. v, pp. 218–20; also Banes, pp. 20–22.

Potomac and marched to Great Falls, in Maryland, a distance of nine miles, where it was halted. October 1st, started at noon and reached Rockville by night. October 2d, marched to Seneca Mills,— part of the time through a heavy rain. The men by this time appeared to be well used to campaigning. October 3d, reached a point four miles beyond Poolesville, Montgomery County, Maryland, where tents were pitched and Colonel Baker gave verbal orders that each company might use ten fence rails for fuel, and no more, as the command would soon move forward.

"Day after day passed, and the first allowance of fence rails had been turned into ashes, along with many others that had not been so formally set aside; still there was no sign of a movement. . . . Colonel Baker personally exercised the officers in the manual of arms as well as in the school of the battalion, in both of which he displayed considerable knowledge and proficiency." [1]

[1] Banes, pp. 22–24.

CHAPTER XVI

BATTLE OF BALL'S BLUFF AND DEATH OF GENERAL BAKER — TRIBUTES TO HIS MEMORY

FOR months after the Battle of Bull Run the energies of the Government were largely devoted to assembling and drilling a great military force near Washington. By autumn the Army of the Potomac extended from a point in Virginia opposite the capital northwesterly as far as Poolesville, Maryland, where the Corps of Observation, to which Colonel Baker's brigade had been attached since early in September, was posted, under the command of Brigadier-General Charles P. Stone. On the nineteenth of October (1861) Major-General McCall, commanding a division stationed southeast of General Stone, advanced his forces to Dranesville, a small town in Virginia. The following day, Sunday, the 20th, General Stone was informed of the movement; was told that *on that day* McCall would send out strong reconnoissances; and was directed to keep a lookout upon Leesburg, a Virginia town opposite Stone's headquarters and near the scope of McCall's operations. The official dispatch added, "Perhaps a slight demonstration on your part would have the effect to move them" [rebel forces in the vicinity]. General Stone promptly sent a small detachment across the Potomac at Conrad's Ferry, which, later joined by a slightly larger body, penetrated to within a short distance of Leesburg and then returned to the river — remaining, however, on the Virginia side, obedient to an order of General Stone. Four miles below, at Edwards Ferry, in front of Stone's headquarters, a "feint" was made with the view of deceiving the enemy into the belief that an advance was actually taking place. This detachment, having thus assisted in the "slight demonstration" called for, returned to its quarters. All that General McClellan requested had been done. McCall, too, completed his task, and early Monday morning left Dranesville and marched his division back to its permanent position.

Up at Ball's Bluff General Stone's little party remained, still in the enemy's territory. Instead of calling them back Sunday, after their work was done, General Stone sent a battalion over, late in the day, to enable them to attack the supposed camp and then select and hold a position. The General must have sat up late that Sunday night, for at an early hour on Monday the bulk of his division had left their camps and marched down to the river. At Edwards Ferry a force of several thousand was placed under command of General Gorman, and a considerable number crossed over to Virginia. An order to Colonel Baker [1] was made

[1] I use the title under which Baker was addressed, although he was in fact a major-general. See page 287. — E. R. K.

out at eleven o'clock, which reached the Colonel at about two o'clock Monday morning. It directed him to have the California Regiment at Conrad's Ferry (about three and a half miles above Gorman's position) at sunrise and the remainder of the brigade breakfasted and ready to march at seven o'clock. These directions were executed with characteristic alacrity. At sunrise the Californians, commanded by Lieutenant-Colonel Wistar, were drawn up at the place designated, awaiting further orders from General Stone. The other regiments arrived shortly after, led by Colonel Baker. He was met by Captain Francis G. Young, one of his staff, who had just returned from headquarters with General Stone's orders for Wistar. When Captain Young told Baker that Stone's order to Wistar was to cross if he heard firing on the Virginia side, the veteran colonel was incredulous and exclaimed, "That can't be!" The absurd inadequacy of the means of transportation had been obvious the previous day and had occasioned derisive comments throughout the brigade. So, when Captain Young declared he was not mistaken, and that the General's order was to cross, Colonel Baker contemptuously demanded, "In what?"

By this time regiments that did not belong to Baker's brigade were also arriving, but General Stone had failed to designate a commander for the force, and the only order received, later than those summoning them to the riverside, was that brought by Captain Young to Lieutenant-Colonel Wistar.

Colonel Baker, therefore, rode down to headquarters. General Stone in "a full conversation" explained his purposes. He communicated the facts ascertained during many weeks of observation — the roads in Virginia, the fortifications, the troops that might, perhaps, be encountered — and much more that shall be discussed later. He explained that the forces collected at Conrad's Ferry, opposite Ball's Bluff, comprised the right wing of a movement, the left wing being under General Gorman. He assured Baker that the left would be reinforced and would support the right. Then he appointed Baker to command the right. The Colonel forthwith galloped speedily up to Conrad's Ferry and ordered the troops to "cross at once." Colonel Baker realized the weak point of the movement, — the inadequate means of transportation. There were a few hundred of Stone's division over at Ball's Bluff, where desultory firing could be heard by the brigade. There were several thousand brave fellows on the Maryland side eager to go to the front. Colonel Devens and Colonel Lee were with the men in Virginia, — quite worthy to be trusted with the command, especially since they were merely to hold the position they had chosen. Colonel Baker understood that transportation was the first and greatest task before him. There was no division quartermaster present nor any one especially capable of loading the few scows supplied by General Stone and embarking the forces, so for some time Colonel Baker remained with the bulk of his troops, himself superintending the work and infusing the men with his energy and enthusiasm. By extraordinary efforts the men succeeded in pulling a boat out of the canal that ran beside the Potomac and dragging it across the land and into the river, thus adding to the scant means of conveyance. By this time nearly a thousand men had been ferried across and Colonel Baker proceeded to the field. It had become evident that the rebels were bringing forward troops that greatly outnumbered the Union force at the front. The scows and the water-logged canal boat were poled tediously back and forth, across one channel of the river to Harrison's Island, a narrow, long property. Then there was a hurried rush to the far side of the island and again a scow ferry over another channel of the river; but the Southern force was at the same time augmented by regiments. Baker had left an order for Cogswell, a West Pointer, colonel of the Tammany Regiment, to take charge of the artillery, and during the afternoon Cogswell arrived on the field with three guns. The musketry firing on the rebel side was kept up constantly, but was generally ineffective. Colonel Baker was cool and unperturbed. He pleasantly remarked, "They mean well enough, but they don't seem to hit us." The sharpshooters, however, were taking good aim and wounding some of the Union men. Meantime the government troops, under the directions of their experienced commander, were lying down to avoid the enemy's bullets, loading, rising to aim and fire, and then dropping back to the ground. The Fifteenth Massachusetts formed the right, the Tammanys the centre, the California Regiment was on the left, and the Twentieth Massachusetts in reserve. The Massachusetts men were poorly armed, and their old-fashioned muskets would not carry far enough to reach the rebel ranks. The two howitzers were of little use, but the six-pounder gun did effective service, although it had not been supplied with the most suitable ammunition. Colonel Baker walked from place to place, instructing the men how best to aim, pointing out sharpshooters whom he wished dislodged, cheering all by word and example. The rebels came out of the woods and advanced several times, but were repulsed. During the action every officer and man attached to the six-pounder gun was either killed or wounded, but Baker, Wistar, and Cogswell took their places and continued the firing, being aided by a number of the men. Lieutenant-Colonel Wistar was badly wounded, his sword arm being disabled, when Colonel Baker took the sword and returned it to its scabbard. Reinforcements were continually coming up from the river, but slowly and in numbers far too small to equal the force of the enemy. At one time nearly two companies of the Tammanys climbed the steep bluff and came cheering into action. It is seldom, I believe, that men are compelled to stand under fire so long a time as Baker's command stood that Monday — for hours. They could not retire; the steep bluff and the rapid, unbridged stream were behind. They could not advance. Still, they held their line, unwavering. Colonel Baker looked for assistance to come from Stone's right wing, under Gorman, four miles below. During the forenoon Stone sent a messenger to Baker informing him that the rebel force was larger than he had supposed at the morning conference. Later, Baker sent word to Stone that he was heavily engaged and expressing the hope that the movement four miles below might be of advantage. Officers and men of the left wing heard the noise of the battle and begged to be allowed to go to the assistance of their comrades. The gallant Lander, by this time brigadier-general, but on this day with no troops subject to his direct command, regretted that he had not "stolen" about three thousand and fought his way up to the right wing. It was the judgment of the Congressional Joint Committee which investigated this battle that if the forces that crossed at Edwards Ferry had gone up on the Virginia side to the aid of Colonel Baker there would undoubtedly have been a decisive Union victory. But the left wing lay inert. During the day a gallant officer of General Stone's staff came on the field and encouraged the men by stating that Gorman was coming up with five thousand reinforcements. As there was no sign or sound of them late in the afternoon Colonel Baker ordered Captain Young to go to General Stone and urge him to hasten help. The greater force of the rebels had enabled them to press slowly forward until the hostile forces were almost close enough for the use of the bayonet. Colonel Baker had designed to call up his reserves at such a juncture and give the rebels the cold steel. But just before five o'clock he was struck by four or five bullets, almost simultaneously, and fell dead. In the words of John Hay, "Edward Dickinson Baker was promoted by one grand brevet of the God of Battles, above the acclaim of the field, above the applause of the world, to the heaven of the martyr and the hero."[1] The rebels rushed in to seize Colonel Baker's body, or his sword, but Captain Beiral and a dozen comrades of the California Regiment sprang forward, drove the rebels off, and bore the hero's body down to the river, where it was soon taken across to the Maryland side.

Up to this time, notwithstanding the disparity in numbers, the fortunes of the day were not decided. Colonel Lee, of the Twentieth Massachusetts, at once took command on the field and proposed to retire to the river and recross to the island as expeditiously as the preposterous fleet of scows could transfer the men. It soon appeared that Colonel Cogswell was the ranking officer, so Colonel Lee relinquished the command to him. Cogswell attempted to move to the south, along the river, with the purpose of fighting his way down to Edwards Ferry, but, being tricked into a trap and fired upon at close quarters, he was compelled to fall back as Colonel Lee had first proposed. Up to this time the force had maintained good order.

[1] *Harper's Magazine*, December, 1861.

Now their officers directed the men to save themselves as best they could. The result naturally was a scramble. In the wild rush one of the scows was overloaded so that it capsized. Many undertook to swim to the island, some of whom were drowned. The rebels, unhindered by any orderly effort to hold them back, stood on the brink of the bluff and fired on the men on the shore below and in the water.

The Union force engaged was officially stated as 1700.[1] The casualties were, 49 killed, 158 wounded, and 714 missing, most of the latter being made prisoners.[2]

President Lincoln mourned the loss of Colonel Baker more deeply, probably, than any other death caused by the war. The funeral in Washington would have been at the White House if the building had not been undergoing repairs. In the brigade he had commanded, says one of his officers, "The loss of General Baker was long felt. All spoke of him with affection and admiration; pictures of him were eagerly sought; many were sent home to family and friends that might sympathize with us and have some idea of the man whose death we mourned; small pictures and medals, arranged as badges, were worn by many of the men for a long time, thus showing their loyalty to their brave old commander, whom we would cheerfully have followed wherever duty called." [3]

[1] *Rebellion Records*, series I, vol. V, p. 291. [2] *Ibid.*, p. 308.

[3] *History of the One Hundred and Sixth Regiment, Pennsylvania Volunteers*, p. 15.

The entire loyal North was cast down by the calamity. There had been the humiliating affair at Big Bethel on the ninth of June; the surprising defeat at Bull Run on the twenty-first of July; and now came this disaster at Ball's Bluff. Some journals, ignorant of Colonel Baker's experience in two wars, and ready to seize any occasion to blame the Lincoln Administration, asserted that the affair was the result of appointing "a political colonel." Baker's friends were able promptly to correct that error. Some of these friends, in their grief and rage, unjustly attacked General Stone, going so far as to accuse him of having purposely sent his Northern soldiers across the Potomac to preconcerted slaughter. Now, General Stone's behavior had been in some respects indiscreet. Mr. Stedman, who had been a war correspondent, in a letter to a friend, thirty-two years after, said, "Speaking of Colonel Charles P. Stone, then commandant at Alexandria, I will say that I was impressed by his *soldierly* bearing but found him so thoroughly a 'martinet,' and so loud in praise of Lee and other West Point (Southern) officers, that I was not surprised when he fell under suspicion after the Ball's Bluff disaster. Very likely he was treated unjustly, but his injudicious speech and manner certainly 'provoked injustice.'" [1]

The tributes to General Baker's memory by editors and orators were remarkable. Indeed, I feel warranted in pronouncing them extraordinary.

[1] *Life and Letters of Edmund Clarence Stedman,* vol. I, p. 225.

In the National House of Representatives men of both political parties were rivals in eulogy. Mr. Phelps, of California, said: "To his unyielding determination, coupled with his undying love for free institutions, his glowing eloquence and unanswerable logic, is California indebted, more than to any other man, for the entire overthrow of the political despotism that so long held her in its traitorous grasp." Mr. Sargent, of the same state, said: "He never asked if a measure was popular as a condition of his support; he only cared if it was right. . . . He was approachable to the humblest, sincere in his friendships, mindful of favors, liberal in return. No enemy could provoke him to hatred, no ally complain of treachery. He was indebted as much to the sincerity of his nature — which was manifest in every word and act — as to his wonderful powers of oratory, for the ascendancy he secured wherever he sought it. . . . Prejudice melted in the sunlight of his smile." Mr. Richardson, of Illinois, had served with Baker in the Black Hawk and Mexican Wars, in both branches of the Illinois Legislature, and in Congress, — always of opposite politics. He declared that Baker "was the manly and courteous opponent, the unselfish friend, the statesman without reproach."

At the commemorative session of the Senate President Lincoln and an unusually distinguished assemblage were present. Mr. Nesmith, Senator Baker's colleague, introduced the resolutions and spoke feelingly. Mr. Latham said: "Always opposed in political opinion through several strifeful years, the pleasantest recollection remains of not one unkind word or act. . . . I never knew a man of more kindness of disposition. . . . An entire absence of vindictive malice, the quick forgetfulness of even an injury or wrong inflicted on him, quiet composure amid trying scenes of an eventful life, all bespoke those gentle qualities which made him a fond father, a good husband, and a devoted friend." Mr. Dixon, of Connecticut, declared that "no selfish motive, no vulgar ambition" prompted their heroic dead to take up arms. "He was," said the Connecticut Senator, "not only a great man, but a good man."

Mr. Browning, of Illinois, who had just come to the Senate, after the death of Judge Douglas, said: "Edward D. Baker was, and had ever been, my personal and political friend. . . . He did not reach intellectual results as other men do, by the slow processes of analysis or induction; but if he could reach them at all he could do it at a bound. And yet it was not jumping at conclusions, for he could always state with almost mathematical clearness and precision the premises from which he made his deductions and guide you along the same path he had traveled to reach the goal. . . . He was incapable of a mean and unmanly envy, and was ever quick to perceive and ready to acknowledge the merit of a rival, and would stifle his own desires and postpone his own aggrandizement for the advancement of a friend. . . . In the domestic circle, amid the social throng, and under friendship's genial and enchanting influences, he was as gentle and confiding in his affections as a woman and as tender and trustful as a child. . . ."

Of Charles Sumner's address, Mr. Isaac N. Arnold, who was present as a Congressman, declares: "It was among the best he ever made. It was perhaps the only occasion upon which he ever cut loose from his manuscript and gave free scope to the inspiration of the scene and the moment. He had not the advantage of long acquaintance with Colonel Baker, but he had evidently been greatly struck with Baker's career in the Senate, and it was to that his remarks chiefly referred." Mr. Sumner said, in part: ". . . His fame as a speaker was so peculiar, even before he appeared among us, that it was sometimes supposed he might lack those solid powers without which the oratorical faculty itself can exercise only a transient influence. But his speech on this floor in reply to a slaveholding conspirator, now an open rebel,[1] showed that his matter was as good as his manner, and that while he was a master of fence he was also a master of ordnance. His controversy was graceful, sharp, and flashing, like a scimitar; but his argument was powerful and sweeping, like a battery. You have not forgotten that speech. . . . As the pretension [of a constitutional right of secession] showed itself anew, our orator undertook again to expose it. How thoroughly he did this, now with historic, and

[1] Judah P. Benjamin.

now with forensic, skill, while his whole effort was elevated by a charming, ever-ready eloquence, which itself was aroused to new power by the interruptions he encountered — all this is present to your minds. . . . Call him, if you please, the Prince Rupert of battle; he was also the Prince Rupert of debate."

The surprise, the thrill, of the occasion was the speech of Mr. McDougall, of California, — "a most eloquent speech," says Mr. Arnold, who has already been quoted; "one of the most touching and beautiful speeches ever heard in the Senate." Mr. McDougall, in the course of his remarks, said: —

"He was a many-sided man. Will, mind, power radiated from one centre within him, in all directions; and while the making of that circle, which, according to the dreams of old philosophy, would constitute a perfect being, is not within human hope, he may be regarded as one who at least illustrated the thought. . . .

"He loved freedom — if you please, Anglo-Saxon freedom; for he was of that great old race. He loved this land, this whole land. He had done much to conquer it from the wilderness, and by his own acts he had made it his land.

"Hero blood is patriot blood. When he witnessed the storm of anarchy with which the madness of depraved ambition sought to overwhelm the land of his choice and love, he heard the battle-call. . . . It was in the spirit of the patriot hero that the gallant soldier, the grave Senator, the white-haired man of counsel, yet full of youth as full of years, gave answer, as does the war-horse, to the trumpet's sound. The wisdom of his conduct has been questioned. Many have thought he should have remained for counsel in this hall. Mr. President, the propriety of a senator taking upon himself the duties of a soldier depends, like many other things, on circumstances; and certainly such conduct has the sanction of great names. Socrates, who was not of the councils of Athens simply because he deemed his office as a teacher of wisdom a higher and nobler one, did not think it unworthy of himself to serve as a common soldier in battle. . . . It is but a brief time since the late Senator was among us, maintaining our country's cause with wise counsel clothed in eloquent words. When, in August last, his duties here as a senator for the time ceased, he devoted himself exclusively to the duties of a soldier. Occupying a subordinate position, commanded where he was most fit to command, he received his orders. He saw and knew the nature of the enterprise he was required to undertake. He saw and knew that he was required to move underneath the shadow of the wings of Azrael. He did not, he would not, question the requirement made of him. His motto on that day was, 'A good heart and no hope.' He knew, as was known at Balaklava, that some one had blundered, yet he said, 'Forward, my brigade, although some one has blundered.'

"Was this reckless rashness? No!

"It may be called sacrifice — self-sacrifice; but I, who knew the man who was the late Senator — the calm, self-possessed perfectness of his valor — and who have studied all the details of the field of his last offering with a sad earnestness, say to you, sir, to this Senate, to the country, and particularly to the people of the land of the West, where most and best he is known and loved, that no rash, reckless regardlessness of danger can be attributed to him. It is but just to say of him that his conduct sprung from a stern, hero, patriot, martyr spirit that enabled him to dare unflinchingly, and with a smile to the green earth, and a smile to the bright heavens, and a cheer to his brave companions, ascend the altar of sacrifice. . . .

"In long future years, when our night of horror shall have passed, and there shall have come again

'The welcome morning with its rays of peace,' —

young seekers after fame and young lovers of freedom throughout all this land, yea, and other and distant lands, will recognize, honor, and imitate our late associate as one of the undying dead."

CHAPTER XVII

GRIEF ON THE PACIFIC COAST — GENERAL BAKER BURIED IN SAN FRANCISCO — AN UNFULFILLED PLEDGE

If loyal men in the North were grieved and incensed at the defeat and slaughter at Ball's Bluff, what shall be said of the feeling in that romantic section that supplied the most illustrious victim? —

"We that had loved him so, followed him, honored him,
Lived in his mild and magnificent eye,
Learned his great language, caught his clear accents,
Made him our pattern to live and to die."

Colonel Baker had shone in the National Senate, and we were proud. He had been transcendent at the Bar in California, and we anticipated greater renown for him from professional triumphs in the East. We were told that his speech in Union Square had thrilled the North, and we believed he would in other cities reflect lustre on the coast. He had raised congressional representation from our section to an influence quite unparalleled, and we exulted. Even Broderick had not equaled Baker's success at the national capital. The subserviency and incorrigibility of his party had left Broderick the inspiration of a faction; Baker had been a commanding figure in a great party charged with the sublime task of preserving the Union and establishing Liberty. Broderick had been snubbed and his counsels ignored by President Buchanan; Baker was the close friend and trusted adviser of President Lincoln. And Baker had come out of the Mexican War with such prestige that we never doubted he would win fresh laurels in this later conflict. We fully expected he would live to enjoy the sweetness of his fame.

The shattering of our hopes came suddenly and in a manner that was peculiarly shocking. The overland telegraph had been completed. The customary messages had passed between officers of the telegraph company and congratulations had been exchanged by government dignitaries on the extreme boundaries of the land. Only those who dwelt beyond the Sierras when it took months to exchange communications with parents and homes in the States can imagine or appreciate the joy and enthusiasm that throbbed in every heart in California and Oregon. In that same hour, by the first news dispatch telegraphed westward across the continent, came tidings of the defeat of a Union army and the death of Colonel Baker.[1] In one of

[1] Bancroft, vol. VII, p. 293, carelessly errs in stating that this was "the first through dispatch on the completed overland telegraph." Besides the exchanges mentioned above, an earlier dispatch was the following: "SAN FRANCISCO, October 24, 8.07 P.M. Editor *Transcript*, Boston. All hail! A new bond of union between the Pacific and Atlantic. The lightning now goeth out of the West and speaks even to the East. Heaven preserve the Republic and bless old Boston from hub to rim. THOMAS STARR KING."

the theatres of San Francisco the news of the completion of the telegraph and the words of the first messages transmitted were read from the stage by Edwin Booth, arousing great enthusiasm. Later in the evening Mr. Booth read the tidings of the death of Colonel Baker. The revulsion of feeling, the stun, the grief, the gloom are indescribable; and afterwards the rage. In several towns disloyalists who expressed gratification were roughly handled; in San Francisco several were hanged for a time to the street gas-posts.

Funeral and commemorative services were held in many cities and mining-camps. The courts everywhere adjourned as a mark of respect, after eloquent tributes from judges and eminent members of the Bar. At Portland, Oregon, Mr. Simeon Francis presided at a memorial meeting — a man who "knew Colonel Baker before he entered public or political life." The Reverend Thomas H. Pearne delivered an address, in the course of which he said, "Facts which transpired in this state recently show that Senator Baker's early faith in the divine origin of Christianity and his respect for its moralities had not wavered or diminished."

The Jacksonville (Oregon) "Sentinel"[1] published the following letter from the Colonel, written a month before his death, when every one was looking to General McClellan to say the word for the Army of the Potomac to advance: —

[1] November 2, 1861.

HEADQUARTERS BAKER'S BRIGADE,
CAMP ADVANCE, CHAIN BRIDGE,
September 22, 1861.

DEAR SIR, — We are on the eve of a very great battle. I shall endeavor so to do my duty that the State of Oregon shall have no cause to blush for me, being in no wise forgetful of my obligations to represent her everywhere with fidelity and courage. As you have learned before this, the President was pleased to appoint me a brigadier-general, an office which my duty to the State of Oregon, in my judgment, compelled me to decline.[1] Yesterday I had conferred upon me the appointment of major-general. Actuated by the same motive, I shall decline that also.[2] I confess, however, considering the present condition of the army and the great command this office would devolve upon me, nothing could induce me to decline it but my deep sense of obligation to the State of Oregon, which it will take me many years of faithful service to repay. As it is, however, although nominally a colonel and elected by a regiment, I have a command of nearly seven thousand men, — infantry, cavalry, and artillery, — mostly raised under my own eye and in whom I have great confidence. If I am fortunate I may strike a blow with these troops which may fall heavily on the rebellion, or do something, at least, to maintain the best government the world ever saw.

E. D. BAKER.

[1] It was considered practicable to accept a commission as colonel from the governor of a state — in this case the governor of Pennsylvania — and still retain the senatorship; but it was held that the acceptance of an appointment from the President of the United States would invalidate Colonel Baker's place in the Senate.

[2] In the absorbing care of his brigade Senator Baker had neglected to decline this appointment, but had retained the commission in his possession. An intention to decline is not a declination; and as the commission was in force it appears that accurate history should name him as a major-general. — E. R. K.

It was expected in Oregon that Senator Baker's body would repose in that state, and there was surprise when it was learned that throughout California there was a strong feeling that the sepulchre should be there. Committees representing the Government and citizens of Oregon visited San Francisco, urged their claims, and promised that the state would erect a suitable monument if the desire of the people should be granted. The contention was earnest but was carried on in a reverent spirit and in faultless taste. Senator Baker's widow was finally prevailed on to have the burial in San Francisco and in Lone Mountain Cemetery, which Colonel Baker, as Starr King said, "devoted in a tender and thrilling speech to its hallowed purpose."

Mr. King, in a letter to Fitz-Hugh Ludlow, gave some particulars of the ceremonies when the hero was laid to rest: "I send you to-day an account of the funeral services of our great and lamented Baker. . . . The sorrow was general and deep and the funeral ceremonies very impressive and imposing. The musical service in Platt's Hall was grand. You will see that I conducted the services at the grave. A great crowd was there, and the afternoon, cloudless and genial, was one of the loveliest that could be combined out of air and light. . . . It was a very impressive and memorable scene. *This coast has lost its crown of glory.*"

The oration at Music Hall was delivered by the Honorable Edward Stanly, a citizen greatly respected, who had at one time been Colonel Baker's law partner. Many of his observations were based on his acquaintance with General Baker.

"He had," said Mr. Stanly, "as much unworldliness as Goldsmith. No love of filthy lucre ever found a resting-place in his heart. For years I have known him well, and part of that time was associated with him in business, and I never heard a profane word or irreverent expression from his lips. He never uttered a word that could impair the celestial comfort of a Christian's hope. . . . I have never known a man in public life whose heart more abounded in generous philanthropy for all mankind. He exhibited this feeling at the Bar, when he was conscious of superiority over a younger or feebler adversary. . . . Excepting Webster, no man of modern times has been so successful as Baker in the forum, in the Senate, and before popular assemblies."

Mr. Stanly said, — referring to the graves of Baker and Broderick, so close to each other, — "Let their monuments arise to meet the eye of the ocean - worn exile as he comes near this haven of rest. Let them tell the traveler, as the landscape fades from his sight on leaving our gorgeous land, that 'the paths of glory lead but to the grave.'"

Mr. King in his address quoted this passage from Colonel Baker's oration at the dedication of the cemetery: "Within these grounds public reverence and gratitude shall build the tombs of warriors and statesmen . . . who have given all their lives and their best thoughts to their country."

The speaker on this present sad occasion proceeded: —

"Could he forecast, seven years ago, any such fulfillment of these words as this hour reveals? . . . Could any slight shadow of his destiny have been thrown across his path as he stood here when these grounds were dedicated, and looked over slopes unfurrowed then by the plowshare of death?

"His words were prophetic. Yes, warrior and statesman, wise in counsel, graceful and electric as few have been in speech, ardent and vigorous in debate, but nobler than for all these qualities by the devotion which prompted thee to give more than thy wisdom, more than thy energy and weight in the hall of senatorial discussion, more than the fervor of thy tongue and the fire of thy eagle eye in the assemblies of the people, — even the blood of thy indomitable heart when thy country called with a cry of peril, — we receive thee with tears and pride. We find thee dearer than when thou camest to speak to us in the full tide of life and vigor. Thy wounds through which thy life was poured are not 'dumb mouths,' but eloquent with the intense and perpetual appeal of thy soul. We receive thee to 'reverence and gratitude' as we lay thee gently to thy sleep; and *we pledge to thee not only a monument that shall hold thy name*, but a memorial in the hearts of a grateful people so long as the Pacific moans near thy resting-place, and a fame eminent among the heroes of the Republic as long as the mountain shall feel the Oregon."

The pledge of one who knew the hearts of that generous people, and who spoke under circumstances of transcendent solemnity, will some day be fulfilled.

THE END

APPENDIX

APPENDIX

I

SENATOR BAKER'S SPEECH IN REPLY TO SENATOR BRECKINRIDGE[1]

MR. PRESIDENT, it has not been my fortune to participate in, at any length, indeed, nor to hear very much of, the discussion which has been going on — more, I think, in the hands of the Senator from Kentucky than anybody else — upon all the propositions connected with this war; and as I really feel as sincerely as he can an earnest desire to preserve the Constitution of the United States for everybody, South as well as North, I have listened for some little time past to what he has said, with an earnest desire to apprehend the point of his objection to this particular bill. And now, — waiving what I think is the elegant but loose declamation in which he chooses to indulge, — I would propose, with my habitual respect for him (for nobody is more courteous and more gentlemanly), to ask him if he will be kind enough to tell me what single particular provision there is in this bill which is in violation of the Constitution of the United States, which I have sworn to support; — one distinct, single proposition in the bill.

Mr. Breckinridge. I will state, in general terms, that every one of them is, in my opinion, flagrantly so, unless it may be the last. I will send the Senator the bill, and he may comment on the sections.

Mr. Baker. Pick out that one which is in your judgment most clearly so.

Mr. Breckinridge. They are all, in my opinion, so equally

[1] In the United States Senate. *Cong. Globe,* 1st Session, 37th Congress, pp. 377, 378, and 379.

atrocious that I dislike to discriminate. I will send the Senator the bill, and I tell him that every section, except the last, in my opinion, violates the Constitution of the United States; and of that last section I express no opinion.

Mr. Baker. I had hoped that that respectful suggestion to the Senator would enable him to point out to me one in his judgment most clearly so, for they are not all alike — they are not equally atrocious.

Mr. Breckinridge. Very nearly. There are ten of them. The Senator can select which he pleases.

Mr. Baker. Let me try, then, if I must generalize as the Senator does, to see if I can get the scope and meaning of this bill. It is a bill providing that the President of the United States may declare, by proclamation, in a certain given state of fact, certain territory within the United States to be in a condition of insurrection and war; which proclamation shall be extensively published within the district to which it relates. That is the first proposition. I ask him if that is unconstitutional? That is a plain question. Is it unconstitutional to give power to the President to declare a portion of the territory of the United States in a state of insurrection or rebellion? He will not dare to say it is.

Mr. Breckinridge. Mr. President, the Senator from Oregon is a very adroit debater, and he discovers, of course, the great advantage he would have if I were to allow him, occupying the floor, to ask me a series of questions, and then have his own criticisms made on them. When he has closed his speech, if I deem it necessary I may make some reply. At present, however, I will answer that question. The State of Illinois, I believe, is a military district; the State of Kentucky is a military district. In my judgment the President has no authority, and, in my judgment, Congress has no right to confer upon the President authority, to declare a state in a condition of insurrection or rebellion.

Mr. Baker. In the first place, the bill does not say a word about states. That is the first answer.

Mr. Breckinridge. Does not the Senator know, in fact, that those states compose military districts? It might as well have said "states" as to describe what is a state.

Mr. Baker. I do; and that is the reason why I suggest to the honorable Senator that this criticism about states does not mean anything at all. That is the very point. The objection certainly ought not to be that he can declare a part of a state in insurrection and not the whole of it. In point of fact, the Constitution of the United States, and the Congress acting upon it, are not treating of states, but of the territory comprising the United States; and I submit once more to his better judgment that it cannot be unconstitutional to allow the President to declare a county or a part of a county, or a town or a part of a town, or part of a state, or the whole of a state, or two states, or five states, in a condition of insurrection if in his judgment that be the fact. That is not wrong.

In the next place, it provides that, that being so, the military commander in that district may make and publish such police rules and regulations as he may deem necessary to suppress the rebellion and restore order and preserve the lives and property of citizens. I submit to him, if the President of the United States has power, or ought to have power, to suppress insurrection and rebellion, is there any better way to do it, or is there any other? A gentleman says, Do it by the civil power. Look at the fact. The civil power is utterly overwhelmed, the courts are closed, the judges banished. Is the President not to execute the law? Is he to do it in person, or by his military commanders? Are they to do it with regulation, or without it? That is the only question.

Mr. President, the honorable Senator says there is a state of war. The Senator from Vermont agrees with him; or rather, he agrees with the Senator from Vermont in that. What then? There is a state of public war; none the less war because it is urged from the other side; not the less war because it is unjust; not the less war because it is a war of insurrection and rebellion; it is still war; and I am willing to say it is public war — public as contradistinguished from private war. What then? Shall we carry that war on? Is it his duty as a Senator to carry it on? If so, how? By armies, under command; by military organization and authority, advancing to suppress insurrection and rebellion. Is that wrong? Is that unconstitutional? Are we not bound to do with whoever levies war against us as we would do if he was a foreigner? There is no distinction as to the mode of carrying on war; we carry on war against an advancing army just the same whether it be from Russia or from South Carolina. Will the honorable Senator tell me it is our duty to stay here, within fifteen miles of the enemy seeking to advance upon us every hour, and talk about nice questions of constitutional construction as to whether it is war or merely insurrection? No, sir. It is our duty to advance, if we can; to suppress insurrection; to put down rebellion; to dissipate the rising; to scatter the enemy; and when we have done so, to preserve, in the terms of the bill, the liberty, lives, and property of the people of the country, by just and fair police regulations. I ask the Senator from Indiana (Mr. Lane), when we took Monterey did we not do it there? When we took Mexico, did we not do it there? Is it not a part, a necessary, an indispensable part, of war itself, that there shall be military regulations over the country conquered and held? Is that unconstitutional?

I think it was a mere play of words that the Senator indulged in when he attempted to answer the Senator from New York. I did not understand the Senator from New York to mean anything else substantially but this, that the Constitution deals generally with a state of peace, and that when war is declared it leaves the condition of public affairs to be determined by the law of war, in the country where the war exists. It is true that the Constitution of the United States does not adopt the laws of war as a part of the instrument itself, during the continuance of war. The Constitution does not provide that spies shall be hung. Is it unconstitutional to hang a spy? There is no provision for it in terms in the Constitution; but nobody denies the right, the power, the justice. Why? Because it is part of the law of war. The Constitution does not provide for the exchange of prisoners; yet it may be done under the law of war. Indeed, the Constitution does not provide that a prisoner may be taken at all; yet his captivity is perfectly just and constitutional. It seems to me that the Senator does not, will not, contest that view of the subject.

Again, sir, when a military commander advances, as I trust, if there are no more unexpected great reverses he will advance, through Virginia, and occupies the country, there, perhaps, as here, the civil law may be silent; there, perhaps, the civil officers may flee, as ours have been compelled to flee. What then? If the civil law is silent, who shall control and regulate the conquered district — who but the military commander? As the Senator from Illinois has well said, shall it be done by regulation or without regulation? Shall the General, or the Colonel, or the Captain, be supreme, or shall he be regulated and ordered by the President of the United States? That is the sole question. The Senator has put it well.

I agree that we ought to do all we can to limit, to restrain, to fetter the abuse of military power. Bayonets are at best illogical arguments. I am not willing, except as a case of sheerest necessity, ever to permit a military commander to exercise authority over life, liberty, and property. But, sir, it is part of the law of war; you cannot carry in the rear of your army your courts; you cannot organize juries; you cannot have trials according to the forms and ceremonial of the common law amid the clangor of arms; and somebody must enforce police regulations in a conquered or occupied district. I ask the Senator from Kentucky again, respectfully, is that unconstitutional; or if in the nature of war it must exist, even if there be no law passed by us to allow it, is it unconstitutional to regulate it? That is the question, to which I do not think he will make a clear and distinct reply.

Now, sir, I have shown him two sections of the bill which I do not think he will repeat earnestly are unconstitutional. I do not think that he will seriously deny that it is perfectly constitutional to limit, to regulate, to control, at the same time to confer and restrain, authority in the hands of military commanders. I think it is wise and judicious to regulate it by virtue of powers to be placed in the hands of the President by law.

Now, a few words, and a few only, as to the Senator's predictions. The Senator from Kentucky stands up here in a manly way, in opposition to what he sees is the overwhelming sentiment of the Senate, and utters reproof, malediction, and prediction combined. Well, sir, it is not every prediction that is prophecy. It is the easiest thing in the world to do; there is nothing easier, except to be mistaken when we have predicted. I confess, Mr. President, that I would not have predicted three weeks ago the disasters which have overtaken our arms; and I do not think (if I were to predict now), that six months hence the Senator will indulge in the same tone of prediction which is his favorite key now. I would ask him, what would you have us do now — a Confederate army within twenty miles of us, advancing, or threatening to advance, to overwhelm your Government; to shake the pillars of the Union; to bring it around your head, if you stay here, in ruins? Are we to stop and talk about an uprising sentiment in the North against the war? Are we to predict evil and retire from what we predict? Is it not the manly part to go on as we have begun, to raise money, and levy armies, to organize them, to prepare to advance; when we do advance, to regulate that advance by all the laws and regulations that civilization and humanity will allow in time of battle? Can we do anything more? To talk to us about stopping is idle; we will never stop. Will the Senator yield to rebellion? Will he shrink from armed insurrection? Will his state justify it? Will its better public opinion allow it? Shall we send a flag of truce? What would he have? Or would he conduct this war so feebly that the whole world would smile at us in derision? What would he have? These speeches of his, sown broadcast over the land, what clear distinct meaning have they? Are they not intended for disorganization in our very midst? Are they not intended to dull our weapons? Are they not intended to destroy our zeal? Are they not intended to animate our enemies? Sir, are they not words of brilliant, polished treason, even in the very Capitol of the Confederacy? (Manifestations of applause in the galleries.)

The Presiding Officer (Mr. Anthony in the chair). Order!

Mr. Baker. What would have been thought if, in another capitol, in another republic, in a yet more martial age, a senator as grave, not more eloquent or dignified than the Senator from Kentucky, yet with the Roman purple flowing over his shoulders, had risen in his place, surrounded by all the illustrations of Roman glory, and declared that advancing Hannibal was just, and that Carthage ought to be dealt with in terms of peace? What would have been thought if, after the battle of Cannæ, a senator there had risen in his place and denounced every levy of the Roman people, every expenditure of its treasure, and every appeal to the old recollections and the old glories? Sir, a Senator, himself learned far more than myself in such lore, tells me, in a voice that I am glad is audible, that he would have been hurled from the Tarpeian Rock.[1] It is a grand commentary upon the American Constitution that we permit these words to be uttered. I ask the Senator to recollect, too, what, save to send aid and comfort to the enemy, do these predictions of his amount to? Every word thus uttered falls as a note of inspiration upon every Confederate ear. Every sound thus uttered is a word (and, falling from his lips, a mighty word), of kindling and triumph to a foe that determines to advance. For me, I have no such words as a Senator to utter. For me, amid temporary defeat, disaster, disgrace, it seems that my duty calls me to utter another word, and that word is, bold, sudden, forward, determined war, according to the laws of war, by armies, by military commanders clothed with full power, advancing

[1] The Senator who injected the remark was Mr. Fessenden, but Mr. Breckinridge supposed it was Mr. Sumner, whom he afterwards attacked in speech.

with all the past glories of the Republic urging them on to conquest.

I do not stop to consider whether it is subjugation or not. It is compulsory obedience; not to my will; not to yours, sir; not to the will of any one man; not to the will of any one state; but compulsory obedience to the Constitution of the whole country. The Senator chose the other day again and again to animadvert on a single expression in a little speech which I delivered before the Senate, in which I took occasion to say that if the people of the rebellious states would not govern themselves as states they ought to be governed as territories. The Senator knew full well then, for I explained it twice, — he knows full well now, — that on this side of the chamber, nay, in this whole chamber, nay, in this whole North and West, nay, in all the loyal states in all their breadth, there is not a man among us all who dreams of causing any man in the South to submit to any rule, either as to life, liberty, or property, that we ourselves do not willingly agree to yield to. Did he ever think of that? Subjugation for what? When we subjugate South Carolina what shall we do? We shall compel its obedience to the Constitution of the United States; that is all. Why play upon words? We do not mean, we have never said, any more. If it be slavery that men should obey the Constitution their fathers fought for, let it be so. If it be freedom, it is freedom equally for them and for us. We propose to subjugate rebellion into loyalty. We propose to subjugate insurrection into peace. We propose to subjugate confederate anarchy into constitutional union liberty. The Senator well knows that we propose no more. I ask him, I appeal to his better judgment now, what does he imagine we intend to do, if fortunately we conquer Tennessee or South Carolina, — call it "conquer," if you will, sir, — what do we propose to do? They will have their courts still; they will have their ballot-boxes still; they will have their elections still; they will have their representatives upon this floor still; they will have taxation and representation still; they will have the writ of *habeas corpus* still; they will have every privilege they ever had and all we desire. When the Confederate armies are scattered; when their leaders are banished from power; when the people return to a late, repentant sense of the wrong they have done to a Government they never felt but in benignancy and blessing, then the Constitution made for all will be felt by all, like the descending rains from heaven which bless all alike. Is that subjugation? To restore what was, as it was, for the benefit of the whole country and of the whole human race, is all we desire and all we can have.

Gentlemen talk about the Northeast. I appeal to Senators from the Northeast, is there a man in all your states who advances upon the South with any other idea but to restore the Constitution of the United States in its spirit and its unity? I never heard that once. I believe no man indulges in any dream of inflicting there any wrong to public liberty; and I respectfully tell the Senator from Kentucky that he persistently, earnestly, I will not say willfully, misrepresents the sentiment of the North and West when he attempts to teach these doctrines to the Confederates of the South.

Sir, while I am predicting, I will tell you another thing. This threat about money and men amounts to nothing. Some of the states which have been named in that connection I know well. I know, as my friend from Illinois will bear me witness, his own state, very well. I am sure that no temporary defeat, no momentary disaster, will swerve that state either from its allegiance to the Union or from its determination to preserve it. It is not with us a question of money or of blood; it is a question involving considerations higher than these. When the Senator from Kentucky speaks of the Pacific, I see another distinguished friend from Illinois, now worthily representing one of the states on the Pacific (Mr. McDougall), who will bear me witness that I know that state too, well. I take the liberty, — I know I but utter his sentiments in advance, — joining with him, to say that that state, quoting from the passage the gentleman himself has quoted, will be true to the Union to the last of her blood and her treasure. There may be there some disaffected; there may be some few men there who would "rather rule in Hell than serve in Heaven." There are such men everywhere. There are a few men there who have left the South for the good of the South; who are perverse, violent, destructive, revolutionary, and opposed to social order. A few, but a very few, thus formed and thus nurtured, in California and in Oregon both, persistently endeavor to create and maintain mischief; but the great portion of our population are loyal to the core and in every chord of their hearts. They are offering through me — more to their own Senators, every day, from California, and indeed from Oregon — to add to the legions of this country, by the hundred and the thousand. They are willing to come thousands of miles with their arms on their shoulders, at their own expense, to share with the best offering of their heart's blood in the great struggle for constitutional liberty. I tell the Senator that his predictions, sometimes for the South, sometimes for the Middle States, sometimes for the Northeast, and then wandering away in airy visions out to the far Pacific, about the dread of our people as for loss of blood and treasure provoking them to disloyalty, are false in sentiment, false in fact, and false in loyalty. The Senator from Kentucky is mistaken in them all. Five hundred million dollars! What then? Great Britain gave more than two thousand million in the great battle for constitutional liberty which she led at one time almost single-handed against the world. Five hundred thousand men! What then? We have them; they are ours; they are the children of the country. They belong to the whole country; they are our sons; our kinsmen; and there are many of us who will give them all up before we will abate one word of our just demand or retreat one inch from the line which divides right from wrong.

Sir, it is not a question of men or of money in that sense. All the money, all the men, are, in our judgment, well bestowed in such a cause. When we give them we know their value. Knowing their value well, we give them with the more pride and the more joy. Sir, how can we retreat? Sir, how can we make peace? Who shall treat? What commissioners? Who would go? Upon what terms? Where is to be your boundary line? Where the end of the principles we shall have to give up? What will become of constitutional government? What will become of public liberty? What of past glories? What of future hopes? Shall we sink into the insignificance of the grave — a degraded, defeated, emasculated people, frightened by the results of one battle, and scared at the visions raised upon this floor by the imagination of the Senator from Kentucky? No, sir; a thousand times, no, sir! We will rally — if, indeed, our words be necessary — we will rally the people, the loyal people, of the whole country. They will pour forth their treasure, their money, their men, without stint, without measure. The most peaceable man in this body may stamp his foot upon this Senate Chamber floor, as of old a warrior and a senator did, and from that single tramp there will spring forth armed legions. Shall one battle determine the fate of empire, — or a dozen? the loss of one thousand men or twenty thousand, or one hundred million dollars or five hundred million dollars? In a year's peace, in ten years, at most, of peaceful progress, we can restore them all. There will be some graves reeking with blood, watered by the tears of affection. There will be some privation; there will be some loss of luxury; there will be somewhat more need for labor to procure the necessaries of life. When that is said, all is said. If we have the country, the whole country, the Union, the Constitution, free government — with these there will return all the blessings of well-ordered civilization; the path of the country will be a career of greatness and of glory such as in the olden time our fathers saw in the dim visions of years to come, and such as would have been ours now, to-day, if it had not been for the treason for which the Senator too often seeks to apologize.

II

BATTLE OF BALL'S BLUFF — WHO WAS RESPONSIBLE FOR THAT DISASTER TO THE UNION ARMS?[1]

COMPARED with subsequent engagements in the Civil War the Battle of Ball's Bluff seems now of little moment. But in 1861 the country was greatly excited and enraged over the affair. Officers in General Stone's division testified that their commander had, under flags of truce, carried on correspondence with persons inside the rebel lines, and that his loyalty was distrusted by many in his command. The General was able to make satisfactory explanations. General Stone had been indiscreet.[2] He knew the art of war, but at first he failed to appreciate its spirit as defined by General Sherman.[3] There is not the slightest ground to suspect his fidelity.

Confronting the prevalent hypothesis, that either he or Colonel Baker was to blame for the disaster at Ball's Bluff, he declared that it was Baker; and being angry at having to meet unjust accusations, in defending himself he became unjust to Baker. The War Department took the side against Stone, and while the controversy was hot the General was relieved of his command and imprisoned in Fort Lafayette. He was not tried. No charges against him were ever formulated. And after several months he was released and subsequently was in active service.

The motive that prompted the writing of this book requires me to review the case and see whether the responsibility for the disaster can be definitely placed.

[1] It is impracticable to append a footnote in each of the many instances of use of an official report and of testimony. All such reports are in *Rebellion Records*, series I, vol. v. The testimony is in the *Report of the Congressional Joint Committee on the Conduct of the War*, part 2. Both books are well indexed. — E. R. K.

[2] See page 277.

[3] "War is Hell."

I. In the autumn of 1861 the Army of the Potomac, commanded by General McClellan, extended, by divisions within supporting distance of one another, from a point in Virginia opposite the national capital in a northwesterly direction as far as Poolesville, in Maryland; thus guarding Washington and threatening Richmond. A vigilant and alert foe confronted our entire line, ready to take advantage of any false move. That commander of a division must have been a rash man who should, unless ordered by General McClellan, break the established alignment and disturb the relation between his force and the divisions lying next to him.

On the 19th of October, a Saturday, Major-General McCall, under orders from General McClellan, pushed his division out beyond his established lines, to Dranesville, "to cover reconnoissances," as General McClellan explained, "and gain information of the nature of the country and the position of the enemy." General Stone, whose division lay to the northwest of McCall's, was told of this movement Sunday morning by the following communication from McClellan's adjutant-general: —

> General McClellan desires me to inform you that General McCall occupied Dranesville yesterday and is still there. Will send out heavy reconnoissances *to-day* [1] in all directions from that point. The General desires that you will keep a good lookout upon Leesburg, to see if this movement has the effect to drive them [rebel troops believed to be there] away. Perhaps a slight demonstration on your part would have the effect to move them.

General McCall sent out his reconnoitring parties, got them safely back the same day, and then, pursuant to McClellan's plan and orders, marched back to his former position. The knowledge required had been obtained. The movement was ended.

On the appointed day — Sunday, the 20th — General Stone made a feint at Edwards Ferry. A considerable force,

[1] The italics are mine. — E. R. K.

in sight of the rebel lookouts, marched from their camp down to the bank of the river, where as many of them as practicable were embarked in boats and scows and paddled or poled toward the Virginia shore. They did not land; having contributed toward the "slight demonstrations"; having, perhaps, helped to scare the rebel force at Leesburg, — between three and four miles distant, — they disembarked and returned to their camp. At the time this force was making its feint a detachment of twenty men, under General Stone's orders, actually crossed over the river at Conrad's Ferry, four miles above Edwards Ferry, and marched into the country in the direction of Leesburg, when, coming in sight of what they thought was a rebel camp, they turned back to report, remaining, however, on the Virginia side. Their work was done and the day was ended. General Stone testified that if he had known General McCall's division had fallen back from Dranesville he would have recalled his little party. Instead, he sent orders to Colonel Devens, Fifteenth Massachusetts Infantry, to cross four companies to Virginia, march toward Leesburg under cover of the night, attack the camp that was supposed to have been discovered, and then return to Maryland; provided, however, that under certain circumstances he was to "hold on" in Virginia and report. Devens acted promptly. He found the supposed tents were merely openings in the trees, so he soon returned to Ball's Bluff, and, the circumstances described having come about, he held on, as he had been ordered to. If General Stone, having done all that had been asked or expected of him, had stopped right there; if he had not "guessed wrong" as to McCall and then based an unauthorized movement on his erroneous guess; if he had recalled Devens to his camp in Maryland, there would not have been any battle of Ball's Bluff.

II. The following day, Monday, October 21, without orders from General McClellan; without even notifying the commanding general of his purpose; without trying to establish communication with McCall, — an effort to do which would have relieved him of his delusion as to McCall's position and so have avoided all the chagrin and blame for Monday's operations, — General Stone left the position to which he had been assigned by General McClellan and undertook a movement in force, with nearly his entire division, into Virginia. Such a movement on Sunday, in compliance with a suggestion for a "slight demonstration," would have been an absurd excess. On Monday it was as unwarranted a move as is recorded in the history of warfare.

General McCall, testifying before the Congressional Committee, said: —

I have never been able to account for Stone's movement, which was certainly a very injudicious one.

General McClellan declared: —

No order that I gave looked to a crossing of the river in force by General Stone.

And General Stone, referring to this Monday demonstration, said: —

It originated from myself.

III. General Stone relied for the success of his demonstration on the nearness and influence and coöperation of McCall's division. He listened for the sound of McCall's guns. He looked for McCall's men to appear. He cautioned his own troops to be on the lookout and not fire into McCall's men when they should come in sight. All based on a bad guess. General Stone, having been informed that General McCall's reconnoitring parties were to be out "to-day," Sunday, assumed that they would be out to-morrow, Monday.

General Stone testified: —

Had I known on Sunday night at ten o'clock, when I gave the order to Colonel Devens to go over and destroy the rebel camp which was supposed to be on the other side, that McCall's division was not at Dranesville, I should have made the order to return, and return quickly, an imperative order.

Well, *why did he not know?* The military telegraph between McClellan's headquarters and Stone's camp was in order. McClellan had positive information ten days before that the rebel force at Leesburg was 11,000. He would assuredly have kept Stone in place and out of trouble if he had been given the chance. In this confession, the import and significance of which have been strangely overlooked, the crux of the question of responsibility is cleared up.

IV. The position to which Colonel Baker was sent by General Stone was difficult of access from the north and easy of access from the south; was reached from the river by a hard climb up a steep bluff, but presented no obstacles to troops approaching from the interior, and had no base of supplies or line of retreat to the north except by a hand-power ferry over a swift-running river. Colonel Hinks, of the Nineteenth Massachusetts, who was in the battle, testified: —

> In my judgment it was the most unfortunate selection to cross the river from the Great Falls to Frederick.

Colonel Jenifer, of the Confederates, — a classmate of Stone's at West Point, — asked of a Union officer who had been taken prisoner, "What damned fool sent you over here?"

Colonel Baker had no more to do with selecting the place than he had with planning the movement.

V. The means for transporting troops and munitions across the river were grossly inadequate. Colonel Lee, of the Twentieth Massachusetts, describes the means as consisting of three scows, one of them capable of carrying fifty men and the others from forty to fifty-five each. There was also a skiff.

> These scows, Colonel Lee said, were poled across. The current was pretty strong, very swift, the rains of the previous few days having swollen the river considerably, and in order to reach the island [a distance exceeding two hundred and fifty yards], it was necessary to pole the scows up the river some distance and then take the downward current and a diagonal course across the river. Sometimes the scows failed to make the landing and had to be poled up again.

Captain Merritt, of the Nineteenth Massachusetts, testified that even these conveyances were not ready for use, so that the soldiers, when they wanted to use the scows that fateful Monday, —

had to cut down very sizable trees, and that made the poles so heavy as to make them almost unmanageable.

The hard work of Monday brought the number of Union troops on the field of Ball's Bluff, at the time of the actual battle, up to seventeen hundred and twenty, a force, according to Stone's message to Baker, less than half that of the Confederates. Meantime several thousand troops were standing around on Harrison's Island and the Maryland bank,[1] in plain hearing of the musket firing, anxious to join their comrades, but unable to get across the water. Colonel Lee, when testifying, was asked this question: —

Then, taking it in that point of view, the whole disaster resulted from insufficiency of transportation, because those troops might have been thrown across to make you equal to the enemy?

To which Colonel Lee answered: —

Yes, sir; there is no question about that.

Colonel James H. Van Allen was allowed to testify as to some matters on which he had no direct knowledge; he was in Washington when the Battle of Ball's Bluff was fought; but since he avowed a bias favorable to General Stone his statement relative to the point now under discussion carries weight. He said: —

I wish I could say that I knew there was sufficient transportation right at hand in the canal. I do say, with all my regard for General Stone, that, if there was not, the order to cross was an improper order, and I don't think General Stone's defense is strong upon that point; for although he says there was a scow and two boats there, and that they could carry so many men in so many minutes, I do not think that is a sufficient justification for sending such an expedition across.

[1] The long, narrow island divided the river into two channels.

General McCall in the course of his testimony said: —

> Stone has misstated, unintentionally of course, one or two things in his report. It proved afterward that he had not the means to cross at all.

General Stone displayed the same fatuity as to means of transportation in relation to the crossing of the left wing of his expedition, at Edwards Ferry. Directly General Banks was informed of the disaster at Ball's Bluff he marched his entire division to Stone's relief, arriving opposite Edwards Ferry in the night. Stone notified McClellan of this and assured the General-in-Chief that his means of transportation were ample for reinforcing his left wing, which, after the rout of the right wing, was in peril. Thus misled, McClellan ordered Stone to intrench and hold his position on the Virginia side. But when General McClellan arrived on the ground, early Tuesday morning, he instantly observed, as he declared, "that our means of crossing and recrossing were very insufficient," and he at once withdrew the entire force.

One important point relative to the failure to provide for getting troops and munitions over to Ball's Bluff was developed by Senator Wade, chairman of the Congressional Committee. When Captain Merritt was before the Committee the following testimony was brought out: —

> *Question.* How long would it take to have made a pontoon bridge there?
>
> *Answer.* I think if we had had the conveniences at hand we could have put a bridge across there so that five thousand troops could have crossed in an hour.
>
> *Question.* How long would it take to have made such a bridge? Take everything just as it was; suppose an enterprise to cross the river had been in contemplation two or three days before.
>
> *Answer.* I think it could have been done in two or three hours.

General Stone's testimony on this point is, in substance, that "it would be a very difficult thing," and that "it would take a considerable time!"

Who was responsible for this state of fatal unpreparedness? Certainly not Colonel Baker; the movement was begun, troops had crossed in two places, and thousands of reinforcements had been marched to the ferrying-place, before Baker had received any intimation that he was to be in the affair in any capacity.

VI. If there is anything related to this whole affair that seems unquestionable and indubitable, — except as General Stone, under fearful accusation, denied it, — it is that the General intended and directed and expected the force assigned to Colonel Baker that Monday morning to cross the Potomac, scale the bluff where Lee and Devens and their fine regiments were already posted, and move cautiously forward toward Leesburg. The General sent a small detachment across Sunday afternoon. That evening, as we know, he sent Colonel Devens over with four companies, gave them something to do, and directed them to remain in Virginia if they should see a position which they could "undoubtedly hold *until reinforced*." The purpose to reinforce was, it is plain, in Stone's mind at 10 o'clock Sunday evening. At 11 o'clock he wrote the order to Baker to march his brigade down to the ferry early the following morning. Other regiments were ordered to the same rendezvous. If they were not to cross, what were they expected to do?

Four miles below, at Edwards Ferry, Stone sent a considerable force across the river. If this force was not to be supported by a coöperating force the rebel troops known to be in the vicinity would be concentrated upon it. In the face of these facts General Stone denied all responsibility for the crossing at Conrad's Ferry and declared that Colonel Baker alone was responsible.[1] This specific matter must, therefore, be examined.

Lieutenant-Colonel Wistar, commander of the California

[1] In view of McClellan's testimony, (p. 309), that he did not expect Stone's troops to cross, what right had Stone to leave to the discretion of Baker, or any one, to do what Stone himself had no right to do? — E. R. K.

Regiment, — Seventy-first Pennsylvania, — told the Committee how he arrived with his men at the ferry opposite Harrison's Island and Ball's Bluff about sunrise and sent his quarter-master, Captain Young, down to General Stone to report the regiment's arrival and to ask for orders. Captain Young testified: —

I galloped down the towpath to Edwards Ferry and there found General Stone on the Maryland side, upon a hill, looking very intently at a company which had crossed at Edwards Ferry and could be seen formed as skirmishers on the Virginia side. . . . I gave him my message and waited, feeding my horse in the mean time. He finally came up to me and said, "Your order is, sir, that the California battalion will stand fast until you hear firing *and then immediately cross*." I waited for some further order and then asked, "General, have you any further order?" He spoke very imperiously and curtly, as he always does, and said, "You have your orders, sir." . . . I got on my horse and went back and delivered my orders to Colonel Wistar. . . . He asked me to repeat the order again, and I repeated it literally. He asked me if I was sure I was right. I said there was no mistake about it.

The scant means of transportation, apparent when the Massachusetts men under Lee and Devens were ferried over, the previous day, had become a subject of derisive joking among the troops, and it is evident Colonel Wistar found it difficult to believe that General Stone intended to order a larger force to cross with the same means. The especial significance of this testimony is, however, the proof that Stone had already sent troops across at Edwards Ferry and conditionally ordered troops to go over to Ball's Bluff, Monday morning, the 21st of October, — before Colonel Baker had been consulted.

Captain Young testified that soon after reporting General Stone's order to Colonel Wistar he met Colonel Baker, who had arrived at the river with his brigade. The Captain told Colonel Baker of Stone's order for Wistar to cross the river. Colonel Baker exclaimed, "That can't be." Captain Young repeated his statement that General Stone's order to Wistar was "to cross." Colonel Baker retorted, "*In what?*" Then he pressed the staff officer to say whether it was possible he might have erred in hearing or in communicating General Stone's order. Although Captain Young insisted he had made no mistake, Baker was still incredulous. This was the mind of Colonel Baker before meeting General Stone: — disbelief that the General intended sending any considerable number of men across, as things then stood, and contempt for the means of transportation at hand. Colonel Baker, after his meeting with Captain Young, was unwilling to trust the staff officer respecting the General's wishes. Obedient to Stone's orders he had brought his regiments down to the river bank; he would go, himself, to find out what work Stone had for him to do; so he "started off on a gallop" for headquarters. It is significant of Stone's purpose that just before Colonel Baker arrived the General had ordered a small detachment of cavalry to cross and coöperate with the troops already at Ball's Bluff.

General Stone, in his report and his testimony, describes the interview between himself and Colonel Baker. In his report, dated the 29th of October, Stone says: —

I decided to send him [Colonel Baker] to Harrison's Island to assume command, and in a full conversation with him explained the position of things as they then stood, according to reports received; told him that General McCall had advanced his troops to Dranesville, and that I was extremely desirous of ascertaining the exact position and force of the enemy in our front, and exploring, as far as it was safe, on the right toward Leesburg and on the left toward the Leesburg and Gum Springs road; that I should continue to reinforce the troops under General Gorman, opposite Edwards Ferry, and try to push them carefully forward to discover the best line from that ferry to the Leesburg and Gum Springs road already mentioned, and pointed out to him the position of the breastworks and hidden battery which barred the movement of troops directly from left to right.

I detailed to him the means of transportation across the river, of the sufficiency of which he was to be the judge; authorized him to make use of the guns of a section each of Vaughn's and Bunting's batteries, together with French's mountain howitzers, all the troops of his brigade, and Cogswell's Tammany Regiment, beside the Nineteenth and part of the Twentieth Regiments Massachusetts Volunteers, and left it to his discretion, after viewing the ground, to retire the troops from the Virginia shore under the cover of his guns and the fire of the large infantry force, or to pass over reinforcements in case he found it practicable and the position on the other side strong and favorable; that I wished no advance made unless the enemy were in inferior force, and under no circumstances to pass beyond Leesburg, or a strong position between it and Goose Creek, on the Gum Spring (Manassas) road.

In testifying before the Committee, General Stone said: —

I then told him [Baker] to go up and take entire command, entire control of the right, four miles from where I stood. He said, "Then am I to have entire command?" "Yes," said I. "Please put that in writing," he said. I then took out my pencil and on my knee wrote that order which has been referred to.

So far as General Stone's statements can aid us, we are now qualified to judge of his purposes as they were imparted to Colonel Baker during the "full conversation," and of the actual purport of the written order on which Stone relied to relieve himself of responsibility and fix it upon Baker. In the first place, we must observe that Colonel Baker was not in the least to blame for General Stone's delusion respecting McCall's nearness.

The General declared himself "extremely desirous of ascertaining the exact position and force of the enemy in our front." How could that be done except by going over into the enemy's country? He recognized this, and was also "extremely desirous" of "exploring as far as it was safe on the right towards Leesburg." Well, the only way to gratify a desire to explore is to explore. He believed General McCall had come within supporting distance, so that it was a good time to launch out. He added largely, including some artillery, to the force already commanded by Colonel Baker. Then he "detailed" the means he had prepared for transporting troops across the river. He told how he had organized a force — a left wing — to coöperate with the troops he had collected up the river. He said he should continue to strengthen the left wing. Finally he said to Colonel Baker, "You go up and take entire command of the right wing." Baker, in the habit of his civil profession, replied, "Please put that in writing." He was being placed over several colonels who did not belong to his brigade; he wanted to be able to show his authority. So General Stone wrote this order: —

> Colonel: In case of heavy firing in front of Harrison's Island you will advance the California Regiment of your brigade or retire the regiments under Colonels Lee and Devens upon the Virginia side of the river, at your discretion, assuming command on arrival.

The discretion is conditional, contingent. Unless there was "heavy firing" when Colonel Baker arrived, he had no right to retire Lee and Devens. Well, there was no "heavy firing" at that time nor for hours afterwards.

In his testimony General Stone described another condition in which, he said, Colonel Baker was to exercise a discretion, a choice. "If this party," said Stone, meaning the troops under Baker, "found there was not a strong force there; if it was a force he could easily drive before him; *he should drive it off*. If it was of such a size that he could not drive it off easily, then he was to fall back." Now, Baker had not previously been charged with the duty of ascertaining the extent of the rebel forces in that part of Virginia and had to rely on Stone for information in that matter. What were the facts? Devens had been engaged in small fights, but had not discovered any force that could be considered formidable in the presence of Baker's brigade. With his few hundred men Devens had fairly held his own. Stone, whose division was called the Corps of Observation, had been for weeks watching the movements of the Confederates, frequently employing balloons to aid in his work, and had no suspicion that an important body of the enemy was in the vicinity. Why should Baker hesitate? Why should the right wing be held back while the left wing was being reinforced? General Stone himself testified that after Devens, in his reconnoissance, "had advanced so far *it was not an unreasonable supposition that they* [the Confederates] *were in small force there.*" Clearly it was Baker's duty to drive off such a force. How could he do it unless he sent his men over into Virginia? What did General Stone expect? He answers in his report: —

> That gallant and energetic officer [Colonel Baker] left me at about 9 or 9.30 and proceeded rapidly up the river to his charge. Reinforcements were rapidly thrown to the Virginia side by *General Gorman at Edwards Ferry.*

It is not to be doubted that, after his explanations and orders, Stone fully counted on Baker's also reinforcing the right wing, at Ball's Bluff.

Here let us return for a moment to General Stone's narrative of his conference with Colonel Baker. "I detailed to him the means of transportation across the river," said Stone, " of the sufficiency of which he was to be the judge." This last assertion seems incredible. General Stone, qualified with the incomparable education of West Point, experienced in camp and field, had been for weeks making preparations to cross his division over the Potomac when the expected order to advance should be received. Now, without orders from General McClellan, but erroneously believing that he should be coöperating in a movement by General McCall, he decided to send forward an expedition composed of two wings. He knew very well that an army with two wings is like a bird, — ineffective unless both wings operate. He dispatched his left wing across under his own observation. He ordered several thousand troops down to the river to comprise his right wing. He knew how many there were of them. He knew, so that, as he testified, he "detailed," precisely the means of transportation he himself had provided. When he gave Baker authority to go up and lead the right wing did he suddenly lose confidence in his own judgment? Did he say to himself, "I have ordered so many men to cross and I have provided such and such means to transport them. I am not sure whether the means are sufficient. I will throw the responsibility of deciding that matter on to Colonel Baker"? Impossible.

I keenly deplore the necessity for writing thus of a graduate of West Point Military University — for so I choose to denominate the best training-school for military officers in the world. Boston, which is undoubtedly different from other great American cities, — and, I think, superior to them in civilization, — has been described as not so much a place as a state of mind. Just so, West Point is not merely an institution for teaching, but a place where the magnificence of nature and the splendors of the history of graduates of former years supply loftiest inspirations. Where instructors and cadets, uplifted by honorable traditions, unite to develop and maintain highest standards of manliness, truthfulness, integrity, courage, chivalry, and patriotism. How it will be in the future is not so certain. It is becoming common for spineless Congressmen to award appointments to West Point as prizes — as "Lives" of Washington, silver-plated butter-dishes, and other articles are awarded — to lads who, in competitive examinations, can best remember the facts they have picked up in cramming for the test. This by no means discovers the boy who will make the best officer. Napoleon was forty-second in scholarship at the military training-school at Brienne. Some of our most unsuccessful officers were near the heads of their classes at West Point. The greatest passed low. The best way is to pick out the finest young fellow in the district and send him to the Point. The authorities there will decide upon his scholarship.

Now to return to the matter in hand. If General Stone

(who, it may be remarked, placed a very high estimate on his own talents as an officer) had ignored his knowledge, relinquished his judgment, evaded his duty to decide this fundamental question, and left to Colonel Baker to decide whether to reinforce Lee and Devens or recall them, and to base his decision on his own judgment of the sufficiency or insufficiency of the means of transportation placed at his service, what would have happened? No more troops would have been sent over to Ball's Bluff; the few hundred already there would have been withdrawn, as far as possible; the imbecility of Patterson would have been repeated;[1] the Confederates, finding the Federals gone from Ball's Bluff, would have concentrated their forces and fallen upon Stone's left wing, less than four miles below; and Colonel Baker would have been denounced as a coward. These conclusions do not rest on conjecture, but are supported by evidence.[2]

We have seen that, previous to his interview with General Stone, Colonel Baker deemed it impossible that the General actually intended to try to send any considerable number of troops across with the wretched means at hand. Had the veteran colonel's opinion been altered by his conversation with General Stone? Not in the least, as we shall presently see. "This gallant and energetic officer," wrote Stone, " left me at

[1] General Scott, before the Congressional Committee, testified, "Although General Patterson was never specifically ordered to attack the enemy, he was certainly told and expected, even if with inferior numbers, to hold the rebel army in his front on the alert and to prevent it from reinforcing Manassas Junction." Patterson failed to do this and Johnston joined Beauregard at Bull Run, thus converting what had appeared at first to be a Union victory into a rout.

[2] Colonel Ward, in his *History of the One Hundred and Sixth Pennsylvania*, and of Baker's regiments, says: "General Stone *was in command of that advance*, and must have known that the troops would have to return, and provision should have been made to provide a safe means of retreat; and if none could have been provided, no advance ought to have been made. . . . Granting that the boat had not been sunk, what chance was there of recrossing about fifteen hundred men if pressed rapidly and closely to the water's edge, when the most that could be get into the boat was about one hundred, and over half an hour was consumed in making a trip from shore to island and back for another load? Yet General Stone telegraphed to General McClellan, 'I have the means of crossing one hundred and twenty-five men once in ten minutes at each of the two points.'" (Pages 13, 14.)

about 9 or 9.30 o'clock and proceeded rapidly up the river to his charge." He had scarcely left Stone's headquarters when he encountered Quartermaster Howe, of the Fifteenth Massachusetts, Devens's regiment, who was on his way to report to General Stone the state of affairs over at Ball's Bluff. Colonel Baker halted him and inquired how matters were going. Howe told Colonel Baker that "the regiment had had a skirmish with the enemy and that we still maintained our position where we had been." Colonel Baker said to Howe, "I am going over immediately, with my whole force, to take command." Was this the mind of a man who had been sent to study conditions and then decide on a course of action? Was Baker misrepresenting Stone's orders? Lieutenant Howe swore that after parting from Colonel Baker he went on and reported to General Stone what Colonel Baker had told him. Was Stone surprised? Did he say that Colonel Baker must have misapprehended his orders? That it was doubtful whether Baker would send any additional troops across? That, indeed, he might even recall Devens and Lee? Did Stone send an officer to overtake Colonel Baker and call him back, so that the General might set him right? No, to all these. Lieutenant Howe testified that General Stone confirmed Colonel Baker's declaration: —

> General Stone told me that Colonel Baker would probably be over in a very few minutes, as Colonel Baker had got his orders and was going over to take charge of the division on the right, while General Gorman was to cross at Edwards Ferry.

Congressman Odell asked Lieutenant Howe this question: —

> You understood General Stone to say that he had given orders to Colonel Baker to cross above?

To which Lieutenant Howe answered: —

> Yes, sir; *given orders to Baker to cross.*

Now, mark how Colonel Baker further manifested his understanding of General Stone's plans and orders, so slightly suggested in the written document, but fully explained in the conversation. Having galloped rapidly to where his gallant Californians were still standing, he ordered them to "cross at once." Was the Colonel excited? Had the veteran "lost his head"?

Captain Young testified: —

The Colonel was very serious and quiet; I never knew him to be more so.

Had Colonel Baker altered his contemptuous opinion of the means of transportation? Certainly not. Directly he arrived at Harrison's Island he set a large force to the task of dragging a boat out of the canal into the river, pathetically declaring, "This is all we have to go over in," — proof enough that Colonel Baker was pushing forward the right wing against his own judgment. Appreciating the weak point of Stone's movement, — lack of numbers in Virginia and lack of transportation, — Colonel Baker remained for some time at the ferry, directing the transfer of the troops.

Further to show the mind of General Stone; further to prove that the General intended the crossing and should bear the responsibility for it; let us read the testimony of Major Mix, of the Third New York Cavalry, who was also an officer in the Regular Army. Before Colonel Baker knew that he was to be in the movement or even that there was to be a movement, on Sunday General Stone told Major Mix that he

might have an opportunity of crossing the river [at Edwards Ferry] and having a dash at the enemy if things went *as he expected them to*. . . . General Stone cautioned me to be careful not to operate against any troops on my right until I ascertained who they were, as *he intended to throw over an infantry force above* [at Ball's Bluff].

There is also the testimony of General Banks. When General Stone became aware of the extent of the disaster to his right wing and realized the danger that might involve his left, he appealed to General Banks. That officer, regardless of the fatigue of his men, marched his division all Monday night to Stone's relief, arriving near Edwards Ferry about three o'clock Tuesday morning. When before the Congressional Committee General Banks said: —

In relating the affair to me, on my arrival, General Stone said that it [the movement of his division] commenced with the purpose to make a thorough reconnoissance of the strength and position of the enemy. . . . I do not think, myself, that Colonel Baker could have done otherwise than he did.

Finally, there is the authoritative statement of the commander-in-chief. General McClellan, when testifying, was asked: —

Can you tell us who was responsible for making the crossing at Harrison's Island; was it General Stone or Colonel Baker?

General McClellan did not possess the knowledge on that subject which is now accessible in the government publications, but his answer is sufficient: —

I only know what I learned from General Stone. My recollection is that General Stone gave discretionary orders to Colonel Baker to cross if certain conditions could be fulfilled. *I think General Stone was responsible to the extent that he ought to have informed himself whether it was possible to fulfill those conditions or not.*

As the whole case against Colonel Baker, thus far, rests on the reports and testimony of General Stone, it is in order to introduce one bit of evidence that proves that the General at different times made contradictory statements of his purpose for his right wing. In a letter dated the 2d of November, shortly after the battle, General Stone declared that "the object of the movement . . . *was intended solely to insure the safe return of Colonel Devens and his command!*" Contrasted with Stone's statements to General Banks and Major Mix; with the facts relating to the operations of the left wing; and in the light of all the testimony summarized on preceding pages; this November declaration arouses painful suggestions.

VII. "It cannot be denied that had reinforcements promptly arrived at Ball's Bluff from Edwards Ferry the result of the battle would, in all probability, have been greatly to our advantage instead of being a melancholy disaster." This was the conclusion of the Congressional Committee that investigated the subject. The study and discussion of the years that have elapsed have confirmed it. Why was not Colonel Baker thus reinforced? Baker's force was not a separate army; it was denominated by General Stone the "right wing" of his advance into Virginia. Now, as has just been remarked, the function of wings, whether of birds or armies, can be exercised only through coöperation, and General Stone's orders looked to mutual support by the wings of his division — if everything went well. "Report frequently," he wrote to Baker, "so that when they [the Confederates] are pushed, Gorman [commander of the left wing] can come in on their flank." But what if "they" were not pushed? If the Confederates should turn the tables and push Baker; — what provision was there for coöperation in that event? None. Down at Edwards Ferry they heard the firing at Ball's Bluff. Lieutenant Rea testified that "a great many officers said that it was a shame for us to remain there and do nothing." Captain De Courcy could see nothing to prevent our forces at the ferry from going up to Ball's Bluff. Captain Brady was asked: —

> How long would it have taken that division of the army to which you belonged [Stone's left wing] to go up to Ball's Bluff and relieve them there if you had been ordered to do so?

To which he replied: —

> I do not think it would have taken over an hour, if that.

The testimony of Major Dimmick is especially interesting. This question was put to him: —

> Could you see any reason why our troops should not have gone up from Edwards Ferry to the assistance of General Baker?

This was his answer: —

> I could see none at all. I think we could have done it and have turned them [the Confederates] on their flank and captured them all. I saw the road then and could see no obstacle in the way. They expected us to come up there to assist them, and that was the reason they made such a desperate resistance there. One of our men made his way up there from Edwards Ferry. How he got up there I do not know; but so anxious was he to get into the fight that he left his regiment and made his way up there and went with the Tammany Regiment, and he told the Tammany boys that General Gorman was coming up with his brigade, and they fought with that expectation all day. I know he got with the Tammany Regiment from our regiment. He wandered off three miles to get into the fight.

Lieutenant Downey begged his captain to let him "take our Company anyhow and go to the relief of Colonel Baker." But no; Baker successful and driving the enemy before him was to receive Gorman's support; surprised by a force greater than General Stone had expected him to encounter, and thus unable to advance, and, owing to insufficient transportation, unable to retreat, he was left to his fate. Stone's disposition of his left wing, as he explained to the Committee, was such that he considered it impossible to employ that half of his division in any way to save his right wing from a crushing defeat. For, according to General Stone's testimony, with his right wing at Ball's Bluff and his left wing between three and four miles away, the two sections were effectively separated from each other by a Confederate fort commanding the road — of the existence of which he said he had been aware long before he ordered his troops to cross into Virginia! Denounced in Congress by leading men; fiercely assailed in public journals; distrusted by many of his own command; accused not only of blundering, but of hideous treason; with his back to the wall, Stone declared that he told Baker it would be impossible to reinforce Ball's Bluff from Edwards Ferry owing to this fort. Alas, he failed to make Baker understand him. When, at noon of the battle day, Stone learned the magnitude of the Confederate force gathering upon his right wing, he sent word to Baker that there were four thousand confronting him. Baker, with seventeen hundred, realized his plight. His scows could not bring him sufficient reinforcements and they were equally incapable of transporting his men back to the Maryland shore or Harrison's Island. So he at once sent a message to Stone in which he said, "I hope your movement below will give advantage." Later, during the fury of the battle, Colonel Baker asked Captain Young, the staff officer who visited Division Headquarters for orders early in the morning, "Do you suppose Stone is going to send reinforcements up on the left?" Baker's message proves that he hoped for a coöperating movement by the left wing, which was immediately under Stone's observation, and the question to Captain Young plainly shows that the possibility that aid might come by the road from Edwards Ferry had not been banished from Baker's mind by Stone's full explanation of his plans. The day following, Tuesday morning, Captain Young met General Stone at Edwards Ferry. The Captain's testimony tells what occurred: —

> I said, "General Stone, why did you not reinforce us on the left from Edwards Ferry?" He said, "No one knew better than Colonel Baker that it was impossible to reinforce you on the left from here, because there is a fortification halfway between the two places and it was impossible to pass it." Said I, "Captain Stewart [Stone's adjutant-general] came on the field and told us you were going to send General Gorman up with five thousand men. How is that?"

General Stone evidently found this a poser.

> He made no reply, but just raised his hat and went off.

General Stone apparently forgot, at times, his assertions that the road between the wings of his army was impassable. Describing the incidents of the battle, in his official report dated October 29, he tells how Colonel Lee at first took command after Baker fell "and prepared to commence throwing our forces to the rear, but Colonel Cogswell, of the Tammany Regiment, being found to be senior in rank, assumed command and ordered dispositions to be made immediately for marching to the left and cutting a way through to Edwards Ferry." And General Stone adds, "Unfortunately, just as the first dispositions were being made the movement was thwarted by a deceptive trick of the enemy." One is disposed to ask why, if a Confederate fort blocked the way, it was "unfortunate" that Cogswell's plan to fight his way down to the left wing was not carried out? If Cogswell could have gone down the road to Edwards Ferry, why was it impossible for the force at Edwards Ferry to go up the same road to Baker and Cogswell?

The testimony relating to that fortification is conflicting. Most of the Union officers were skeptical as to its existence, or, if it existed, as to there being any guns in it. Colonel Patrick, of the Sixtieth Pennsylvania, testified as follows: —

Question. How far did you go up the river towards Ball's Bluff?

Answer. I went up about a mile above my lines; about a mile above the ferry.

Question. Did you see any batteries there, or anything to prevent your going up to Ball's Bluff?

Answer. I saw nothing of the kind.

The testimony of Major Dimmick, Second New York State Militia, is of interest. Speaking of the fortification he expressed the opinion that it was no obstacle at the time of the battle, as there had been no guns mounted then.

Question. Did you satisfy yourself that there were no guns there at the time of the Ball's Bluff disaster?

Answer. Yes, sir; on the day after.

Question. How near did you go to it?

Answer. Within three hundred yards.

It is worth while to consider some of the testimony of Colonel Tompkins, of the Second New York, which was at Edwards Ferry: —

Question. Were there any obstacles in the way of your going up to Ball's Bluff?

Answer. None at all. No doubt we would have had to fight a little on our way up. But I think by going up that way, on that side, we could have drawn their attention towards us and engaged them so that Colonel Baker's forces would have had an opportunity to have got a better foothold than they had.

The testimony of General Lander is especially strong relative to the point under consideration: —

Question. Was there any insuperable obstacle in the way of throwing a body of men in their rear and capturing the attacking force? [The force that was fighting Baker.]

Answer. That was the arrangement of General Stone.

Question. Why was not that move made?

Answer. That I cannot tell; from the checking of the first advance of Davies, I suppose. [A misprint for Devens.]

Question. Suppose these men [Union soldiers in Virginia at Edwards Ferry] had advanced at double quick and attacked the enemy in the rear?

Answer. It is said there was a masked battery between, but that could not interfere with skirmishers and sharpshooters. They could not lose over a hundred men in passing them. I think the junction could have been made.

Question. You do not consider the obstacle insuperable?

Answer. Not at all; not by any means.

. . . .

Question. Did you see any batteries there that were an obstacle to moving up to relieve Baker?

Answer. I told my lieutenant-colonel I was of a great mind to steal three thousand men and take the town of Leesburg. [Nearly all of Lander's brigade had been, for this movement of Stone's, assigned to Baker or Gorman, so that Lander's own command was very small the day of the battle.] . . . I could have done it, I think. At least, that shows I did not think much of their batteries.

Following all this came the testimony of General McClellan. Four months after the battle; long after all the reports of officers had been presented and studied; after the controversy between General Stone and his defenders and the friends of Colonel Baker had been talked over and thoroughly discussed in camp and at Headquarters; the commander of the Army of the Potomac, being before the Committee of Congress and on his oath, declared: —

> My belief is that there was no serious obstacle to a communication between Edwards Ferry and Ball's Bluff. I do not think the enemy had any large force or any strong works between those two points near the river that would have interfered with that communication.

The last quoted statement of General Lander contains an extremely important suggestion. If, as General Stone insisted, — contrary to the weight of evidence, — a Confederate fortification made it impossible to march troops from Edwards Ferry to Ball's Bluff by the direct road, why did he not attempt some other measure for the benefit of his right wing? The left wing had been sent across the Potomac at the same time as the right in order that a joint movement might be executed; why did General Stone allow half his division to lie still all that eventful Monday? The General said Colonel Baker failed to send him word of his need. Well, until Baker received word from Stone that the Confederate force was greater than they had supposed during their morning conference the Colonel had no reason to suppose he would require help. And when, promptly upon receiving information of the enemy's strength, Baker sent his message to Stone, it did no good — there was no movement by the forces at the Ferry. Stone had heard firing up at the Bluff all the morning. It was shortly before noon when he learned of the strength of the enemy. It was proper to immediately notify Baker, but there was no occasion to wait for a response. Stone should at once have put his left wing into the game. There were at least two moves practicable: —

(*a*) Lander would have made a dash toward Leesburg. Undoubtedly this would have relieved Baker. Nearly every white man, woman, and child of the vicinage was ardent for the Southern cause. Such a move as that suggested would scarcely have begun when a score of Virginians accustomed to the saddle would have been speeding toward their friends near Ball's Bluff. And General Evans, the Confederate commander, thus informed that his base was to be captured, his line of retreat to be cut off, and his troops confronting Baker menaced by a force in their rear, would have fallen back from the river and joined in a race for Leesburg. Or, if it is conceivable that he would have persisted in his move on Ball's Bluff and his attack on Baker, he would have been attacked in his rear, shut in between the two wings of Stone's division, and most of his force would have been captured.

(*b*) If there was an armed fortification in the road it might have been flanked. Many officers said so. Nobody questioned it. A reading of General Stone's testimony on this point leaves the impression that he was more inclined to make excuses and fog than candid explanations. However, his admissions are important. He was asked: —

Suppose your force [the left wing] had been thrown around there [beyond the fort] with the appearance of coming in their rear, would not they have been compelled to leave their intrenchments?

To which he answered: —

Yes, sir, if I had chosen to expose fifteen hundred men [far short of the number of his left wing] to extraordinary risk, — an unusual military risk, — the attempt could have been made.

Then Senator Chandler put this question: —

If those batteries had not been there, or if being there they had been flanked in any way, would it not have been a comparatively easy task to have captured their whole force?

General Stone answered: —

No, sir, because they [Stone's troops at the ferry] could not have marched that distance in twice the time that the action at Ball's Bluff lasted.

Let us see about this element of time. The actual battle began between two and three o'clock and raged until nearly five — more than two hours. "Twice the time" is at least four hours. But General Stone must have known this was a misleading measure. Even before he sent Baker to take command, Devens's force, which led the movement, had been engaged. Baker left Stone about half-past nine, and as he rode up toward Ball's Bluff Devens and Lee were exchanging shots with the Confederates. Sharp firing continued from time to time during the day and was heard at Stone's headquarters. His men over on the Virginia side at Edwards Ferry heard the guns and begged to be led up to where they knew Baker was engaged. An alert general would have ridden the distance, less than four miles, or at least have sent a member of his staff, — as later in the day, too late, Stone did, — to find out how the fight was going. At about half-past eleven Stone learned that the Confederate force confronting Baker was larger than he had supposed. That was the time to do something. It was more than five hours from that time to the moment when Baker fell and the rout began; five hours in which the left wing, lying inert at the ferry, might — although at much risk, Stone said — have marched out into the country, beyond that dreaded battery, and then come in toward the river again, higher up, and given Evans and his yelling Confederates a surprise; five hours to march — how far? Let us revert to the testimony. After eliciting the statement that there was not time to send relief to Baker on account of the distance, Mr. Chandler asked, "What distance?" To that General Stone made this answer: —

> *The distance they* [the troops of Stone's left wing] *would have been obliged to march would have been at least eight or nine miles! And after such a march as that they would have come into action tired and fatigued!* [1]

Then, General Stone, apparently oblivious to the disclosure

[1] The italics and exclamation points are mine. — E. R. K.

he had made, but evidently realizing that he had been guilty of exaggeration in describing the distance, continued: —

> Remember that all this was unknown ground. There is a range of hills there that cuts off the view of what is behind. And for troops to march seven or eight miles [a moment before it was eight or nine "at least"] around, over unknown ground, without knowledge of the force of the enemy,[1] is very brave work indeed; but I do not think it would have been soldierlike.

Yet when Stone learned of the disaster to his right wing and realized that the victorious Confederates might come down upon his left and overwhelm it, and sent to the nearest force for help, General Banks marched his division in the night nearly fourteen miles to Edwards Ferry and made no complaint of the fatigue.

It was after these statements of General Stone that General McClellan testified before the Congressional Committee: —

> I think they [the troops of the left wing] should either have been thrown upon Leesburg or sent to assist Colonel Baker.

VIII. The conditions that led to the Battle of Ball's Bluff and the causes of the Union defeat have now been fully set forth and responsibility for the disaster has been placed. Charges made directly after the event forced General Stone into an attitude of strenuous self-defense. Some of the published statements were unfounded. So the General lost his temper, and, asserting that Baker's "friends" were attacking him, with the illogicalness of an angry man he turned upon the dead Colonel and charged him with losing the battle through unskillful handling of his troops. Whoever has read the history of the Civil War knows that such a charge would have early lain against many officers who later became distinguished for their victories. Many men were at first inexperienced; many were out of practice. If the correctness of General Stone's charge were conceded, Baker's fame would be but slightly dimmed and his claim upon the gratitude of

[1] General Stone had notified Baker that the rebel force was four thousand.

the country he served so well would continue unimpaired. Lord Rosebery truly says, "With Pitt, as with Nelson, his country will not count flaws. What do they matter? How are they visible in the sunlight of achievement? A country must cherish and guard its heroes." [1]

But the justice of General Stone's charge is not conceded; it is denied. And the effectiveness of the charge is weakened, if not destroyed, by the inconsistencies and contradictions of the complainant. In his first official report, dated eight days after the engagement, General Stone said: —

> Had an efficient officer with one company remained at each landing, guarding the boats, their full capacity would have been made serviceable, and sufficient men would have been passed on to secure the success of his [Baker's] operation.

In an indorsement on the report of the action by Captain Young, General Stone wrote that if there had been regularity and order in the movement of the boats "there would have been no disaster." It would seem that at this time General Stone had no idea of charging Colonel Baker with unskillful handling of his troops. But in his angry letter of the 2d of November to General Williams, Stone declared that "as the troops were arranged on the field I feel that increased force would only have given us increased loss." Then, by the 5th of January, 1862, having cooled off to some extent, he testified that if the scows had been well managed, Baker might have got enough men across "to have crushed out the force there." Thus, while Stone blamed Baker for losing the battle through unskillfulness in handling the troops, he plainly and repeatedly showed that he believed Baker would have won a victory if there had been troops enough on the field. And although he frequently maintained that the means of transportation were ample, he blamed Baker for deciding to cross the river with the facilities provided, — a decision, it is now contended, Baker did not make.

[1] *Lord Chatham*, 1910. Harper and Brothers.

Again, General Stone blamed Colonel Baker for spending some time on Harrison's Island directly superintending the work of ferrying reinforcements over to Ball's Bluff. Yet it was the judgment of every officer who testified before the investigating committee that the greatest need of the day was reinforcement. Stone would have had the work of reinforcing left to a subordinate. Baker, appreciating the supreme need of the expedition, as long as possible attended to it himself. Devens, selected for the post by General Stone, could safely be intrusted with the command on the Virginia side an hour or two longer. The inexperienced volunteers on the island could not as efficiently manage the transportation difficulties. Indeed, after Colonel Baker left them the work fell into confusion. Stone, without proof, assumed that Baker put no one in charge of the work, although he was conscious of its supreme importance.

Baker was dead and unable to tell his side of the story, but it is difficult to believe that a talented veteran officer could, after giving the matter his own supervision, abandon it and make no provision for any one to take his place. Indeed, Mr. Abbott states that "Captain Ritman was put in charge of forwarding the men from the island to the Virginia side." [1] It is highly probable that some other was charged with a similar duty on the Maryland shore. Possibly the brave fellows assigned to that specific duty were after a time swept away by their enthusiasm and went forward into actual fighting, leaving to others the inglorious drudgery of loading and starting the uninspiring scows. I place this guess against General Stone's; I think it the better of the two.

This word more should be said: when Colonel Baker went over to Ball's Bluff he left instructions concerning the artillery. He well knew that transportation, quite as much, needed attention. It is highly probable that he left orders as to that.

[1] Abbott, chapter VIII. The precise page has escaped me. It was, I think, between pp. 217 and 220. — E. R. K.

General Stone condemned Colonel Baker for allowing the horses to be taken along when the artillery was ferried across, complaining that the space taken by the horses would have been better used if it had been filled with infantry. But Colonel Cogswell was in charge of the artillery, by Baker's order, and it was this trained West Pointer who saw guns and horses ferried over, while Baker was on the firing-line; and the effective work of the six-pounder amply justified Cogswell for ferrying it across. General Stone also condemned Colonel Baker's disposition of his troops on the battlefield. In a letter dated December 2, 1861, Stone said, with unpardonable exaggeration, "The troops were so arranged on the field as to expose them all to fire, while but few could fire on the enemy." A month later, before the Committee, he modified his charge, and testified, "The Fifteenth and Twentieth Massachusetts, by the way they were posted, could deliver only about half their fire upon the enemy." The "but few" of the entire force of the first statement has got down to "about half" of the two Massachusetts regiments in the January testimony, and the California Regiment, the most numerous organization in the action, and the Tammany Regiment, are not referred to. Nor does Stone state the reason why some of the Massachusetts men were at first not put into the fight, which was that they were prudently posted as reserves.

If a comparison of these two statements does not discredit General Stone as an accuser, the substance, the gravamen, of his charge is disproved by the official reports of killed and wounded in the affair. A great part, if not the greater part, of the Union loss occurred after the retreat and rout, while an extremely small part of the Southern loss was inflicted by the Union soldiers after they left the battlefield; yet the Confederates had 153 killed and wounded and the Union loss was but 207, — proof that while the Government troops remained on the field their fire was effective, and, in view of the much greater number of the Southern muskets, better than that of their adversaries.

The last communications that were exchanged between General Stone and Colonel Baker are reprinted here. Stone's note, written hours after he had sent Baker to Ball's Bluff, is as follows: —

COLONEL: I am informed that the force of the enemy is about 4000 all told. If you can push them you may do so as far as to have a strong position near Leesburg, if you can keep them before you, avoiding their batteries. If they pass Leesburg and take the Gum Spring road you will not follow far, but seize the first good position to cover the road. Their design is to draw us on, if they are obliged to retreat, as far as Goose Creek, where they can be reinforced from Manassas and have a strong position. Report frequently, so that when they are pushed Gorman can come in on their flank.

How was this understood by those who first received it? Captain Young testified that he was on the island when Colonel Cogswell, who was on the Maryland shore, held up a paper and shouted that it was an order from General Stone to Colonel Baker, just received. Captain Young called out to Cogswell to open and read it. "He did so," says Young, "and said *it was to go ahead.*"

How did Colonel Baker understand it? After that long conversation earlier in the day, when Stone explained the topography of the contiguous part of Virginia, and

told him that General McCall had advanced his troops to Dranesville, and that I was *extremely desirous* of ascertaining the exact position and force of the enemy in our front, and *exploring* as far as it was safe on the right towards Leesburg and on the left towards the Leesburg and Gum Spring road; and that I should continue to reinforce the troops under General Gorman opposite Edwards Ferry, *and try to push them carefully forward* [1] to discover the best line from that ferry to the Leesburg and Gum Spring road, etc.,

how could Colonel Baker understand this midday communication as anything but a suggestion "to go ahead"? What if,

[1] The italics are mine. — E. R. K.

when Gorman arrived at "the Leesburg and Gum Spring road," he should find no Union troops to coöperate with him, but should encounter the Confederates? Baker undoubtedly thought of that and determined that he would not fail Gorman nor disappoint Stone. So in reply to Stone's order he sent this message: —

GENERAL: I acknowledge your order of 11.50 announcing their force at 4000. I have lifted a large boat out of the canal into the river. I shall, as soon as I feel strong enough, advance steadily, guarding my flanks carefully. I will communicate with you often. I shall cross some guns, Rhode Island and New York, directly. As you know, I have ordered down my brigade and Cogswell, who will cross as rapidly as possible. I shall feel cautiously for them. I hope your movement below will give advantage. Please communicate with me often.

These two dispatches and the circumstances under which they were written tell a plain tale. General Stone still wanted information of conditions over in Virginia and still expected Baker to push forward and obtain it. Colonel Baker, obedient and faithful, the true soldier, would do what his chief expected of him. Now that he knew the numbers confronting him he realized that both wings of the army must work together to make a success of the General's plan. The right wing would not falter; but there is a tone of appealing pathos in the Colonel's closing words: "I hope your movement below will give advantage. Please communicate with me often."

When General Stone published his defense he omitted the text of these two documents, but he represented them to be as follows: —

I warned him [Baker], when I ascertained it, that I believed 4000 troops would be opposed to him; there was still time to retire; and when he replied, "I shall not retire," I had no doubt, and I have now no doubt, that he felt perfectly able to meet that force.

Is this a fair summary of those two communications? General Stone did, in his 11.50 note, inform Colonel Baker of the estimated number of the enemy; but is there anything in the language or sentiment of the note that justified characterizing it as a warning? "If you can push them you may do so"; is that the language of warning? Was General Stone's statement designed to convey the impression that in his message to Colonel Baker he said something to suggest that "there was still time to retire"? And is there anything in the note that could by any possibility be construed as such a suggestion? General Stone told the American people that Colonel Baker replied, "I shall not retire." Is this a fair representation of the real answer? Was General Stone justified in putting such a declaration in quotation marks?

One thing remains for discussion. In the judgment of some officers Colonel Baker erred in forming his line of battle near the brink of the bluff. They would have had him advance to the wooded ground a short distance from the river. If Baker was wrong, —

> "it was a grievous fault,
> And grievously hath Cæsar answered it."

But is it quite certain that Baker erred? The advantage of the wooded position suggested by Colonel Cogswell as a defensive position was obvious. But, on the other hand, if General Evans, whose force greatly outnumbered Baker's, had slipped around one end of Baker's line, got in his rear, and cut off the Union troops from their base, Baker would have been compelled to change front under fire and make a dubious fight to recover his first position. However slow and irregular the scows may have been, they were the only means of supplying the supreme needs of the day, more troops and more ammunition. For Colonel Baker to have allowed the rebels to separate him from the ferry would probably have alarmed and demoralized the men. To have risked such a move would have been a mistake. General Stone made other criticisms of Colonel Baker's handling of his troops, inspired by the desperation of his position and in angry retaliation upon the dead hero for the attacks some of his friends had made upon Stone. They seem to require no discussion here.

Finally. Before Colonel Baker was killed he apparently realized that the day was probably lost. He was not strong enough to advance and he had no bridge over which he could retire. But, although outnumbered, he was able to stand his ground. His practical suggestions to his men for diminishing their peril and adding to their effectiveness in delivering their fire, his encouraging remarks, his inspiring example of serene, cheerful demeanor, and his fearless, conspicuous example of undaunted courage, were "worth a host of men." While requiring his men to lie down, he walked from regiment to regiment, arousing their wildest enthusiasm. Yet he knew that the only hope for victory was in the arrival of Gorman's troops. We used to read, in picturesque narratives of the Battle of Waterloo, how Wellington, hard-pressed by the fierce onsets of the French, exclaimed, "Oh, that Blücher or night would come!" For Wellington, Blücher arrived in time. But Stone did not move his left wing. The last command Baker ever gave was to Captain Young, whom he ordered to report to General Stone that troops could not be ferried over in sufficient numbers and that reinforcements must come up on the left.

General Stone said, in a dispatch to General McClellan, written several hours after Baker fell, — several days before he appreciated the necessity for a scapegoat, — "All was reported going well up to Baker's death." A Southern historian says, "Shortly after the action became general Colonel Baker, passing in front of his command, was killed by a sharpshooter, which so demoralized the Federals that the surviving officers conferred and decided to retreat." [1]

While Baker lived there was no rout, no disorder, no defeat.

[1] *Confederate Military History*, edited by General Clement A. Evans, vol. III, p. 191.

III

BITTERNESS OF CALIFORNIA DISLOYALISTS

Letter from Mr. James R. Morse

Dear Mr. Kennedy, — Referring to our conversation regarding California experiences and Southern sympathizers leaving that state to join the Confederacy, I am sorry to say I cannot give names, with one exception, for it has been many years since I have even thought of the incident.

As I told you, I went from Wisconsin to the Pacific Coast in company with my father and brother in 1862. We crossed the Plains with ox teams. When out two or three days from Bear River, Utah, on our way to Nevada, a party of six men rode into our camp, and from the leader, Captain Jackson, we learned they were from Marysville, California, and that when they started they numbered fifteen, all well armed and well mounted. They undertook this ride of some three thousand miles across the Plains, to "offer their services to Jeff Davis," as they expressed it. One morning, early in August, at a place called "City of Rocks," just as they were about to break camp they were visited by an unusually large party of professedly friendly Paiute or Shoshone Indians, who offered them fresh beef in exchange for tobacco and spirits. Captain Jackson, who possessed a wonderful knowledge of Indian character, at once suspected treachery, and quietly passed the word to his men to prepare for a running fight. While engaging the chief in conversation about hunting in the neighborhood, all preparations were made; his men mounted and slowly began to move out of camp. Captain Jackson thanked the chief for the information given him, bade him good-bye, mounted, and followed his men. Almost immediately the Indians began to close in on him, with the intention, no doubt, of cutting him off from his comrades. He drew his revolver, shot two of the Indians, put spurs to his horse, and soon joined his men, when a running fight was begun and kept up until late in the afternoon. In the mean time Jackson was obliged to abandon his packhorses, and thus all their provisions were lost. Just before dusk he was also obliged to give orders to dismount (their saddle horses having become exhausted), and take to the rocks. Up to this moment not a man had received even a scratch, but within fifteen minutes from the time they reached the hills they were surrounded, six of them killed, and three badly wounded. Under cover of darkness Jackson, with five comrades, succeeded in removing the three wounded men to a thick growth of willows in the valley, on the banks of the Feather River, made them as comfortable as circumstances would permit, left them well armed, with plenty of ammunition, but no food, and promised to return with a rescuing party if spared to get through to a settlement about one hundred miles distant. After a rest of a few hours Jackson and his five comrades made their start, and three days later came staggering into our camp about ten o'clock at night. We were a party of about sixty men, women, and children, with from thirty to thirty-five wagons well supplied with provisions, arms, and ammunition. The following morning, before daybreak, Jackson, as guide and in command, with twelve volunteers from our party, started on his return to the Feather River to rescue his wounded comrades. Twenty-four hours later two of these wounded men came crawling into our camp, more dead than alive, and reported the third man alive when they left him. They had missed Jackson and his party, as they traveled only at night, and were in hiding and off the main road during the day. On the third day from the time Jackson left us we were met a short distance from the Feather River by one of the rescuing party, who reported Jackson and the others camped where they had originally left the wounded, and that the third wounded man was alive and doing well. All this time he had subsisted on wild rosebuds, as did those who were with him. The wounded men reported that for several nights after their battle the Indians would occasionally approach within a short distance and throw stones into the willows, finally disappearing altogether. Jackson and his party accompanied us as far as Starr City, Humboldt County, Nevada. My recollection is that the wounded men entirely recovered.

To illustrate their intense hatred for Union men, one of them, who had been shot five times by the Indians, and who was then carrying the balls within his body, and being nursed and cared for by a Unionist, remarked that he would much rather kill a Union man than an Indian.

Yours very truly,

James R. Morse.

AUTHORITIES REFERRED TO

Abraham Lincoln. John G. Nicolay and John Hay. The Century Company.

A Belle of the Fifties: Memories of Mrs. Clay of Alabama. Put into narrative form by Ada Sterling. Doubleday, Page & Co.

A Senator of the Fifties. Jeremiah Lynch. A. M. Robertson.

Bench and Bar in California. Oscar T. Shuck. The Occident Printing House.

California (American Commonwealths Series). Josiah Royce. Houghton Mifflin Company.

Checkered Life: In the Old and New World. Rev. J. L. Ver Mehr. A. L. Bancroft & Co.

History of California. Theodore H. Hittell. Pacific Press Publishing House and Occidental Publishing Company.

History of the Pacific States of North America: California. Hubert Howe Bancroft. The History Company.

History of the Civil War in America. John S. C. Abbott.

History of the Philadelphia Brigade. Brevet Lieutenant-Colonel Charles H. Banes. J. B. Lippincott and Company.

History of the One Hundred and Sixth Regiment, Pennsylvania Volunteers. Colonel Joseph R. C. Ward. F. McManus, Jr. & Co.

House of Representatives, Report of the Joint Committee on Conduct of the War. In three parts. Part 2. Government Printing Office.

Life and Letters of Edmund Clarence Stedman. Laura Stedman and George M. Gould, M.D. Moffat, Yard, & Co.

Lights and Shadows of Life on the Pacific Coast. S. D. Woods. Funk & Wagnalls Company.

Lincoln, Master of Men. Alonzo Rothschild. Houghton Mifflin Company.

Masterpieces of E. D. Baker. Edited by Oscar T. Shuck. The Editor.

Personal Reminiscences of Early Days in California. Stephen J. Field. Printed for a few friends. Not Published.

Representative and Leading Men of the Pacific. Edited by Oscar T. Shuck. Bacon & Co.

Sketch of the Life and Public Services of Edward D. Baker. Joseph Wallace. Springfield, Ill., 1870.

The Congressional Globe. Prepared by John C. Rives.

The History of California. Frank Tuthill.

The Illini. Clark E. Carr. A. C. McClurg & Co.

The Life of Abraham Lincoln. Isaac N. Arnold.

The Life and Works of Rufus Choate. Samuel Gilman Brown. Little, Brown, & Co.

The War of the Rebellion. A compilation of the Official Records of the Union and Confederate Armies, prepared under the direction of the Secretary of War. By Brevet Lieutenant-Colonel Robert N. Scott. Government Printing Office.

Twenty Years of Congress. James G. Blaine. The Henry Bill Publishing Company.

Three Years in California. Rev. Walter Colton, U.S.N. A. S. Barnes & Co.

INDEX

INDEX

The Riverside Press
CAMBRIDGE . MASSACHUSETTS
U . S . A